Women in Iberian Filmic Culture

N.º
Nome
Proc. N.º

Women in Iberian Filmic Culture

A Feminist Approach to the Cinemas of Portugal and Spain

Edited by Elena Cordero-Hoyo and Begoña Soto-Vázquez

intellect
Bristol, UK / Chicago, USA

First published in the UK in 2020 by
Intellect, The Mill, Parnall Road, Fishponds, Bristol, BS16 3JG, UK

First published in the USA in 2020 by
Intellect, The University of Chicago Press, 1427 E. 60th Street,
Chicago, IL 60637, USA

A catalogue record for this book is available from the British Library.

Copy editor: Lorraine Slipper
Cover designer: Alexsandra Szumlas
Cover image: Catarina Mourão
Production manager: Laura Christopher
Typesetting: Contentra Technologies

Print ISBN 978-1-78938-152-8 (hardback)
Print ISBN 978-1-78938-171-9 (paperback)
ePDF ISBN 978-1-78938-173-3
ePUB ISBN 978-1-78938-172-6

This is a peer-reviewed publication.

This work is funded by Portuguese national funds through FCT – Fundação para a Ciência e a Tecnologia, I.P., in the scope of the project UID/ELT/00509/2019 and by Spanish national funds through the project PRECINEMUJER HAR2015-66262-P (MINECO/FEDER,UE).

Contents

Introduction: Women in Iberian filmic culture: A tour of Spain and Portugal

Elena Cordero-Hoyo and Begoña Soto-Vázquez

In addition to their geographical location, Portugal and Spain share periods of history which are, if not indivisible (we will not go so far back in time), at least have run in parallel. This is the case with the histories of their respective cinemas. The first cinema screenings in the two countries happened in the same year, with the same available projector travelling with the film to show identical animated images in the capital cities of both Spain and Portugal. E. Rousby presented an Animatograph in Madrid on 12 May 1896 and in Lisbon on 18 June of the same year (Guadaño 2014: 11). The development of the first film shoots in each country was also similar: starting out using foreign equipment and camera operators and later Spanish and Portuguese work teams. In this way, the films (most of which are lost) distributed by Robert W. Paul as *A Tour in Spain and Portugal*[1] can be used as a basis for discussing this parallel development.

The film industries and cultures of Portugal and Spain were also both culturally and politically isolated during much of the twentieth century due to the dictatorships in place in the two countries. Following a military coup in 1926, the regime of the Estado Novo was imposed in Portugal from 1933, first under António de Oliveira Salazar and then Marcelo Caetano, ending in the Carnation Revolution of 1974. In Spain the military dictatorship was preceded by a *coup d'état* in 1936 and a devastating civil war (1936–39), and continued until 1975, when a period of transition to democracy began after the death of the dictator Francisco Franco. The strict censorship enforced in both countries during this time limited themes and artistic practices adopted in cinema, and made some filmmakers seek alternatives to the imposed official discourse and pre-conceived definitions of supposed national identities. By contrast, from the 1970s onwards Spain and Portugal experienced a great change in their societies: the arrival of democracy widened not just the panorama of film production and criticism, but also opened the film industry to participation by women in areas historically assigned to men. Although each case has, obviously, its own particularities, all of the above meant that the Iberian film industries faced during their history – and continue to face today – common problems related to being on the peripheries of the main cinematographic production centres.

Despite the fact that these historical events and the development of both national cinemas occurred in contexts which are geographically, culturally and linguistically close, the relationships and exchanges between the two countries are not as fluid as one might expect. This is the case with many academic fields, where collaboration is absolutely necessary and should be effective. From our perspective, we see this lack of exchange as a problem in the area of cinema research.[2] One of the reasons for this situation is probably that Spain and Portugal are rarely seen as a joint subject of study. As a result, in film studies both countries are studied either as separate entities (Spain together with the Spanish-speaking countries in Central and South America, Portugal in the much more disperse geographical area of lusophone countries), or are bundled together as part of Ibero and Latin American studies. In fact, since 2010 the interest in gender studies has sparked the appearance of several academic publications focused on female filmmakers from these regions (Nair and Gutiérrez-Albilla 2013; Feenstra, Gimeno Ugalde and Sartingen 2014; Martin and Shaw 2017; Álvarez and Scholz 2018). However, there is a scarcity of publication focusing only on the cinematic cultures of the two Iberian states, one of the few examples being Mira's book *The Cinema of Spain and Portugal* (2005).[3] This reality may be a result of the fact that the differences between these two countries are more important than the similarities, suggesting that addressing their particular contexts together is not as logical as it seems; or that the links between them are difficult to interpret and analyse.

This collective volume brings together research into a variety of subjects, methodologies and theoretical approaches. Our objective is to enlarge the debate around the position of women in Iberian cinemas from the standpoint of such diverse fields as film analysis, cinema history, comparative studies, cultural studies, feminist theory and postcolonial studies, while being constantly aware that this variety and diversity is an essential part of the debate. We hope that these axes could create multiple intersections and link interdisciplinary works that allow the reader to reflect on the existing (dis-)connections between these cinematic traditions, while we contribute to the development of future comparative cinema studies in the region. It seems to us that one of the best places from which to tackle this initial comparison of national experiences is women in cinema, precisely because of their peripheral role within the dominant cinema culture. *Women in Iberian Filmic Culture* does not and cannot aim to be exhaustive in its scope, but it does hope to integrate or start a conversation between distant and scattered voices. It does not aim to establish a map of the whole territory, but to sketch out a roadmap from which such a project might be undertaken.

We have established various coordinates on this roadmap, and not only in the title of this book. We believe that the practical use of the term and concept *women* (in the plural) within any academic (or political) context is still useful and necessary. Although the relativization of the gender binary – including in film studies – has become evident (Feenstra, Gimeno Ugalde and Sartingen 2014: 29), the inequalities in the representation of women in audiovisual discourse and women's access to professions in cinema are still considerable. Therefore, in this book the term *women* is understood to be a historical category of analysis which meets the practical needs of academic reflection, film analysis and political action.[4] We have also chosen the geographical term *Iberian*. It is not our intention to homogenize the complex cultural and national experiences of both countries, or to question, or even to contextualize and minimize ideologically, a term with so much geopolitical potential and such considerable scope and connotations in its structural and cultural construction. Our main idea is solely to establish a much more fruitful comparative analysis in practice and theory than if we looked at the nation-states of Spain and Portugal as two separate entities. Last, our scope of reference is 'film culture', understood as all the practices that construct the experience of cinema in different territories in its extensive form, and not only those that involve films as the only point of focus, and the context of film direction and production as the only parameters worthy of analysis.

Despite comprising a perhaps overly diverse collection of essays in their methodologies and approaches to cinema and filmmakers, we conceived this volume as a project which explores cinema as the meeting point for various ways of representing and doing, focusing on its capacity to create discourse about women and women's ability to create discourse. In respect to the latter, this volume does not only deal with women exclusively as filmmakers in the restrictive sense of the term, but examines their role within a cinema culture that questions the concept of creative authorship itself – a concept which is not in the least bit favourable to the visibility of women – as the only model of involvement. Finally, the word feminist in the subtitle of the volume should also be considered in its broader sense, independent from how each chapter addresses the issue because of each author's different background, nationality, generation or, political engagement, among other factors. In any case, one of our aims was to explore the heterogeneity within feminist film studies, taking into account that the feminist discussion is almost a newcomer to the Iberian academia in general, and to film studies in particular, in comparison with other European academic contexts. For those reasons there are some chapters in which this approach could be more evident and explicit than in others.

This edited peer-reviewed book arose from a meeting of people and ideas being exposed and discussed at the international conference *Women in Iberian Cinema* held at the University of Lisbon and organised by the research group Cinema and the World – Studies on Space and Cinema (THELEME, Centre for Comparative Studies) in 2017. The symposium's very existence made obvious how seldom women's contribution to cinema has been the subject of research in articles and publications in the field of Spanish and Portuguese film studies. In this sense, and from a feminist perspective, our sole aim is not only to analyse and expose this reality, but also to contribute changing it. Within this dynamic, it is important to point out that this volume contains slightly more Portuguese authors and topics than Spanish, which is unusual in this type of comparative study where the imbalances tend to be the other way around. From the open debates that arose around the reality of women in the Iberian context sprang the desire to bring some of the most important ideas together in a book.

Although we have laid the first stone in the comparison of Iberian cinemas from a feminist perspective, there is still much work to do. Therefore, a desideratum for future projects could include some other in-depth studies of local, regional or intranational subjects, like the one by Barreiro González about the Galician example, and also to explore cinemas in different Iberian languages or dialects. In addition, the comparatist approach taken by Estela Vieira in her chapter surpasses our idea of establishing a dialogue between the texts of each section. This comparative chapter could be an inspiration for future works aligned with other articles devoted to cinema published in specialized Iberian studies publications such as *The Routledge Companion to Iberian Studies* (Amago 2017; Epps 2017), *Looking at Iberia: A Comparative European Perspective* (Gimeno Ugalde 2013) and the work of Villarmea in issue 69 of *Iberoamericana*, volume 18 (2018).

In any case, making this volume possible has been a continuous learning experience for several reasons. First, publishing a book was not a pre-conceived idea, but it followed a logical development, coming from the identification of a gap in scholarship that needed to be filled and the necessity to approach the subject from different perspectives. Second, we have experienced challenges because this is – let's say it – our first experience as editors of this type of publication and moreover in a language which is not our mother tongue. And last, we have had to deal with the confluence of the Portuguese and Spanish experience that we have lived. Both of us are of Spanish origin but have had academic, professional and personal careers in both Portugal and Spain which have overlapped and intermingled in intense but uneven ways because of work, life and the generational differences between us. We hope that this learning process has left a clear mark on the final result of our efforts, as we feel that the journey and the process should remain essential elements of our work.

This book is composed of four sections (each of which comprises three chapters), which touch upon topics that are currently the subject of debate and in which we have a personal interest: the invisibility of women in the film industry and film history; the concept of authorship and the influence that it has on the study of women's work; the value given to different non-hegemonic professions within the process of film creation; and the plurality of relationships between the production of non-fiction, archive and memory, spheres in which women are making greater inroads. Although the texts can all be read individually and in any order, we hope that dividing the chapters into four sections will serve as conversation points for further reflection. Not trying to unify the different lengths or number of figures and footnotes of the chapters has been a conscious editorial decision in order to embrace the heterogeneity intrinsic to the volume, not only in the treatment given to the themes but also in the academic writing style of the scholars coming from different backgrounds. For that reason, we believe that this apparent 'imbalance' is a strength of a volume that is making an effort to establish interdisciplinary dialogues between different theoretical fields.

The first section 'The presence of women in Iberian cinemas', proposes a theoretical approach to the position of women as professionals in Portuguese and Spanish cinema, examining the relationship between visibility and invisibility. The three chapters in this section reflect the experience of female filmmakers in both the present and the past, supported with quantitative and historical data. The virtual absence of Portuguese and Spanish women in the history of cinema is noteworthy for the double marginalization to which these women are subject: first due to social, political and economic factors related to their condition as women, and second because of the fact that they work outside the mainstream film industries.

The first chapter in the section, 'Fiction as a place of power: The presence of female directors throughout the history of Portuguese cinema' by Ana Catarina Pereira, reflects on the historical transition that female Portuguese fiction filmmakers have been through at a national level, from occupying a position of total 'otherness' to directing, having benefited from the battles won by the feminist movement. This transformation of their professional role has allowed them to, among other things, choose the themes of their work, observe from their own points of view and direct their own stories. In this way the author uses both quantitative and qualitative data to outline the principal fiction feature films directed by women, thereby creating the perfect context in which to understand their situation in Portuguese cinema.

Annette Scholz´s contribution 'The invisible women of Spanish cinema' was published in 2018 in the book *Cineastas Emergentes: Mujeres del siglo XXI*. This translation into English fills an important gap by examining the proportion of women who trained in the various professions in Spanish film schools and training institutions in comparison to women in other European countries, and the proportion of women who then went on to work in the film industry in Spain. After drawing up her own statistics, she measures in quantitative terms the number of women working on Spanish film productions and is able to highlight the reasons that underlie the inequality of their representation in the industry, despite the fact that there were more women training to work in Spanish cinema than in other European countries. Last, she analyses how the scant recognition that women filmmakers and their work have received in terms of prizes is part of the problem, and she proposes some possible actions for moving towards equality.

The third chapter in the section, '*Três dias sem Deus* by Bárbara Virgínia: A different form of representation', centres on one of the most paradigmatic cases in the history of Portuguese cinema, the film *Três dias sem Deus* (1946) by Bárbara Virgínia, considered to be the first Portuguese sound production to be directed by a woman. What remains of this film consists of a 26 minute fragment and some production documents (plot and storyboards) preserved in the Arquivo Nacional da Imagem em Movimento (ANIM – National Archive of the Moving Image) at the Cinemateca Portuguesa. Ricardo Vieira Lisboa uses these preserved resources to analyse the representation of women in the film, focusing on the figure of semi-authority embodied by a teacher in a rural school. From this case study, he explores her double role, as transmitter of the values of the dictatorship and as an example of the professional emancipation of women in Salazar's Portugal.

The second section, 'Killing the muse: Women as creator', is dedicated to women creators based on two very specific cases: Spain's Isabel Coixet and Portugal's Margarida Cardoso. Both of these contemporary filmmakers are recognized internationally for their work and have received prizes in their countries of origin, making them exceptional examples of directors in their respective film industries. Coixet has received three Goya Awards[5] as screenwriter (2003, 2005 and 2018) and two as director (2005 and 2018), while Margarida Cardoso has received a Sophia Award for best director (2016). The work of these filmmakers is the subject of the pieces by Estela Vieira, Katarzyna Paszkiewicz and Adriana Martins, whose three chapters have personal perspectives but together establish a fruitful dialogue that exceeds the limits of analysing the films of these two directors. The authors of the chapters are able to use these perspectives to reflect on the recent history of both countries, and on the need that these directors have to deconstruct their epic national stories by recovering a female voice and a female gaze.

In 'Gender violence and historical memory in Margarida Cardoso and Isabel Coixet', Estela Vieira juxtaposes the films *A costa dos murmúrios* (2004) by Margarida Cardoso and *La vida secreta de las palabras* (2005) by Isabel Coixet. Both films are an attempt by the directors to reconsider gender violence and its link to historical memory through the eyes of their female characters. Vieira supports her reflection on how the colonial past and war crimes have been represented in film with the work of these two filmmakers. In this way, her arguments contribute to the ethical debate of whether violence against women can or should be seen by spectators and how cinematographic language can or should be used to depict it.

The fifth chapter, '"People don't understand [the] world": The limits of transnational authorship in the cinema of Isabel Coixet', continues with the analysis of Coixet's recognized transnational oeuvre and career. Analysing the film *Nadie quiere la noche* (2015), Katarzyna Paszkiewicz presents the debates around the notions of authorship, and more specifically female authorship. In addition, she uses this case study to analyse the way in which Coixet critiques imperialist narratives and questions her own position as a white author and an individualist and exclusionary model in postcolonial experience.

In 'Murmuring colonial ghosts in Margarida Cardoso's filmography', Adriana Martins points out Margarida Cardoso's uniqueness in Portuguese cinema in the way that she confronts Portugal's colonial past. To do this, she applies a comparative methodology to the films *A costa dos murmúrios* (2004) and *Yvonne Kane* (2014), which she sees as a path towards a better understanding of Cardoso's filmography and her representation and critique of the power relationships between colonizers and colonized. Martins centres her analysis on the filmmaker's interest in contrasting cultural and marginal historical memory presented through the perspective of female characters.

The third section, 'Beyond the author: Recognizing other cinematographic professions', explores other professions connected with cinema culture, attempting to step away from a limiting focus on film direction and establish a broader perspective that takes into account the various roles involved in filmmaking. This is why the section comprises three chapters dedicated to three under-appreciated and, until now, very rarely studied trades where women had or still have a predominant position: film criticism, institutional film censorship and costume design.

The seventh chapter, 'Weaving a cinematographic culture and writing about film, or how to reconstruct the subject of women in Spanish silent cinema', is fundamental for the understanding of this book, as it develops the concept of cinema culture that guides a large part of this tome. Here, Begoña Soto-Vázquez discusses the many women writing about cinema in Spain in the early decades of the twentieth century and the invisibility surrounding the important role they played in the construction of cinema culture in the history of Spanish cinema. The author points out two key aspects as possible reasons for their lack of visibility: on the one hand, a lack of interest in and knowledge about the, mainly female, cinema-going public, and on the other, historians' weakness for the two apparently inseparable concepts of 'oeuvre' and 'author' (most commonly conjugated as masculine and singular).

Ana Bela Morais introduces the reader to one of the least explored and most unpopular professions in the social and political history of cinema: film censorship over a seven-year period during the Portuguese dictatorship (1968–74). This profession is of capital importance (on an aesthetic, political, industrial and cultural level) in the construction of the cinema created in the Iberian countries due to their very lengthy dictatorships, but has been largely ignored in the field of film studies. In 'A woman censor during the Portuguese dictatorship (1968–74)', Morais delves into the subjectivity of the censors within apparently institutional and objective parameters, illustrating her hypothesis with the writings of Portuguese censor Mariana Rita Nova Goa.

The last chapter in this section, 'Costume designers in Portugal: A trade between art and technique relegated to the status of "a woman's thing"' by Caterina Cucinotta, is devoted to a profession where the majority of workers are women and which the author knows well, as she is herself a film costume designer. This being one of the few texts about this activity in Portugal, Cucinotta exposes the lack of recognition received by those working in the profession, a situation exemplified by the lack of consensus over its official name and the general disregard for the skill needed to do this work. The author also notes that one possible reason why costume design is so undervalued within the industry and history of film is that it is mainly women who work in this area, and proposes that the authorship of cinema production should be understood from a wider and more inclusive perspective.

Finally, the fourth section, 'Historical memory and the gendered archive', connects family, regional and national history with film documentation as a witness of the passage of time. The three chapters in this section raise questions around dualities such as those between the individual and the social, the domestic and the political, and the contemporary and the historical. In this way, one of its common themes is how problematic it is to see the archive as a plastic concept that speaks directly of the land and of memory, and how women creators take advantage of these points of reference to develop their own vision in their non-fiction works.

Érica Faleiro Rodrigues centres her chapter 'Paradigms: Women filmmakers in 1970s revolutionary Portugal – Delgado, Nordlund, Cordeiro and Serra' on four documentaries directed by women shortly after the Carnation Revolution which ended the dictatorship in Portugal in 1974. The films analysed – Noémia Delgado's *Máscaras* from 1976; Solveig Nordlund's *A lei da terra* from 1977; António Reis and Margarida Cordeiro's *Trás-os-Montes* from 1976; and Manuela Serra's *O movimento das coisas* from 1979 to 1985 – are examples of the reflections of female Portuguese filmmakers on the turbulence of the times. Rodrigues also analyses their careers as individuals, within cooperatives and in partnerships, as well as their preference for documentaries about rural communities, through which they attempted to capture and rediscover the Portuguese agricultural experience before its inevitable change as a consequence of the post-revolutionary agrarian reform brought about by modernity and democracy.

Galician migration as a trauma or wound is the main theme of the chapter by María Soliña Barreiro González, 'The mother awaits: Woman and landscape in Galician non-fiction cinema'. She explores the relationship between the archetype of the mother 'who awaits' and the landscape of Galicia, a region in the north west of the Iberian Peninsula, in various non-fiction films (migrant films, documentaries and promotional films). These audiovisual formats, historically undervalued in the field of film studies, play a fundamental role in the experience of migrants by means of the construction of the image of the immutable mother/land which will not betray their memory or question their right to return.

Finally, in the last chapter, 'Exploring the Portuguese memory through appropriation film: *A toca do lobo* (Mourão, 2015)', Elena Cordero-Hoyo reflects on the fragmentation of family memory, and on its relationship with national Portuguese memory from the perspective of filmmaker Catarina Mourão in her documentary *A toca do lobo* (2015). As a parameter for comparison, the author borrows Laura Mulvey's notions of 'palimpsest' – understood as the inscription of a new text onto a previous one – 'gleaning' – the process of collecting, accumulating and recycling pre-existing materials – and 'detournement' – the act of inscribing a new meaning to existing material that supplants the original one – which are used to analyse the compilation film *Un'ora sola ti vorrei* (2002) by the Italian Alina Marazzi. Mulvey's feminist perspective helps Cordero-Hoyo to understand how the documentary is created by interweaving archive material with family history to discuss the political structures of a country, the circularity of memory and the passing of time.

Acknowledgements

Before ending this introduction we must give thanks for the confidence invested in us by Intellect Books and their team in accepting our editorial project without hesitation, as well as for their guidance during the entire journey. In addition, we would like to thank Catarina Mourão for generously providing the image for the cover (from her film *A toca do lobo*, 2015).

Likewise, we would like to express our gratitude to the generous and essential work of our three scientific editors, Ana Cabral Martins, Marina Díaz and Alejandra Rosenberg, without whose help this book would not be of the quality that it is today. As English is not the mother tongue of either of the editors, we have relied on the help of all the authors and the patience and work of Teresa Ortiz, Aileen Robinson and Robin Driver. We are also thankful to all the researchers for their hard work in producing really interesting contributions, and for their patience during the revision process.

We will end at the beginning, where it all started, by thanking the main organisers of the conference from which the idea for this project arose: Filipa Rosário and Mariana Liz, who gave the green light to making this book a reality. And of course, our thanks also go to the institutions which have supported us economically, organizationally and administratively in this long process, from the moment the idea was conceived to it finally becoming a book: The Centre for Comparative Studies of University of Lisbon's School of Arts and Humanities and the University of Girona from the research project: *Presencias y representaciones de la mujer en el cine de los orígenes* (Presence and Representation of Women in Early Cinema).

They have all helped us on this journey, which we hope many will now enjoy and which, above all, we hope will help readers to learn as much as we have.

Elena Cordero-Hoyo and Begoña Soto-Vázquez
Madrid, Lisbon, June 2019

REFERENCES

Álvarez, Marta and Scholz, Annette (eds) (2018), *Cineastas emergentes: Mujeres en el cine del siglo XXI*, Madrid and Frankfurt: Iberoamericana Vervuet.

Amago, Samuel (2017), 'Reflexivity in Iberian documentary film', in J. Muñoz-Basols, L. Lonsdale and M. Delgado (eds), *The Routledge Companion to Iberian Studies*, London: Routledge, pp. 639–51.

Christie, Ian (n.d.), 'Spanish detective work', Paul's Animatograph Works, https://paulsanimatographworks.wordpress.com. Accessed 29 December 2018.

Epps, Brad (2017), '(Inter)national spectres: cinema in mid-twentieth-century Iberia', in J. Muñoz-Basols, L. Lonsdale and M. Delgado (eds), *The Routledge Companion to Iberian Studies*, London: Routledge, pp. 516–27.

Feenstra, Pietsie, Gimeno Ugalde, Esther and Sartingen, Kathrin (eds) (2014), *Directoras de cine en España y América Latina: Nuevas voces y miradas*, Frankfurt: Peter Lang Edition.

Gimeno Ugalde, Esther (2013), 'Polyglot Iberia – or what is the place for Iberian languages in current cinema? Presence (and absence) of Iberian languages in cinema', in S. Pérez Isasi and Â. Fernandes (eds), *Looking at Iberia: A Comparative European Perspective*, Oxford: Peter Lang, pp. 265–92.

Guadaño, Luis (2014), 'Edwin Rousby: Un misterio desvelado', *FILMHISTORIA Online*, XXIV: 2, pp. 1–31.

Martin, Deborah and Shaw, Deborah (2017), *Latin American Women Filmmakers: Production, Politics, Poetics*, London and New York: I. B. Tauris.

Mira, Alberto (2005), *The Cinema of Spain and Portugal*, London: Wallflower Press.

Nair, Parvati and Gutiérrez-Albilla, Julián Daniel (eds) (2013), *Hispanic and Lusophone Women Filmmakers: Theory, Practice and Difference*, Manchester: Manchester University Press.

Scholz, Annette (2018), 'Las invisibles del cine español', in M. Álvarez and A. Scholz (eds), *Cineastas emergentes: Mujeres en el cine del siglo XXI*, Madrid and Frankfurt: Iberoamericana Vervuet, pp. 45–69.

Soto Vázquez, Begoña (2004), 'Lo que de real tiene el mar: Sobre *A Tour in Spain and Portugal* (R. W. Paul/H. W. Short, 1896)', in *El documental carcoma de la ficción: X Congreso de la Asociación española de Historiadores del Cine*, Granada, 12–15 February, Córdoba: Filmoteca de Andalucía, pp. 205, 211.

Talavera Mila, Julio (2014), *Female Directors in European Films: State of Play and Evolution between 2003 and 2012*, Brussels: European Audiovisual Observatory.

Villarmea, Iván (2018), 'Rostros y espacios de la austeridad en los cines ibéricos (2007–2016)', *Iberoamericana*, 18:69, pp. 13–36.

NOTES

1. *A Tour in Spain and Portugal* or *A Tour through Spain and Portugal* (Christie, n.d.) is the name under which a series of fourteen films were distributed (although a total of eighteen were filmed). Shot in 1896 by Henry Short, who was sent to film in Spain (Cadiz, Seville and Madrid) and Portugal (Lisbon, Algés and Cascais) by Robert W. Paul, these seem to be, if not strictly the first, some of the earliest images filmed in both countries (Soto Vázquez 2004: 209).
2. Perhaps the only exception to this rule is research centred on the relationship between the cinema of both countries during the civil war and the immediate post-war period. See work by Alberto Pena Rodríguez and Fernando González.
3. We find it significant that this one example is by a British publisher and therefore aimed at an English-speaking audience.
4. Both countries have a low ratio of women directors to national film production. Portugal is below the European average and Spain only just reaches the average. See Talavera Mira (2014) for more data on female directors in the European context.
5. The Goya Awards are the annual prizes that have been awarded by the Academia de las Artes y las Ciencias Cinematográficas de España (the Spanish Academy of Cinematic Film Arts and Sciences) since 1986. The Sophia Awards are the annual prizes that have been awarded by the Academia Portuguesa de Cinema (the Portuguese Academy of Cinema) since 2011.

PART I

The presence of women in Iberian cinemas

Fiction as a place of power: The presence of female directors throughout the history of Portuguese cinema

Ana Catarina Pereira

To reflect upon the evolution of the women who have directed fiction films in Portugal is to carry out a study of women who have reversed a dominant tendency throughout the twentieth century: that of occupying other jobs in cinema, far from the possibility of effectively assuming the direction of a film. In this way, the reflection that we initiate here intends to analyse a certain abandonment of the place of the *other* (turning to the feminist and existentialist terminology proposed by Simone de Beauvoir[1]), as well as the process of constructing a device in which the woman is elected, observed or understood by herself.

Any historical and/or sociological study concerning Portugal, or specific moments in its history, cannot, of course, ignore the fact that the conditions for ensuring equal opportunities between the genders would be different before and after the establishment of democracy. The dictatorial period (designated as the Estado Novo or New State), beginning with the 1926 military coup and ending on 25 April 1974, led to innumerable legal, moral, educational and social consequences for the feminine condition. The possibility of more women being able to dedicate themselves to a profession such as filmmaking should also, therefore, be read in light of these dates.

In relation to methodology, we should highlight the continuity of this study, which began as part of a Ph.D. thesis[2] that also advanced a sociological and quantitative approach, comprising a panoramic examination of more than a century of history. The collected data allows us to carry out different readings, in the sense of expected evolutions that did not actually come about. We will therefore focus on identifying women who have directed full-length feature films in Portugal. The impossibility of covering all Portuguese film production from the end of the nineteenth century until the present day is a combination of several factors, which include: (a) the difficulty of cataloguing all the short and long films directed and produced to date in Portugal, as a result of the sheer number of records on short films held by Portuguese Cinematheque and the National Archive for Moving Images (ANIM);[3] (b) the space-time dimension of our research; (c) the required financial investment, which is substantially higher in relation to full-length films[4] than for short films, and for fiction films rather than for documentaries.[5] For the reasons outlined above, a case study of full-length feature films is relevant from the perspective of gender studies: being the most expensive genre, it is also the most inaccessible to a gender that may be discriminated against in terms of equal opportunities.

In historical terms, we now know that during the Estado Novo there was only one full-length feature film directed by a woman in Portugal (Castro 2000; Matos-Cruz 1999; Pereira 2016). Released on 30 August 1945 at the Cine Ginásio in Lisbon, *Três dias sem Deus* by Bárbara Virgínia is an adaptation of the book *Mundo perdido* by Gentil Marques.[6] The film focuses on a young schoolteacher who goes to a small village in the mountains to teach. A few days after her arrival in the lost and secluded place, Lídia is informed by the doctor that he and the priest will be absent from the village to go to the city: there will as a result be 'three days without God', according to popular wisdom. In the meantime, the teacher becomes acquainted with Paulo Belforte, whom the villagers accuse of having a 'pact with the devil' for the alleged murder of his wife and attempting to set the local church on fire. *Três dias sem Deus* (Virgínia, 1945) therefore represents the debut of Portuguese women in directing fiction films, and also provides the first example of the gothic cinematographic genre in Portugal; the work of light and shadow that can be perceived in the remaining images from the film suggest this aesthetic choice.

On 20 September 1946 Cannes hosted the first International Film Festival. This first instance of the festival presented in competition films such as *Roma, città aperta* (Rossellini, 1945), *Brief Encounter* (Lean, 1945), *Gilda* (Vidor, 1946) and also two Portuguese films – *Camões* by José Leitão de Barros and *Três dias sem Deus* by Bárbara Virgínia. Of the latter, only about 25 minutes of film, which have never been restored, remain at the National Archive for Moving Images. Therefore, the film is significant in terms of cinema history less for its narrative and visual construction than for the director's pioneer spirit. As it is not possible to perform a cinematographic analysis of the film from a contemporary point of view, this case study is restricted to the director's testimonies, collected at the time and in the following years, without the possibility of accessing the images that could retell the story and the vision that she intended to transmit.

From the invisibility to which the history of Portuguese cinema has consigned the director, Bárbara Virgínia has, in recent years, come to receive sporadic but valuable tributes. In 2015, from 5 to 7 June, a documentary exhibition (consisting essentially of video testimonies and some photographs of the director) was shown during the second Olhares do Mediterrâneo Film Festival at the São Jorge Cinema in Lisbon.[7] In October 2017 Luísa Sequeira premiered *Quem é Bárbara Virgínia?* (2017) at the Doclisboa Film Festival. The synopsis reads: '[t]his is a work of human and emotional archeology that brings to light the life and work of a woman who did much for lusophone culture and who was forgotten'. The film won the Best Documentary award in that year's Caminhos do Cinema Português and at the first Porto Femme Film Festival in June 2018. It continues to be regularly screened at festivals, mainly in Portugal and Brazil, contributing, in this way, to the efforts to ascribe Bárbara Virgínia her rightful place in cinema history and to the reconstruction of her biography.

The work of Bárbara Virgínia has not been the subject of much analysis and reflection in the literature; Marisa Vieira (2009) dedicated her final degree thesis to the subject, as did Ricardo Vieira Lisboa (2017) with his master's dissertation. The last interview given by Bárbara Virgínia[8] during her lifetime was published by Ana Catarina Pereira and Wiliam Pianco in the second issue of the *International Journal of Cinema* (2017). From among nostalgic recollections and, on occasion, instances of unsound reasoning – caused by a degenerative neurological disease that was already in an advanced stage – some outbursts of protest made by the pioneer who broke into an exclusively masculine universe stand out: 'Women never sought cinema like this [as film directors]. You see that even today, in the world, we have very few women directing cinema. Women, I believe, have never taken themselves seriously in this respect. I don't know' (Virgínia 2017: 23).[9] From the discourse briefly quoted here, what comes to the fore is the fact that Bárbara Virgínia occupied a pioneering and solipsistic position, with the resulting absence of colleagues with whom she could exchange experiences, and also accompanied by a low female self-confidence, enhanced by the patriarchal structures of society which would not allow women to occupy positions previously exclusive to the male sphere.

The lack of awareness of Bárbara Virgínia's story, even among film studies researchers, dialogues with the 'archive fever'[10] that Jacques Derrida (2001) associates with the institutionalization of certain authors and the power relations assigned to the same process. His essay of the same name, it is worth mentioning, critically links the concepts of 'history', 'truth' and 'power' with that of the archive. In this sense, the author questions the relevance of that support, which, besides registering statements, hierarchically orders them in their various discursive series, motivating more critical and detailed analysis of the historical knowledge passed to future generations both for tradition as well as for institutions of knowledge. From the same perspective, Michel Foucault matches the archive to the 'law of what can be said; the system that governs the emergence of statements as singular events'[11] (Foucault 1987: 149). In this brief study, which intends to systematically analyse the number of women who have had the opportunity to direct fiction films in Portugal, it is not for us to question the neglect of and recent tributes to Bárbara Virgínia in the history of Portuguese cinema; we do, although, highlight the phenomenon as a possible encouragement to future researchers.

The historical importance of other female representatives in the restricted cinematographic market should not, however, remain hidden – a fact which demands their rescue. In support of this, the book *Cineastas portuguesas: 1874–1956* by Ilda Castro (2000) assumes a fundamental importance, being essentially a biographical and encyclopaedic register as far as the filmmakers of the first half of the twentieth century are concerned. The information collected in it can also be cross-referenced with other encyclopaedic works, as we did with *O cais do olhar – O cinema português de longa-metragem e a ficção muda* compiled by José de Matos-Cruz and edited by the Portuguese Cinematheque (1999).

When reading both of these works, it becomes clear that Virgínia de Castro e Almeida is the first woman to play a significant role in the history of cinema in Portugal. She was also a writer (of numerous children's literature books), translator and founder of the production company Fortuna Filmes, established in 1922. Her first production was *A sereia de pedra*[12] (Lion, 1923), which was followed by *Os olhos da alma* (Lion, 1923), both French–Portuguese co-productions (Castro 2000; Matos-Cruz 1999). She never assumed the role of director. Maria Emília Castelo Branco, on the other hand, was an actress, producer and director. In 1930 she produced *O Castelo das Berlengas* (Leitão, 1930) and in 1957 she directed the documentary *Roteiros líricos do Douro*. In *Cineastas portuguesas* she is presented as 'the beautiful girl of Portuguese Cinema during the silent cinema period' (Castro 2000: 24) due to her participation in the two films produced by Virgínia de Castro e Almeida, as well as in *O diabo em Lisboa* (Lupo, 1926), *Táxi 9297* (Ferreira, 1927) and *Zé do Telhado* (Lupo, 1929).

Maria Helena Matos is the first woman to whom reference is made in terms of co-writing a screenplay. She was also an actress and assistant in the film *Campinos do Ribatejo* (Lopes, 1932) (Matos-Cruz 1999). Two decades later, the film *A luz vem do alto* (Campos, 1959), a drama in which two friends confront their deep religiosity and atheism, was produced by Maria Dulce, while Maria Teresa Ramos was the director's assistant. This film received the Grand Prize of the SNI (Secretariado Nacional de Informação/National Information Secretariat), the Best Actor award (Mário Pereira) and the Best Cinematographic Adaptation award (Fernando Fragoso) (Matos-Cruz 1999).

Another impressive accomplishment was achieved by the writer and director Maria Luísa Bivar who, between 1962 and 1964 (a period of only three years), directed 70 documentaries for the Junta de Acção Social (the Board of Social Action), including *Folhas de ouro* (1962), *Barros de Estremoz* (1962), *Trabalhos de cortiça* (1963) and *Figuras do mar* (1963), among many others.[13]

Teresa Olga would later be the first female director for Portuguese television. With strong connections to the cinema world, she was able to fulfil technical roles in several films of the Novo Cinema Português (New Portuguese Cinema). She was production assistant for *Domingo à tarde* (Macedo, 1966) and *Mudar de vida* (Rocha, 1966), and edited *Uma abelha na chuva* (Lopes, 1972) and *Pedro Só* (Tropa, 1972). In the 1990s she directed two documentaries for RTP: *Aristides de Sousa Mendes – O consul injustiçado* (1992) and *Humberto Delgado – Obviamente assassinaram-no* (1995).

The 1970 film *Nem amantes, nem amigos* (Vitorino, 1979) features notable participation from Ivone de Moura: in the technical roles list, her name appears as director's assistant, next to Afonso de Sousa and Nuno Vitorino, but it also appears as 'collaborator in direction'. The work tells the story of a woman in love with the characters that a man plays in the theatre and is an adaptation of a novel written by the director himself. Having been censored, it did not premiere at the Portuguese Cinematheque until 28 April 1983 (Matos-Cruz 1999).

In an attempt to establish a relationship between these women's pioneering efforts with the career path taken by others in literature, we are able to perceive, once again, the increased difficulties and the place of power that cinema in general, and fictional cinema in particular, represents in an artistic context. It can be considered that the process of emancipation of the Portuguese woman as a writer was able to begin even in an adverse context such as the Estado Novo. Names like Ana de Castro Osório, Judith Teixeira, Maria Lamas, Irene Lisboa, Virgínia de Castro e Almeida, Florbela Espanca, Maria Archer and Ilse Losa, who had already established literary careers, inspired authors in the 1960s, such as Sophia de Mello Breyner, Maria Velho da Costa, Maria Teresa Horta, Maria Isabel Barreno, Natália Correia, Luiza Neto Jorge and Fiama Hasse Pais Brandão. The 1960s and 1970s were thus determinant for Portuguese literature. Our list is not exhaustive, but only illustrative of the political movement that advocated the emergence of more women writers, who are today read and recognized nationally and internationally. The same movement did not materialize in cinema, and particularly in the world of fictional films – and based on the data which we will presently examine, we dare to say that this is still the case today. The high costs, as well as the slowness of the production processes and the management of large teams, might be some of the reasons for this persistent discrimination.

Already in a democratic context, and returning to our central case study, the second full-length feature film directed by a woman in Portugal dates back to 1976. *Trás-os-Montes*, co-directed by António Reis and Margarida Cordeiro, was also the only one made in the 1970s. In the anthropological portrait created by the directors, a rural, north-eastern province of Portugal is evoked, where the absence of the departed is as striking as the presence of those who insist on compliance with centuries-old traditions. The tradition of ethnographic cinema – of which *Acto da Primavera* (Oliveira, 1962), *Festa, trabalho e pão em Grijó da Parada* (Costa e Silva, 1973) and *Falamos de Rio de Onor* (Campos, 1974) are examples – was further enriched with this film. It should be remembered, however, that these gazes come from a Lisbon that was experiencing a kind of revolutionary fever that was eager to show the rural, isolated Portugal that the Salazarist dictatorship tried to hide – poetry attentive to politics, as well as to life conditions in rural areas, memory, earth and landscape. Jean Rouch and other French critics would widely praise the film ('Ce film est pour moi la révélation d'un nouveau langage cinématographique'[14]), in contrast to the silence about and ignorance of the couple's work in Portugal. Their films continue to be seen and discussed in an academic context, without any further action being taken for them to reach the general public.[15] Nevertheless, the little importance attributed to Margarida Cordeiro as a colleague and companion of António Reis – a situation that would cause the filmmaker to isolate herself, refusing interviews, public testimonies or participation in exhibition of her films after Reis' death – has also not yet been duly justified or studied, which leaves considerable space for future reflection.

Besides the two films already mentioned, another 38 feature-length films were produced before the end of 2009. As demonstrated in Figure 1, the first 'strong decade' in terms of female production can be seen in the 1980s, with the premiere of seven films. It is after this that women's difficult entry into an art form previously reserved for men begins, with the likes of Margarida Gil, Monique Rutler and Solveig Nordlund – who we might consider to be the first generation of female filmmakers in Portugal.

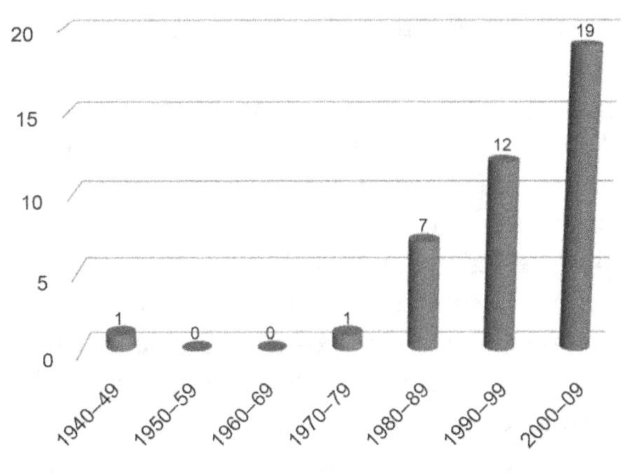

FIGURE 1: Evolution of the number of feature-length films made by women in Portugal. Source: Pereira, 2016.

As Figure 1 shows, the 1990s followed the growing trend, corresponding to a remarkable period in the history of Portuguese cinema on several levels. Following the recent establishment of democracy in Portugal in 1974 and the country's entry into the European Union in 1986, the attempt to promulgate measures that would foster equal opportunities generated debate and criticism. Some of the more complex films released at that time – by Teresa Villaverde (*Três Irmãos*, 1994 and *Os Mutantes*, 1998), Pedro Costa (*Ossos*, 1997), Margarida Gil (*Rosa Negra*, 1992 and *O Anjo da Guarda*, 1998), Solveig Nordlund (*Até amanhã, Mário*, 1994) and João César Monteiro (*A comédia de Deus*, 1995 and *As bodas de Deus*, 1999) – unveil divisive distances, while denouncing the many problems that suffocate certain segments of society. The images of children and teenagers growing up in a country of marginalized suburbs, uncertainty in the face of that which is new, and perennial injustices would be dominant motifs in the cinematography of those years and continue into the early years of the new millennium.

In this context, Monique Rutler decided to make a period film. Looking to the past, she questioned the present and envisaged a future that could go backwards in terms of human rights if the ruling powers were not held to account for consenting in the discriminatory treatment of women and the working classes. After intense research, the Franco-Portuguese filmmaker made a film/complaint about the history of Adelaide Coelho da Cunha (1863–1942) – the daughter of the founder of the newspaper *Diário de Notícias* and the first wife of one of its directors – who was hospitalized and subjected to improper psychiatric care for having decided to embark on an adulterous love affair.

Solo de Violino (1992) takes place in the period following the establishment of the Portuguese Republic (5 October 1910). Revealing the beginning of Adelaide's passion for Manuel, the bourgeois family's driver who was 23 years younger than her, the film highlights the process of her forced hospitalization by her husband without any respect for the principles that govern the careful development of a diagnosis of mental ill-health. The film portrays Egas Moniz (the only Portuguese person to be awarded the Nobel Prize for Medicine in 1949), Júlio de Matos (the then director of Hospital Miguel Bombarda) and Sobral Cid (professor of psychiatry at the University of Coimbra, who came to assume the functions of civil governor of the district of Coimbra and Minister of Public Instruction in two of the governments of the First Portuguese Republic). Due to its choice of subject matter, the film, with Fernanda Lapa and André Gago in the main roles, might have been expected to generate greater consternation, arousing a parallel interest in the public. However, having its theatrical release in only three theatres throughout the whole country, its total audience was only 2,706 according to the data provided by the Cinema and Audio-visual Institute (ICA).

Rosa Negra by Margarida Gil premiered in the same year. With an established career in film direction and television production, as well as her work as a professor at the Universidade Nova de Lisboa and the direction of the Portuguese Association of Filmmakers, she is one of the most canonical filmmakers mentioned in our study. As a filmmaker, she is part of a generation that includes Alberto Seixas Santos, Fernando Lopes, Paulo Rocha, João César Monteiro and Rita Azevedo Gomes, among others, who have incessantly sought to create a connection between national cinema and art house films, and between Portuguese literature and Portuguese cinema. In terms of the films of Margarida Gil, the script of *Relação fiel e verdadeira* (1987), for example, was written with Luísa Neto Jorge and that of *Rosa Negra* (1992) with Maria Velho da Costa. Born in Covilhã in the 1950s, the director returns to her origins four decades later to film a story of memories and disagreements, unveiling a Serra da Estrela permanently afflicted by wildfires. The film dialogues offer the mimesis of a closed city with which the filmmaker seems to have a score to settle. 'Adeus, terra adormecida, adeus, que me vou embora' ('Goodbye, sleeping land, goodbye, I'm leaving') sings Teresa Salgueiro in the purposeful composition by João Gil that features in this film. Running throughout the narrative is the sharing of experiences of the feminine condition, synthesized in the speech of one of the characters: 'I [...] before me, my mother, daughter of another woman' – generations that convey melancholy, a lack of support and the will for something which seems always harder to achieve due to a particular condition, like the train that comes from Lisbon and, travelling through idyllic landscapes, takes so long to arrive. Mário Viegas and Zita Duarte would also play their last roles in this film.

The end of the 1990s saw the first screening of Teresa Villaverde's *Os Mutantes*. The third feature of this filmmaker, after *A idade maior* (1991) and *Três irmãos* (1994), represents her ultimate consecration, nationally and internationally. Villaverde's initial idea, which she described in several interviews, was to film a documentary about children and teenagers raised in foster homes. Due to the impossibility of capturing real-life images and testimonies, her decision to opt instead for fiction resulted in the creation of a character – Andreia – who constantly escapes from social reintegration centres and wanders the streets of Lisbon looking for the boy who got her pregnant. Pedro and Ricardo, in a similar situation, try everything in order to survive, including petty thefts and posing for photos for perverted Dutchmen. The three adolescents are 'mutants': fragile and exhausted beings, maladjusted to a reality that does not offer them alternatives to the violence in which they were raised.

At the beginning of the twenty-first century, almost half of the 40 films that constitute the totality of our case study had been released. A further nineteen feature films date from 2000 to 2009, with the names of Catarina Ruivo, Cláudia Tomaz and Raquel Freire among the newest generation of Portuguese filmmakers. We then tried to determine if the distribution of films was equitable among these filmmakers, drawing the conclusions detailed in Figure 2.

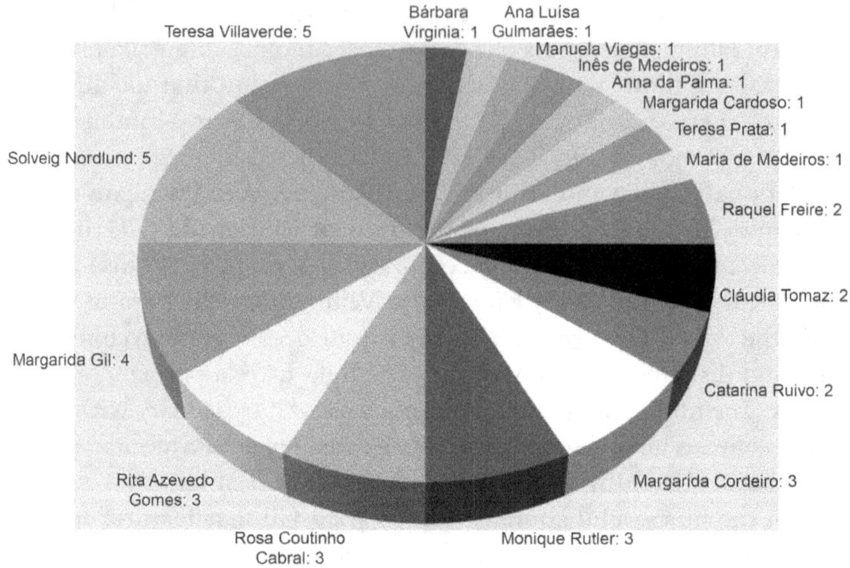

FIGURE 2: Distribution of number of films per director for the period 2000–09. Source: Pereira, 2016.

Teresa Villaverde and Solveig Nordlund are the filmmakers who have directed the largest number of feature films (five each), followed by Margarida Gil with four. At the same time, eight of the filmmakers listed have made only one full-length feature. It should also be noted that although the period 2000 to 2009 shows a significant increase in production, this was counterbalanced by a parallel increase in the number of films made by men. In percentage terms, the conclusions we wish to present here can be demonstrated by the data shown in Figure 3.

The data in Figure 3 confirms that Portuguese women filmmakers have directed 14 per cent of the feature films that gained a theatrical release between 1980 and 2009. Nevertheless, if we were to count all the feature-length films made by women since the beginning of the history of Portuguese cinema, this percentage would be significantly reduced.

In the necessary updating of this data in order to assess its evolution, we are, of course, tracking the contemporary course of the present decade since 2010. Nevertheless, we sought, along with the ICA, to determine the number of feature films directed by women filmmakers and premiered in Portugal while retaining the distinction between majority and minority national production.[16] According to the new data from the ICA, 31 national feature-length films were premiered in 2017. Among these, only one was directed by a woman: *O divã de Estaline* by Fanny Ardant. It is a minority national production, directed by the French actress

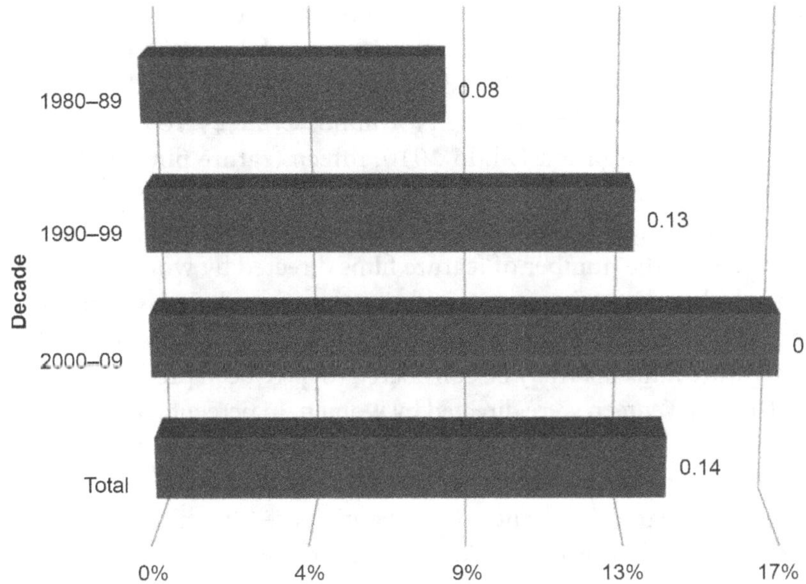

FIGURE 3: Percentage of Portuguese films directed by women from 1980 to 2009, constructed from the list drawn up by the ICA.

and director. The year before, in 2016, eighteen feature films were released. Of these, only *Jogo de damas*, by Patrícia Sequeira, can be included in the films that this study focuses on. In 2015, of the nineteen feature films directed and released in Portugal, only three were directed by women, namely: *Alda e Maria, Por Aqui Tudo Bem* by Pocas Pascoal, *Bobô* by Inês Oliveira and *Yvone Kane* by Margarida Cardoso.

Back in 2014, 24 feature films were released, but only two of them can be included in our case study and both in the national minority production category. We are referring to *Cadences obstinées*, again by Fanny Ardant, and *Bridges of Sarajevo*, a collaboration by Leonardo di Costanzo, Jean-Luc Godard, Kamen Kalev, Isild Le Besco, Sergei Loznitsa, Vincenzo Marra, Ursula Meier, Vladimir Perisic, Cristi Puiu, Marc Recha, Angela Schanelec, Aida Begic and Teresa Villaverde. In 2013 the number of full-length fictional features premiered in theatres totalled sixteen. Only *Em segunda mão*, by Catarina Ruivo, can be counted in this study. In 2012, 24 feature-length films were released, five of which are relevant to our discussion: *A vingança de uma mulher* by Rita Azevedo Gomes; *Capitães de areia*, a Brazilian production with some Portuguese funding co-directed by Cecília Amado and Guy Gonçalves; *As linhas de Wellington* by Valeria Sarmiento; *Paixão* by Margarida Gil; and another collaboration: *O que há de novo no amor?* by Hugo Alves, Mónica Santana Baptista, Hugo Martins, Tiago Nunes, Rui Santos and Patrícia Raposo.

In 2011 only sixteen national feature films were released, among which are three major national productions relevant to our study, coincidentally directed by the three filmmakers with the highest production in the previous decades. They are: *A morte de Carlos Gardel* by Solveig Nordlund, *Cisne* by Teresa Villaverde and *Perdida Mente* by Margarida Gil. In 2010, fifteen feature films were premiered, with only *Cinerama* by Inês Oliveira being eligible for this case study.

Although the decade beginning in 2010 has not yet concluded, there has been a decreasing trend in the number of feature films directed by women, a trend which deserves much closer attention from institutions and foundations capable of funding these films. Our research shows – and emphasizing the seriousness of this fact – that of the 163 feature films that may be considered to have been produced nationally in this period, only seventeen were directed by women. In percentage terms, this corresponds to only 10.4 per cent. It should be remembered that in the first decade of the twenty-first century this percentage was more promising, reaching 17 per cent. The prospect of greater representativeness anticipated by the data relating to the period 2000 to 2009 is now contradicted by a decrease in the number of films made by women since 2010, which continues to configure the feature film as a sphere of power within a structure which is still eminently patriarchal.

In this sense, we also have a linear conclusion of an essentially performative nature: if a film's meaning is produced at the moment of reception, it is necessary for films to be watched for this to take place. From this fact arises a new urgency: we must work on encouraging audiences to request, provoke and react to films made by women. In the specific case study of our research, getting audiences to watch films directed by women – so that they can identify with a different perspective than the usual – implies a huge task in creating alternative structures for commercial exhibition circuits. The list of required tasks may include film presentations in the presence of filmmakers and special sessions in classrooms, film clubs or associations dedicated to the promotion of egalitarian and feminist social causes.

Several other suggestions have been made in order to reverse or get around the commercial logic of distributors. The use of independent producers, preferably those dedicated to art house films, the widespread distribution of digital versions of films, or even directors assuming production themselves through other types of support – online, for example – are all possible strategies. In addition, we also consider that it is important to create a women's film festival in Portugal (as has been done in other countries of the European Union and the United States of America) where their films could be screened.

In this connection, we consider it pertinent also to present some data collected with the help of two private organizations – Women Make Movies and Women in the Director's Chair – underlining the difficulty (if not the impossibility) of devising a conclusive list of women's film festivals, since many initiatives are emerging at the same time as others are suspended or concluded. Although we did not have access to updated data from these two organizations, we cross-checked the information collected with that available on the Festival Focus website and with parallel surveys conducted online.

We emphasize that we have made a methodological choice not to refer to specialized festivals, such as the numerous events dedicated to women of a single race or ethnicity (for example, the International Black Women's Film Festival in Oakland, USA) or those for women with a specific sexual orientation (such as Cineffable – Festival International du film lesbien et féministe de Paris). We also excluded a festival dedicated solely to animation films by women – Tricky Women Film Festival in Vienna – because it was limited to this genre. The festivals mentioned in our final list (Pereira 2016: appendices) are thus aimed at women directors regardless of their race, religion, country of origin, sexual orientation or even the cinematographic genre to which they are dedicated.

In statistical terms, there were 53 women's film festivals in 2012 (the conclusion date of the first part of our study): we emphasize that we refer to films made by women, and not restricted participation by women in other categories worldwide. Of these, 24 events – corresponding to 45 per cent – occurred in the United States of America and more than half (62 per cent) took place on the American continent. Fourteen events with similar purposes were held in Europe, five in Asia, only one in Oceania and none on the African continent.

Portugal was included in a list of countries – which included countries with much larger population sizes, such as Russia and China – without any women's film festivals. It is worth pointing out that, on the other side of the Iberian Peninsula, in Spain, there are two events of this nature (Mufest in Santiago de Compostela and Mujeres en dirección in Cuenca). In performative terms, we argued at the time of the conclusion of our thesis that the existence of a festival of this kind could encourage a greater number of filmmakers to make films, as well as to promote the debate on issues related to equal opportunities in democracy. Right on time, Ana Castro and Rita Capucho, cultural programmers and film club attendees, joined forces to create the team that in 2018 directed and organized the first Porto Femme International Film Festival. The genesis of the project came two years earlier, with the creation of the XX Element Project – Cultural Association, which aims to 'promote the artistic work done by women and also demonstrate through them and the development of cultural, civic and social activities, the rights of women and gender equality'.[17] The association thus intended to create privileged spaces for the dissemination of these works, where the main focus would be on cinema and the exhibition of different types of women's films (such as student films, extensions of festivals and foreign shows, among others), in the *Maus Hábitos* space in Porto. Furthermore, renewing the spirit of cine clubs, films are discussed after their exhibition, in the presence of the filmmakers or members of the technical teams whenever possible.

From 30 May to 3 June 2018 Porto Femme had two international competitions – one for films directed by women and the other for films in which at least one woman played a fundamental role – and a national competition, to which, according to information published on the festival's website, a total of almost seventy films were submitted across different categories. The festival also awarded the Women's Rights Prize for the best film 'on the subject of women's rights and gender violence'. Across locations including the Auditorium of the Almeida Garrett Municipal Library, the Cinema Trindade, the Casa das Associações do Porto and the Barracuda, the first Porto Femme received 393 films from 42 countries, according to information published in the newspaper *Público* on 21 May 2018.[18]

In conclusion, we consider that the political and social context that we now live in, almost ten years after the beginning of our study, is more favourable to the debate. One of the final considerations that we put in our thesis concerned a certain discomfort on the majority of the filmmakers interviewed in relation to the possibility of a feminist reading of their work, ignoring the importance of this and of the permanently polysemic status of the film (Pereira 2016: 341–50). In 2019, facing an international mediatic environment that gives prominence to the subject of feminism, thus facilitating its understanding, the discussion seems to have revived, giving rise not only to phenomena such as Porto Femme, but also to a greater interest from students in higher education who introduce new perspectives, alongside experimental and innovative proposals. This new path is welcome, but we must also reiterate that it is accompanied by a worrying decrease in the production of fiction films directed by women. If the debate and its visibility are increasing, the possibility of film direction by women seems to be decreasing. In the struggle for equal opportunities no victory can be taken for granted.

REFERENCES

Beauvoir, Simone de (1976), *O segundo sexo* (trans. S. Milliet), vol. 1, Venda Nova: Bertrand Editora.

Campos, António (1974), *Falamos de Rio de Onor*, Portugal: António Campos.

Castro, Ilda (2000), *Cineastas portuguesas 1874–1956*, Lisbon: Câmara Municipal de Lisboa.

Costa e Silva, Manuel (1973), *Festa, trabalho e pão em Grijó da Parada*, Portugal: Instituto de Tecnologia Educativa (ITE).

Derrida, Jacques (2001), *Mal de arquivo: Uma impressão freudiana* (trans. C. de Moraes Rego), Rio de Janeiro: Relume Dumará.

Foucault, Michel (1987), *A arqueologia do saber* (trans. L. F. Baeta Neves), Rio de Janeiro: Editora Forense-Universitária.

Lisboa, Ricardo Vieira (forthcoming), *O restauro cinematográfico como recoreografia, o caso de 'Três dias sem Deus' de Bárbara Virgínia*, Lisbon: Instituto Politécnico de Lisboa: Escola Superior de Teatro e Cinema.

Matos-Cruz, José de (1999), *O Cais do olhar: O cinema português de longa-metragem e a ficção muda*, Lisbon: Cinemateca Portuguesa.

Oliveira, Manoel de (1962), *Acto da Primavera,* Portugal: Federação Nacional dos Industriais de Moagem (FNIM).

Pereira, Ana Catarina (2016), *A Mulher-Cineasta: Da arte pela arte a uma estética da diferenciação*, LabCom.IFP Books Colecção Ars, Covilhã: Universidade da Beira Interior.

Sequeira, Luísa (2017), *Quem é Bárbara Virgínia?*, Lisbon: Instituto do Cinema e do Ausiovisual.

Vieira, Marisa (forthcoming), *Três dias sem Deus: Tese de Licenciatura,* Lisbon: Faculdade de Letras da Universidade Clássica.

Virgínia, Bárbara (2016), interview with Ana Catarina Pereira and William Pianco, 'Bárbara Virgínia – A primeira realizadora de cinema, em Portugal', *International Journal of Cinema*, 2, pp. 18–29.

NOTES

1. In the essay *The Second Sex*, originally published in 1949, Simone de Beauvoir discusses the double incapacity of men to regard women as autonomous and of women to assume an identity of their own: 'she (the woman) is nothing more than what man decides she is. [...] The female is the non-essential before the essential. Man is the Being, the Absolute, she is the Other' (Beauvoir 1976: 12) (my translation of the original: 'ela (a mulher) não é senão o que o homem decide que seja. [...] A fêmea é o não essencial perante o essencial. O homem é o Ser, o Absoluto, ela é o Outro').
2. This Ph.D. began in 2009 and finished in 2014. The thesis results were reviewed and edited in 2016 in the book *A Mulher-Cineasta: Da arte pela arte a uma estética da diferenciação* ('The Woman-Filmmaker: From Art through Art to an Aesthetics of Differentiation') (Pereira 2016).
3. This difficulty is assumed in the initial note to the book *O cais do olhar* (Matos-Cruz 1999), written by João Bénard da Costa, then director of the Portuguese Cinematheque: 'All Portuguese production from 1896 until today? Unfortunately, it is not yet possible to cover it with the same degree of exhaustion that characterizes this volume and with the same certainties' (Costa in Matos-Cruz 1999: 7) (my translation of the original: 'Toda a produção portuguesa desde 1896 até hoje? Infelizmente, não é ainda possível cobri-la com o mesmo grau de exaustão que caracteriza este volume e com as mesmas certezas').
4. Decree-Law No. 124/2013 of 30 August, published in *Diário da República*, defines in Chapter I, Article 2: '(b) "Short film" means a cinematographic work that lasts less than sixty minutes; [...] (j) "Long-feature film" means a cinematographic work lasting sixty minutes or more.' Legislation available at: https://dre.pt/application/dir/pdf1s/2013/08/16700/0526405279.pdf (my translation of the original: '(b) "Curta-metragem", a obra cinematográfica que tenha uma duração inferior a sessenta minutos; [...] (j) "Longa-metragem", a obra cinematográfica que tenha uma duração igual ou superior a sessenta minutos').
5. A brief comparative study of the funding available for short films and long feature films, both documentaries and fiction films, denounces these disparities. As an example, the competition run by the Cinema and Audio-visual Institute for 2018 (available at http://

www.ica-ip.pt/pt/concursos/2018/) distinguishes between the three levels in the same way as our analysis does. The competition 'Support for Cinema – First Feature-Length Fiction Films' provides financial support of €1,800,000. The contest 'Support for Cinema – Short Fiction Films' provides financial support of €600,000. Finally, the competition 'Support for Cinema – First Film Documentaries' provides financial support of €450,000.

6. The cast included Bárbara Virgínia herself, Linda Rosa, João Perry, Alfredo Ruas and Maria Clementina.
7. The exhibition was curated by Ana Mafalda Reis and Matilde Carmo, in parallel with a panel discussion including: Ana Catarina Pereira and Wiliam Pianco, both researchers; Helena Matos, journalist; Luísa Sequeira, cinema director; and Tiago Baptista from the Portuguese Cinematheque. More information about the event can be found at: http://www.olharesdomediterraneo.org/barbara-virginia-primeira-realizadora-portuguesa/.
8. In the interview, Bárbara Virgínia revisits her places of memory, her experience as an actress declaiming poetry for the national radio broadcaster, as well as her work as a writer of and collaborator on several publications in Portugal and Brazil, to where she moved in the 1960s and where she would live until her death on 7 March 2015.
9. My translation of the original: 'Mulheres nunca procuraram assim (como realizadoras) o cinema. Tanto que você vê que ainda hoje, no mundo, temos pouquíssimas mulheres a dirigir cinema. A mulher, acho, nunca se tomou a sério a esse respeito, não sei.'
10. The expression is the most common in English translations of Derrida's essay. The original expression, *mal d'archive*, is closer to the common Portuguese translation, *mal de arquivo*.
11. My translation of the original: 'lei do que pode ser dito; o sistema que rege o aparecimento dos enunciados como acontecimentos singulares'.
12. Some of the films mentioned do not have any equivalent in English, as no official translation was found. This happens mainly with films that had no distribution outside Portugal or among the first films of the history of cinema in Portugal.
13. A full list is available on the IMDb website.
14. Excerpt from Jean Rouch's letter to the director of the Portuguese Film Centre in 1976. The 276th edition of *Cahiers du Cinéma* (May 1977) devotes eight pages to António Reis (including an interview with Serge Daney and Jean-Pierre Oudart and also a text by Daney on *Trás-os-Montes*). Copies of both can be found on the António Reis blog, and particularly in the following post: http://antonioreis.blogspot.com/2006/04/143-trs-os-montes-carta-de-jean-rouch.html. Accessed 9 September 2018.
15. It is important to note that, even today, the *Trás-os-Montes* trilogy has not been restored and there are no DVD copies of the films.
16. Minority national productions are distinguished by the fact that the majority of the film finance does not come from Portugal, in addition to most of members of the technical and artistic teams coming from outside Portugal.
17. More information can be found at: https://portofemme.com/en/.
18. See http://p3.publico.pt/cultura/filmes/26126/porto-femme-um-festival-para-divulgar-o-cinema-feito-por-elas.

The invisible women of Spanish cinema

Annette Scholz[1]

Where are the women?

The popular Spanish actress and singer Ana Belén drew attention to the situation of women in cinema in her acceptance speech upon receiving the Honorary Goya Award[2] in 2017:

> Nor do I understand why women still have such a hard time getting the same level of recognition as men, especially in a profession as liberal and open as ours [...] It is beyond me why there are still so few women in cinema. Sometimes I think that if we didn't need women to play women on screen, those that there are wouldn't even be there.
>
> (Filipino 2017)

At that ceremony, held on 4 February 2017, several speeches mentioned the situation of women in the film industry. It was the starting point for a long series of actions set to bring the inequalities between male and female filmmakers into sharp focus. In fact, not only do women lack the visibility of men in the industry, they are also far fewer in number in the film world in general, including in Spain, the country referenced in this chapter.

Since 2016 the issue of the gender gap in the world of cinema has become a recurring topic of conversation in the news media; focusing on the issue is considered a must and it seems to be omnipresent at film festivals across Spain. From San Sebastian to Seminci and Alcine to the Jameson Notodofilmfest,[3] spaces have been established to showcase films made by women, thematic meetings have been organized to discuss the situation of women in film and, in light of Hollywood scandals and the rise of the #MeToo[4] movement, debates have been held on the problem of sexual harassment in the audio-visual industry.

In addition to the increasing visibility of the struggle for equality at film festivals, several Spanish universities are now devoting resources to research into the current situation of women working in the audio-visual industry.[5] There are, however, two obstacles to looking into the subject in greater detail: first, the lack of valuable statistical information on the situation in general, and second, the lack of a standardized approach to its production. In addition to the GECA research group at the Complutense University of Madrid and two reports drawn up by CIMA (the association of women filmmakers) in 2015 and 2016 (Cuenca 2017), some personal research projects (Pousa 2016) have documented the number of women working in some very specific fields related to filmmaking.

For the purposes of this chapter, the number of women who worked on films classified by the Ministry of Culture from 2007 to 2015 has been assessed using the yearbooks of Spanish film edited by the Spanish Institute of Film and Audiovisual Arts (ICAA); the years 2016 and 2017 were not included due to a lack of data. The yearbooks contain all the films classified by the Ministry in that year.[6] They are the most comprehensive and the only official documents providing detailed information on Spanish films in this way. However, there is neither a database nor any report that brings together information concerning all the films made in Spain in any year. The production of various statistics is further complicated for a number of reasons: first, the lack of unification between film entries in the yearbook – the same categories/departments do not appear in each film, which often makes it impossible to clearly assign each person to the categories under investigation. Second, it can be impossible to immediately assign a gender to the people listed, because it can be difficult to know if a name is masculine or feminine.

In the absence of any other data, if not specified otherwise, this chapter always refers to data taken from the yearbooks of the ICAA because they are deemed to be the most comprehensive documents. The Annual Report of CIMA 2015, for example, takes into account 143 feature films, while the ICAA report considers 255; both include fictional films, animated films and documentaries. The Goya Awards only accept films premiered at film theatres and the ICAA yearbooks only consider those classified by the Ministry, although a large number of films are not premiered or classified and, therefore, are not registered in any archive. Being premiered in a film theatre seems a somewhat anachronistic and relative criterion today; because of the increasing number of platforms and digital channels for viewing films, recent films are often premiered directly on the platform or digital television channel (e.g. Netflix, Movistar Plus, etc.) that has contributed to their production.

The data in Table 1 is based on a wide-ranging study that details the presence of women in Spanish film. In order to provide a percentage comparison without having to take into account the disparate nature of the entries in the Spanish film yearbook edited by the ICAA, the women listed in each film were counted and associated with the number of films classified in each genre. The statistics therefore provide approximate and not real values, because in most cases the yearbook entries do not include comprehensive information on all the personnel working on each film. The statistics are restricted to quantifying female participation in each production over nine years and detailed by film genre. The count took into consideration the most significant departments, that is those that have decision-making power, and did not attempt to include every single department – for instance production assistants and aides were not counted, but producers were. The data produced constitute the basis and a possible starting point for research that this chapter aims to initiate but which is far from being concluded. The goal is simply to provide some significant data.

As the figures in Table 1 show, the presence of women in Spanish cinema over almost ten years is concentrated above all in the Technical-Aesthetic Group,[7] which comprises the departments of Costume Design, and Makeup and Hairdressing. These are the only professions in which female participation is close to 50 per cent in the fiction genre every year. Also worthy of mention is the area of Production in which the average female participation recorded over the nine-year period is around 30 per cent in both the fiction and documentary genres. The same percentage was recorded in the Production Supervision area in the Organization Group.

It is surprising that women, who have a relatively significant representation in the Technical-Artistic Group, with an average of almost 30 per cent in Artistic Direction in Fiction and in Documentary Editing, are, in contrast, under-represented in the areas of Cinematography, Sound and Musical Composition. In the Technical-Specialist Group, relating to Special Effects and including the animation department, female participation is negligible, or to put it more bluntly, virtually non-existent. The importance of women in the casting department is also significant. Despite the fact that none of the previous reports take this department into account, the decision as to which actors take part in fiction films can be considered to be important. Although statistics show female participation does not exceed 30 per cent, that figure could well be higher because not all the year-book entries take into consideration the people responsible for casting the films.

Female representation in the Leadership Group, which is where most of the decisions are taken that will ultimately affect the content of the feature film, varies over the years in accordance with the film genre. First, it is worth noting that there is an increase in female participation in the directing and scriptwriting of documentaries; there are therefore more women in decision-making roles in the documentary genre, although the 30 per cent threshold is not exceeded here either. According to the CIMA 2016 report, the increased representation of female directors in documentaries is the result of lower costs in this genre of film: 'As costs increase, the presence of female directors falls' (Cuenca 2017: 30). This would explain the fact that there are fewer women in decision-making positions in fiction films, since these films usually require a larger budget to be made.

Year		2007	2008	2009	2010	2011	2012	2013	2014	2015	Media
Directing	Fiction	11.36	15.45	18.85	6.3	5	14.55	15.11	7.32	10.64	11.62
	Documentary	15.15	7.55	20	20.97	25.71	16.92	21.84	45.45	26.85	22.27
	Animation	0	10	0	9.09	0	14.29	20	12.5	0	7.32
Scriptwriting	Fiction	14.39	23.64	22.13	15.75	21.67	30	19.42	21.34	21.99	21.15
	Documentary	12.12	16.98	30	35.48	30	23.08	32.18	68.18	36.11	**31.57**
	Animation	0	50	0	18.18	22.22	14.29	20	12.5	16.67	17.10
Production	Fiction	24.24	36.36	38.52	18.18	25.83	30	33.81	25.61	29.79	29.15
	Documentary	33.33	32.08	21.67	29.03	18.57	33.85	26.44	68.18	28.7	**32.43**
	Animation	0	10	25	18.18	0	0	40	12.5	16.67	13.59
Production Supervision	Fiction	19.7	39.09	27.87	20.47	38.33	40.91	31.65	29.27	52.48	**33.31**
	Documentary	21.21	13.21	26.67	11.29	10	53.85	51.72	79.55	50.93	**35.38**
	Animation	42.86	30	0	27.27	33.33	71.43	0	37.5	50	**32.49**
Editing	Fiction	21.97	18.18	25.41	15.75	25	22.73	20.14	12.8	21.28	20.36
	Documentary	36.36	13.21	16.67	35.48	27.14	35.38	20.69	56.82	22.22	29.33
	Animation	0	20	0	0	11.11	0	0	12.5	0	4.85
Sound	Fiction	6.06	10.91	9.84	7.87	4.17	9.09	7.91	7.32	12.06	8.36
	Documentary	18.18	11.32	8.33	14.52	17.14	12.31	10.34	11.36	13.89	13.04
	Animation	28.57	10	0	0	0	0	0	0	0	4.29

Cinematography	**Fiction**	6.06	5.45	7.38	4.72	3.33	7.27	7.19	3.05	7.8	5.81
	Documentary	3.03	5.66	5	8.06	8.57	12.31	6.9	45.45	19.44	12.71
	Animation	0	10	0	9.09	0	0	20	25	16.67	8.97
Artistic Direction	**Fiction**	26.52	30.91	27.05	25.98	31.67	27.27	38.85	21.34	38.3	29.77
	Documentary	3.03	7.55	5	6.45	5.71	7.69	5.75	11.36	3.7	6.25
	Animation	0	10	25	9.09	11.11	0	40	0	16.67	12.43
Musical Composition	**Fiction**	3.03	3.64	5.74	1.57	6.67	5.45	4.32	6.71	8.51	5.07
	Documentary	3.03	1.89	5	9.68	8.57	4.62	11.49	13.64	6.48	7.16
	Animation	0	10	5.38	9.09	0	14.29	0	0	16.67	6.16
Costume Design	**Fiction**	66.67	58.18	51.64	58.27	49.17	47.27	57.55	43.29	54.61	**54.07**
	Documentary	3.03	11.32	6.67	3.23	2.86	3.08	8.05	15.91	2.78	6.33
	Animation	0	0	0	0.79	0	0	0	12.5	0	1.48
Make-up and Hairdressing	**Fiction**	68.18	95.45	63.11	56.69	62.5	54.55	51.08	39.63	70.92	**62.46**
	Documentary	3.03	16.98	11.67	4.72	12.86	3.08	4.6	15.91	4.63	8.61
Special Effects	**Fiction**	0.76	0	1.64	3.23	1.67	0.91	3.6	1.22	2.13	1.68
	Documentary	0	1.89	0	9.09	0	0	2.3	2.27	0.93	1.83
	Animation	0	0	0	0	0	0	0	0	0	0.00
Casting	**Fiction**	30.3	29.09	30.33	61.29	26.67	21.82	27.34	12.8	26.24	29.54
Animation	**Documentary**	0	0	0	0	0	1.54	1.15	0	0.93	0.40
	Animation	0	30	0	0	0	0	0	12.5	0	4.72

TABLE 1: Percentage of women working in the audio-visual sector (produced with the invaluable help of Anne Sophie Brandt).

Table 1 shows that '[over several years] women are subordinated to positions that are further removed from decision-making power and the fields in which they have the highest representation are associated with the gender traits attributed to feminine values' (Cuenca 2017: 53). It is interesting, therefore, to take into consideration data concerning film students in order to ascertain whether there are also fewer women even considering working in the Leadership Group in their formative years. If there were far fewer female students of directing, scriptwriting and production, it would be logical to assume there would also be fewer women eventually working in these departments.

Film students

Table 2 makes a gender comparison between the students of different fields in the audio-visual sector in the two most important film schools in Spain – the ECAM (Escuela de Cinematografía y del Audiovisual in Madrid) and the ESCAC (Escuela Superior de Cine y Audiovisuales in Catalonia) – and people who go on to work in the corresponding professions. Despite the fact that there are many more film schools than the two considered here and Table 2 cannot, therefore, be taken as a definitive statistical statement on the subject, it does provide a rough idea of the percentage of women who study film in relation to the percentage who end up working professionally in the sector.

Table 2 shows an average of the number of women working in each area in the years examined; reference is made to the same years as those used in the information provided by the film schools. It would be interesting to investigate subsequent years to find out how many students have managed to get a job in the industry and work in the profession they studied.

It is striking that there is a difference of no more than 10 per cent between the percentages of women enrolled on each degree course in both schools, except for the specialist areas of sound and cinematography. There are 15 per cent more women enrolled for cinematography at the ESCAC, and 27 per cent more women are enrolled for sound at ECAM. It is also worth noting that in both of these areas there is a greater fall in this percentage between students and women actually working in the audio-visual sector: in the industry their representation is less than 10 per cent in both areas. Perhaps this phenomenon could be attributed to the fact that these technical sectors are still dominated by men and that it can be especially difficult for a woman to make her way in a world controlled by the opposite gender, imbued as it is with highly complex prejudices that are taken as given by society. Nely Reguera says the following in this regard:

> There are still many executives in positions of power who do not trust men and women in the same way and this is noticeable, so yes, women do have less access

> than men [...] I felt more discriminated against for being a woman as a technician than as a director. So as a female technician, when dealing with male technicians the fact that you were a woman generated more distrust or meant they did not value your work in the same way. They didn't relate to you with the same respect, or in the same way they would relate to a man [...] There were also many cases of men who did not have this attitude. That's how things are.[8]

It is also noteworthy that the percentages of women studying production and artistic direction are higher than those of men enrolled on the same degree courses. However, the percentage of women who go on to work in this sector is quite a lot lower than the percentage of men; from film school to profession, the statistics are reversed. This

Film school		ECAM	ESCAC	Industry
Year		2011–16 %	2011–15 %	2011–15 %
Directing	Men	64.00	70.00	89.42
	Women	36.00	30.00	10.52
Scriptwriting	Men	67.00	75.00	78.85
	Women	33.00	25.00	21.15
Production	Men	40.00	45.00	70.85
	Women	60.00	55.00	29.15
Editing	Men	64.00	65.00	79.64
	Women	36.00	35.00	20.36
Sound	Men	38.00	65.00	91.64
	Women	62.00	35.00	8.36
Cinematography	Men	80.00	65.00	94.27
	Women	20.00	35.00	5.73
Artistic direction	Men	22.00	12.00	70.23
	Women	78.00	88.00	29.77
Documentaries	Men	61.00	57.00	72.65
	Women	39.00	43.00	27.35

TABLE 2: Comparison between number of film students and audio-visual sector workers. Source: Data provided by ECAM and ESCAC and the data included in Table 1.

is a phenomenon that deserves more attention than can be given in this text, which will restrict its scope to discussing women directors of fiction films in greater depth.

The comparison between students of directing at ECAM and ESCAC and women who go on to direct fiction films shows a drop of 20 per cent. It is, however, also necessary to bear in mind the fact that the film industry employs men and women between the ages of approximately 20 and 70. These film schools have been in existence for a limited period of time: 24 years in the case of ESCAC and 20 years in the case of ECAM. The percentage of professionals joining the industry in the last 20 years may be representative, but this is not the case for all professionals working today, especially those who joined the industry before the schools came into being.

When various filmmakers currently working in Spain were asked whether they had felt ready to work in the audio-visual industry at the end of their studies, the majority answered 'no'. They highlighted a gap between graduation from film school and gaining entry into the profession. Belén Funes summarizes the problem as follows:

> At film school I was taught to love cinema, to respect the profession and above all that the most important thing is your team: your people, with whom you will end up shooting films. But I think you learn how to make films by doing it or, at the least, by watching others do it. That's why I think it's important to train and get out into the professional world as soon as possible.

The data in Table 3 shows that, in comparison to students of directing in other European countries, the number of female students in Spain is below the average of 38 per cent, but above the percentage of female students in neighbouring France, a country which is so often cited as a model for emulation. With the exception of Sweden, which achieved an exemplary figure of 50 per cent women directors in 2015 as a result of the equality policy implemented by Anna Serner, the head of the Swedish Film Institute (García 2017), other European countries still have a way to go to reach equality in the number of male and female directors.

Film school		Spain	Germany	Austria	Hungary	France	Italy	UK	Sweden
Directing	Men %	67.00	60.00	61.00	62.00	73.00	62.00	55.00	56.00
	Women %	33.00	40.00	39.00	38.00	27.00	38.00	45.00	44.00

TABLE 3: Women at European film schools. Source: Statistics for Spain are based on data provided by ESCAC and ECAM. Statistics for all other countries were prepared by EWA – European Women's Audiovisual Network (2017) for the period 2006–13.

Female directors of fiction films

Examining the number of women who have directed fiction films over the last 10 years in Spain, the percentage has never exceeded the 20 per cent threshold, and no more than 25 films a year have been made by women with or without the collaboration of male directors. Although the number of films made per year has increased in recent years, the number of female directors has not risen proportionately. The highest figure for women responsible for making a film was achieved in 2009 (see Table 4).

Year	2007	2008	2009	2010	2011	2012	2013	2014	2015
Total feature films	172	173	186	200	199	182	231	216	255
Fiction films	**132**	**110**	**122**	**127**	**120**	**110**	**139**	**164**	**141**
Directed by women or in collaboration	15	17	23	8	6	16	21	12	15
Women directing fiction films %	11.36	15.45	18.85	6.30	5.00	14.55	15.11	7.32	10.64

TABLE 4: Proportion of fiction films directed by women. Source: ICAA yearbooks.

The aforementioned research uses the Goya Awards as a representative indicator of what is happening in the Spanish audio-visual industry, and the films entered as candidates for the different categories of that award provide a corpus for the preparation of various reports.[9] On reviewing the 32 years' worth of nominations for the Goya Awards, it is clear that the Spanish Academy of Film Arts and Sciences itself considers Best Film, Best Director and Best New Director to be the most important categories, because they are the last awards to be presented at the ceremony and take pride of place on the Academy's website (Premios Goya n.d.). On this basis, Table 5 lists the number of female nominations and award-winners in these three main categories. In this regard it is necessary to bear in mind that the Best Film category only includes fiction films and not documentaries or animated films, which have their own 'inferior' category. It goes without saying, however, that the word 'film' encompasses documentaries, animation and short films, despite 'film' and 'fiction film' still being viewed as synonyms in some contexts in a simplistic and simplifying manner.

As can be observed, only twelve women have won in the Best Film, Best Director and Best New Director categories. Female winners in these three categories equate to no more than 4 per cent of nominations in the entire 32-year existence of the awards.

Year	Best Film			Best Director			Best New Director		
	Total nominations	Women nominated	Female winners	Total nominations	Women nominated	Female winners	Total nominations	Women nominated	Female winners
1987	3			3	1	1			
1988	3			3					
1989	3			3					
1990	5	1		5	1		5	1	
1991	3			3			3	1	1
1992	3			3	1		3	1	
1993	3			3			3	1	
1994	3			3			3	1	
1995	3			3			3		
1996	3			3			3	1	
1997	3	1	1	3			3		
1998	3			3			3	1	
1999	4			4			4		
2000	4	1		4	1		4	1	
2001	4			4			4	1	
2002	4			4			4		
2003	4			4			4	1	
2004	4	2	1	4	2	1	4	1	1
2005	4			4			4		

2006	4	1	1	4	1	1	4		
2007	4			4			4		
2008	4	1		4	2		4		
2009	4			4			4	1	
2010	4			4			4	1	1
2011	4	1		4	1		4	1	
2012	4			4			4	1	
2013	4			4			4	1	
2014	5	1		4	1		4	1	
2015	5			4			4	1	
2016	5	2		4	2		4	1	
2017	5			4			4	1	
2018	5	2	1	4	1	1	4	1	1
TOTAL	**123**	**13**	**4**	**118**	**14**	**4**	**109**	**21**	**4**
%		**10.57**	**3.25**		**11.86**	**3.39**		**19.27**	**3.67**

TABLE 5: Female nominees and winners at the Goya Awards over their 32-year existence. Source: Premios Goya (n.d.).[10]

It is also worth noting that only in the Best New Director category did the number of female nominees almost reach 20 per cent, which is at least well above approximately 12 per cent in the Best Director category. This discrepancy confirms the theory expounded by Zurian: a large number of filmmakers, despite getting their debut work finished, do not actually manage to establish a foothold, or manage to stand out, in the audio-visual industry (Zurian 2017: 21) – a phenomenon that characterizes the Spanish film sector in general, regardless of the director's gender. There are several female directors who have been nominated for the Best New Director Goya whose names never again appear on the list of nominations for the Spanish film awards. Roser Aguilar confirms this situation: '[i]t's not difficult to arrive; what's difficult is keeping going.'[11] However, there are a few recurring names on the lists: four of the awards presented to women and several of the nominations were for the work of the same director: Isabel Coixet.

It is fair to say that only a few female directors stand out due to a prolonged presence in the industry and on the lists of nominees for the Goya Awards in the Best Film and Best Director categories: Isabel Coixet, Icíar Bollaín, Gracia Querejeta and Pilar Miró. Except for Pilar Miró, the first woman to receive a Goya Award who died in 1997, they are all female directors over the age of 50 with a proven professional track record, which means that, after their debut film they have continued to regularly premiere new work and have an audience that goes to the cinema to see it.

It is also striking that until 1997, at the tenth Goya award ceremony, no woman had won the Best Film award. Of the four awards won by women in each cate-

Year	Category	Director	Film
2018	Best Film, Best Director (and Best Adapted Screenplay)	Isabel Coixet	*The Bookshop*
	Best New Director	Carla Simón	*Estiu 1993*
2010	Best New Director	Mar Coll	*Tres dies amb la familia*
2006	Best Film, Best Director (and Best Script)	Isabel Coixet	*La vida secreta de las palabras*
2004	Best Film, Best Director (and Best Script)	Icíar Bollaín	*Te doy mis ojos*
	Best New Director	Ángeles González-Sinde	*La suerte dormida*
1997	Best Director	Pilar Miró	*El perro de hortelano*
1991	Best New Director	Rosa Vergés	*Boom, boom*

TABLE 6: Goya Awards won by women filmmakers. Source: Premios Goya (n.d.).

gory, three have been won only since 2004. That is why it is important to highlight 2004 and 2018, which were very special years in the history of the Goya Awards because of the success of women filmmakers, who won all three categories – Best Film, Best Director and Best New Director – as detailed in Table 6.

The visible women of Spanish cinema

It would be interesting to carry out a wide-ranging sociological study to ascertain the causes of the numerical decline in the ratio of female students to women filmmakers. This chapter can mention only a few theories as to the factors that appear to give rise to this phenomenon. Judith Colell suggests that the causes behind this lack of equality could have been internalized to such an extent that we are not even aware of them: '[i]t is something that forms part of our customs, it's educational; historically there has been a clear intention to bury women away, to ensure they were not included in the history of art. The fact it is so internalized makes it very difficult to shake off' (cited in Sierra López 2016).

According to the declarations of the women filmmakers interviewed who are making their way in the audio-visual sector, personal initiative and perseverance are essential in order to take those first steps: getting to know the industry while working in various spheres, getting a foothold, making friends, seeking out opportunities. At university one learns the theory and at film school one learns the trade, but in order to become a director one must have talent, something that only comes to light when one makes films.[12] 'We lack confidence in ourselves. All filmmakers are insecure, but in the case of women, it's three times as bad. We were educated to have children, not to be leaders', says Isabel de Ocampo, who was nominated for Best New Director in 2011 (cited in Koch 2018).

The report in Arranz (2011) also suggests sociological factors that might explain the reasons why the number of women falls when the time comes to take those first professional steps (Callejo 2007). Many women are conditioned by a desire to have a family and find there is no legal support for this in the industry, a fact which is coupled with difficulties inherent to the industry itself as regards a balance between personal desires and professional ambitions.

According to the survey carried out for this text, women working in various professions in the audio-visual sector are especially concerned about finding a balance between family life and work. Working in the world of cinema requires a great deal of dedication in terms of time and effort, which is almost impossible to balance with a family life with children, who also require a lot of attention. The concerns are such that some of those interviewed have had to choose between these two facets of their life. For Ana Pfaff, a Catalan editor of numerous well-known films, it is the 'big issue', because she feels that society, the industry and those working creatively in the audio-visual sector have a long way to go before the obstacles to making their professional and family lives compatible are removed and conditions become acceptable. Elena Trapé highlighted the role that society still confers on mothers as an aggravating factor, pointing out issues such as having to be the ones who worry about the children, as well as the ones who take charge and organize childcare if it is essential to make a business trip. Men still just announce the fact they are off, says the director, to show the difference between women and men working in the audio-visual sector. Belén Funes sums it up: 'I am concerned because I think as women we have to design our personal lives so they have the least possible impact on our professional lives. It is a riddle that my partner, for example, will never have to solve.'[13]

Campaigning at award ceremonies and feminist statements such as *#Másmujeres*,[14] set up by CIMA, 'are nothing new: since the fifties, every decade has witnessed its own, according to *The Hollywood Reporter*, and they have always ended in nothing' (Koch 2017). However, in view of the demonstrations, strikes and political and cultural action and communications that took place on 8 March 2018 in Spain, on International Women's Day, it does appear that a new page has been turned in terms of raising awareness that it is necessary to reassess the situation of women in Spanish society in general, and also the specific case of the audio-visual sector. Mar Coll shares this opinion:

> I think that there is still a huge gap between the number of women who would like to work in the audio-visual world in positions of responsibility and those who get there in the end. The audiovisual industry is mostly led by men, which results in an inertia that is difficult to stop. Fortunately, awareness is being raised as to this situation, which we hope will lead to the creation of the tools needed to put it into reverse and achieve equality of access.[15]

Hopefully this is true and the next time a ceremony that wishes to champion the rights of women in the world of film is organized, a woman will be hired to write the script. At the 2018 awards ceremony held by the Spanish Academy of Cinematographic Arts and Sciences, despite drawing attention to the salary imbalance and glass ceiling that appears to be preventing an increase in the participation of women in certain areas, the two people chosen to present the 2018 Goya Awards and for telling jokes, sometimes in bad taste, were two well-known male Spanish comedians. There is still a lack of women in decision-making roles. If this is not the case, then how is it that the Honorary Goya Award, in recognition of a professional career and won by Ana Belén in 2017, has over 32 years been awarded to 26 men and only six women. Out of the six female winners only one did not work in front of the cameras – Josefa Molina who won in 2012 for her work as a director and scriptwriter (Cuenca 2017: 44). A woman's physical appearance still seems to be more important than her creative vision or the skills she can contribute.

Although there are few female role models in the Spanish audio-visual sector in the field of directing, over the last year a gentle breeze has blown in from Catalonia. The list of winning female directors at the national film awards reveals that most of them have their roots in that region, above all Isabel Coixet, who has won four accolades and is a role model and producer for many young female filmmakers, and Mar Coll, who won the Best New Director Goya in 2010 for her first feature film.

Carla Simón is not alone in standing out with her debut work *Estiu 1993* (2017), which was well received by the press and general public alike after screenings at the most prestigious Spanish and international festivals, and triumphs at various Spanish film awards ceremonies. Among others, she has won awards for Best Film, debut work and Best Director at the Berlinale, the Festival de Málaga, the Goya Awards and the Premios Gaudí. New female Spanish film artists, most having learnt their trade at ESCAC, have set tongues wagging with their first feature films and/or short films, heralding an important and bright future in film. To mention but a few: Elena Trapé was recently awarded the *Biznaga de oro* at the Festival of Málaga for her second feature film *Les Distanciès* (2018); Elena Martín's debut work *Julia ist* (2017) has done the rounds at various Spanish and international festivals; as has Nely Reguera's *María y los demás* (2016); after *Lo mejor de mí* (2007), Roser Aguilar has premiered her second film *Brava* (2017). This progress is surely due to, on the one hand, training received at the Catalonian film school and, on the other, the production companies Escándalo Films and ESCAC Films that were set up at ESCAC to facilitate the production conditions for students' first films. Perhaps Catalonian film institutions are also more aware of the situation of women in film and are taking small steps to improve it.

The short films of the following women, who are also based in Catalonia, have stood out at numerous festivals, such as Sundance, Cannes, Valladolid, Málaga and Alcalá de Henares: Laura Ferrés with *Los Desheredados* (2017), Clara Roquet with *Les bones nenes* (2016) and Belén Funes with *La inútil* (2017) – the last two are currently preparing their first feature films. Furthermore, the recent discovery from the official short film section at the Festival of Málaga, who surely has a hugely promising future ahead of her, is Bárbara Farrè with *La última virgen* (2017). Laura Ferrés confirms this opinion:

> Several new female directors came onto the scene in 2017 and 2018, alongside more consolidated female directors who premiered new films in the same period. I feel the landscape of film is going through a gradual process of renewal. There is no doubt that new viewpoints are required to reflect the complexity of

> the country and also to ensure cinema itself evolves. What is more, if younger generations have women as role models who are associated with leadership, it is clear that will lead to an increasing number of women filmmakers.[16]

Most of these female directors seem to belong to a generation of women educated in a different way – a far cry from the feminine ideals promoted by the Francoist dictatorship, in a way that transmits self-confidence. They are female directors who mostly make films that deal with their own first-hand experiences, women who know how to promote their work and make use of new media, and who do not appear to be afraid of the patriarchy dominating the sector. Unfortunately, outside the confines of the festival circuit their films, despite constituting a critical milestone in terms of their visibility in certain circles, have made a very limited impact on the industry in terms of audience numbers and box-office receipts. In order for this to change, there is still a lot to do. It is to be hoped that the public authorities and production and television companies which currently determine the films that are made, as well as the sector's own production and other companies, sign up to this generational change.

> There is no lack of ideas. The proposals of scores of voices including film schools, production companies, female directors, academics, actors and politicians point to common solutions: the creation of gender-equal commissions to award subsidies and select entries for festivals; positive discrimination when awarding grants, based on the successful Swedish model; the promotion of feminine role models in traditionally masculine professions; increased budgets for films directed by women, to help them escape the ghetto of intimist cinema; or subsidies for filmmakers with children. Enough ingredients to cook up a recipe capable of ridding us of the bitter taste of discrimination that still reigns in the seventh art in Spain.
> (Koch 2018)

As a result of the unstoppable awareness-raising work being undertaken by the association of women filmmakers of Catalonia, Dones Visuals (2018), there is real hope that the precarious situation of women in film might change in the medium to long term, at least in one part of Spain. Not only does Dones Visuals collect data on women working in film, it also has an action plan to increase the number of women working in the wider industry. From a creative retreat, a new producer accompaniment plan and grants for professionals who lack market opportunities to a directory of women film professionals, they are seeking out solutions for various problems that make it difficult for women to access the film industry. As differences between Catalonia and the rest of Spain come into ever sharper focus, it is to be expected that such differences will also find their echoes in the world of film.

REFERENCES

Alcine – Festival de Cine de Alcalá de Henares/Comunidad de Madrid Official Website (2018), 'Ediciones anteriores, Alcine47', http://47.alcine.org/. Accessed 14 October 2018.

Arranz, Fátima (2010), 'La situación de las mujeres y los hombres en el sector audiovisual español: estudios sociológico y legislativo', http://www.cineenvioleta.org/wp-content/uploads/2010/02/1255974265-ARCHIVO.pdf. Accessed 22 April 2018.

——— (2011), *Cine y Género en España*, Valencia: Cátedra.

Callejo, Javier (2007), 'La formación de estudiantado universitario en comunicación audiovisual: las expectativas profesionales', in F. Arranz (ed.), *Cine y Género en España*, Madrid: Feminisimos.

Cuenca, Sara (2016), 'Informe Anual CIMA 2015: La presencia de las mujeres en el sector cinematográfico', https://cimamujerescineastas.es/wp-content/uploads/2018/01/INFORME-FINAL-ESTUDIO-2016.pdf. Accessed 3 April 2018.

——— (2017), 'Informe CIMA 2016: La representatividad de la mujeres en el sector cinematográfico español', https://cimamujerescineastas.es/wp-content/uploads/2018/01/INFORME-FINAL-ESTUDIO-2016.pdf. Accessed 3 April 2018.

Dones Visuals Official Website (2018), 'Home page', https://www.donesvisuals.cat/. Accessed 14 October 2018.

EWA – European Women's Audiovisual Network Official Website (2017), 'Advocacy, EWA Study, where are the women directors in European films?' https://www.ewawomen.com/resources/. Accessed 25 March 2018.

Festival Internacional de Cine de San Sebastián Official Website (2018), 'Home page', https://www.sansebastianfestival.com/es/. Accessed 14 October 2018.

Filipino, Mariano (2017), 'Ana Belén en los Premios Goya', YouTube, https://www.youtube.com/watch?time_continue=27&v=ZUhVJ1PwK_M. Accessed 1 April 2018.

García, Rocío (2017), 'Suecia, el paraíso de las mujeres cineastas', El País, https://elpais.com/cultura/2017/09/28/actualidad/1506615467_446714.html. Accessed 22 April 2018.

Jameson Notodofilmfest Official Website (n. d.), 'Home page', http://www.jamesonnotodofilmfest.com/. Accessed 14 October 2018.

Koch, Tommaso (2018), 'Más mujeres en el cine, sí, pero ¿cómo?', El País, https://elpais.com/cultura/2018/03/08/actualidad/1520517249_369285.html. Accessed 22 April 2018.

L'apunt Blog Informatiu de la UVic (n.d.), 'Home page', http://mon.uvic.cat/lapunt/les-jornades-dones-i-cinema-embrio-dun-projecte-interuniversitari-per-investigar-en-aquest-ambit/?home. Accessed 14 October 2018.

Pousa, Laura (2016), 'Las mujeres que estudian hoy en las escuelas de cine ¿serán directoras?', working paper, Barcelona: UIC Barcelona.

Premios Goya Official Website, 'Home page', https://www.premiosgoya.com/32-edicion/nominaciones/por-categoria/. Accessed 3 April 2018.

Seminci, Semana Internacional de Cine de Valladolid Official Website (2018), 'Histórico, Secciones y Ciclos, Supernovas', http://seminci.es/historico-de-secciones-y-ciclos-seccion-y-ciclos/?itemselec=4&ano=2017&catid=201719. Accessed 14 October 2018.

Sierra López, Cristina (2016), 'Mujeres y cine, entre el drama y la ciencia ficción', El País, https://elpais.com/elpais/2016/09/12/mujeres/1473698857_413992.html. Accessed 22 April 2018.

Universidad Complutense Madrid, Website Género, Estética y Cultura Audiovisual (GECA) (2018), 'Home page', https://www.ucm.es/geca. Accessed 8 April 2018.

Zurian, Francisco A., Pérez Sañudo, David and Vázquez Rodríguez, Lucía G. (2017), 'El falso *boom* de las mujeres directoras: realizadoras españolas con un solo largometraje de ficción (2000–2015)', in F. Zurian (ed.), *Miradas de mujer: Cineastas españolas para el siglo XXI*, Madrid: Fundamentos, pp. 21–37.

Appendix

Questions for emerging filmmakers[17]

1. Where did your interest in filmmaking come from?
2. Did you feel ready for work in the audio-visual industry after graduating?
3. Do you view your short film as a stepping stone to feature films? Is it a highly personal work?
4. Do you think Spanish cinema has made space for itself in the international film industry? Does it have worldwide recognition?
5. On the specific topic of support for women filmmakers, how do you view the current situation of Spanish films made by women – in terms of training, access to work, access to financing and collaborative networks?
6. Have you ever felt that your entry into the film industry was more difficult because you are a woman? In other words, have you felt discriminated against because you are a woman?
7. Are you worried about finding a balance between your family and professional lives? Do you see any difference in comparison with your male colleagues in the profession?
8. How do you think the film scene has changed for women in Spain since you began making short films?
9. If you had to place your work within a cinematographic tradition, from which artistic trends or movements would you say it has descended? Do you feel your work is in dialogue with the work of any other directors? Are any of them women?
10. How many women are there in the teams involved in the production, shooting or post-production of your work?
11. As a woman filmmaker who includes female characters in your films, do you consider your films to be feminine?
12. Do you think your work would have been received differently if you were a man?

13. In your opinion, what measures would help women to get a foothold in the Spanish film industry? What would you recommend women to do to get a foot in the door of the film world?

NOTES

1. Translation by Jeremy Aldis of Scholz, Annette 'Las invisibles del cine español', in Annette Scholz and Marta Álvarez (eds) (2018) *Cineastas emergentes: Mujeres en el cine del siglo XXI*, Madrid: Iberoamricana Vervuert. Colección: Aproximaciones a las Culturas Hispánicas, 4. pp. 45–69.
2. The Goya Awards are held on an annual basis by the Academia de las Artes y las Ciencias Cinematográficas de España (The Spanish Academy of Film Arts and Sciences) in order to recognize the best professionals in each specialist area of Spanish cinema. The Honorary Goya is awarded to a filmmaker from any area in recognition of their career in the film industry.
3. Around 500 film festivals of varying sizes and importance are held all over Spain. There is only one in category A, on a par in terms of size and importance with Cannes, Berlin or Venice, which is the San Sebastian International Film Festival. La Seminci, Semana Internacional de Cine de Valladolid is, with 63 years under its belt, one of Spain's oldest festivals. In 2017 women filmmakers received special visibility with the season *Supernovas*. Alcine – Alcalá de Henares/Community of Madrid Film Festival specializes in short films and in discovering new talent in film. In 2017 it devoted its 47th year of the festival to women. Jameson Notodofilmfest is an internet-based Spanish short-film festival created in 2001 by the http://notodo.com website based on an idea of the filmmaker Javier Fesser, which has had a major impact among young filmmakers.
4. #MeToo is the name of a feminist campaign that went viral as a hashtag on social networks in October 2017. Its aim was to denounce sexual aggression and sexual harassment, as a consequence of accusations levelled against the US film producer and executive Harvey Weinstein. It led to the founding of the Time's Up movement against sexual harassment on 1 January 2018 by Hollywood celebrities.
5. The MYC Project came into being at the University of Vic, grouping researchers from various universities and institutions devoted to investigating various aspects of the situation of women in film. There is also the GECA research group at the Complutense University, which in Spanish stands for gender, aesthetics and audiovisual culture.
6. The classification by age groups of films and film trailers for commercialization, dissemination or marketing in movie theatres is requested by production companies or distributors and granted by the general direction of the Film and Audiovisual Arts Institute.
7. In the Annual Report of CIMA 2016, Sara Cuenca revisits and modifies a model for organizing positions that establish the structural hierarchy of the film sector drawn up by Fátima Arranz in her publication *Cine y Género en España* (2011). It is based on the study entitled

'La situación de las mujeres y los hombres en el sector audiovisual español: Estudios sociológico y legislativo' (Arranz 2010), which investigates the situation of women in the Spanish audio-visual sector from 2002 to 2006. Using this as a base, Cuenca sets up five hierarchical groups: the Leadership Group (Directing, Script-writing, Production), the Technical-Artistic Group (Editing, Artistic Direction, Cinematography, Musical Composition and Sound), the Organization Group (Production Supervision), the Technical-Aesthetic Group (Costume Design, Makeup, Hairdressing) and the Technical-Specialist Group (Special Effects), which serve as a reference in this chapter.

8. In order to write this chapter, a survey was carried out among a series of emerging filmmakers. The following filmmakers kindly responded: Roser Aguilar, Mar Coll, Laura Ferrés, Belén Funes, Ana Pfaff, Nely Reguera, Clara Roquet, Elena Trapé and Gemma Vidal. They gave their opinions on the situation of women in the Spanish audio-visual sector. Since the analysis of this chapter of the situation of women in Spanish film is based on the responses of women filmmakers, it is inevitable that the situation is reflected from their viewpoint, which is the viewpoint of the subject matter of this chapter. The questionnaire that formed this survey is reproduced in the Appendix and translations of their responses are by Jeremy Aldis.
9. See the reports prepared by CIMA in 2015 and 2016.
10. As a result of a lack of a more accessible balance sheet of legitimate titles, the qualitative study of the films and the participation of women in them refers to information taken from the website of the Goya Awards of the Film Academy. However, it is worth noting that the Academy is still a professional association, or lobby, and its selection of titles is determined by a sector of Spanish cinema that is not aligned with the most commercial side of cinema, or with independent cinema (the members of which are not in the Academy). Socially and culturally, the Goya Awards constitute one possible interpretation of the industry. Its connection with society at large is relative. The awards are decided by the votes of the associate members.
11. See note 10.
12. See note 10.
13. See note 10.
14. At the 32nd Goya Awards ceremony for Spanish cinema, CIMA professionals handed out red fans with the hashtag *#Masmujeres* to denounce inequality and to announce its determination to correct the situation.
15. See note 10.
16. See note 10.
17. Translation of the questionnaire from the original Spanish is mine.

Três dias sem Deus by Bárbara Virgínia: A different form of representation

Ricardo Vieira Lisboa[1]

Bárbara Virgínia[2] is considered to be the first woman to make a sound feature film in Portugal: *Três dias sem Deus* is that film, and Virgínia both directed and starred in it at the age of 22. The film premiered at the Cinema Ginásio Theatre on 30 August 1946 and, on 5 October in that same year, was shown at the first official staging of the Cannes Film Festival, along with *Camões* by José Leitão de Barros (Matos-Cruz 1999: 79–80). *Três dias sem Deus* would be Bárbara Virgínia's first and last film as a director.[3] Although the project originally belonged to another filmmaker (Raúl Faria da Fonseca), in this chapter I will analyse, mainly using preserved production documents (plot and storyboards) and preserved film fragments (the film is partially lost), how Bárbara Virgínia modified the project as a female filmmaker in that era. In particular, I will focus on the way she portrayed the character of the primary school teacher – just a few years after the first courses for primary teaching had opened – as opposed to figures of authority, such as the priest, the doctor, the nobleman and the mystical healer. This portrayal constitutes, as I will try to assert, an unusual fictional testimony of a remarkable moment in the emancipation of Portuguese women in the world of work and one of its first filmic representations.

The film and its documents

Only a small portion of the image reels from *Três dias sem Deus* remain; the entire soundtrack has been lost. A total of 26 minutes are left to us, divided between two reels archived in the Arquivo Nacional da Imagem em Movimento (ANIM) and measuring a total of 868 metres (Matos-Cruz 1999: 79–80). Of the 102 minutes of film that premiered in 1946, less than a quarter has been preserved. The loss of the film is indirectly related to the role played by the production company, Invicta

Filmes Independente, as the adventurous incursion of Felisberto Felismino into the film industry. Felismino, who was a 'well-known Lisbon merchant' and importer of Conklin permanent ink pens (Ribeiro 1983: 544), nonetheless managed to recover his investment during the four weeks in which the film was exhibited in Lisbon, ending on 26 September (Matos-Cruz 1999: 80).

The film is an adaptation of the novel by Gentil Marques[4] titled *Mundo Perdido*, and several production documents are preserved at the Biblioteca da Cinemateca Portuguesa – Museu do Cinema (CPMC): the *sequência dialogada, base de planificação* ('dialogue sequence, storyboard basis') (1945) penned by Raúl Faria da Fonseca, the author of the original adaptation, a storyboard reviewed by the censor (IFPI 1946) and another storyboard filled with work annotations (IFPI 1945).

The first document (dialogue sequence, storyboard basis) is what is now called a full-length synopsis, a fifteen-page document divided into three acts describing the content of the main plot of the film. Both storyboard documents have been arranged horizontally in columns, describing the scale of each shot, its duration, the action that occurs in it, the lenses that should be used, the dialogue and special sound effects or camera movements. One of these documents corresponds to the version of the film that was submitted to the Direction of Censorship Services, with each page marked with an approval stamp. The other is a work storyboard, annotated with several changes made during the shoot (changes in dialogue, scene cuts and other changes).

In order to better explain how the film became a reality, I have developed a chronology (Appendix A) composed from short articles in newspapers and specialty magazines, mainly from *Filmagem* magazine, but also from *7.ª Arte: revista mundial de cinema*, *Cinema*, *O.K.*, *Eva* and the daily newspaper *O Século*.

From this chronology of short articles and excerpts from longer ones, a series of important events becomes evident:

(a) Raúl Faria da Fonseca is the author of the original storyboard of the film and was to be the director of *Três dias sem Deus*.
(b) Due to his duties with the Metro-Goldwyn-Mayer 16mm department, Faria da Fonseca was required to travel to the United States for specialized training, which prevented him from being present during the shooting of the film.
(c) Shooting was delayed several months by the aforementioned situation but also by the lack of new 35mm film throughout Europe in the months after the end of the Second World War.
(d) Bárbara Virgínia was originally slated to act in the role of the film's protagonist, and it was probably only due to Faria da Fonseca's unavailability that she was invited to take his place in the director's chair, taking on both roles.

(e) The shooting of *Três dias sem Deus* must have taken place sometime between 18 February and 10 March 1946, and certainly not consecutively, including the exteriors.
(f) The premiere of the film was rescheduled, perhaps because of its international premiere in Cannes in October (it should be noted that although it was reported that Bárbara Virgínia would be present at Cannes, this did not happen).
(g) Despite a positive reception from Portuguese audiences (and a mixed reception from Portuguese film critics),[5] the poor reception at Cannes led to Virgínia regretting having been selected to represent her country at the festival.

Dialogue sequence, storyboard basis

A close reading of the 'dialogue sequence, storyboard basis' reveals the plot of the film in three acts, which is summarized below (all citations are from Fonseca 1945).

In the first act we are introduced to Lídia, a young woman who has just graduated as a primary schoolteacher and finds a job in a small rural village. On the first day of class she is interrupted by the village doctor, who informs her that he, along with the town's priest, will have to leave the village for three days – the three days from the film's title: 'Three long days in which emotions seem to have no end.' Immediately afterwards, Paulo Belforte – a man whom 'the whole village hated, as if he were the devil' – arrives at the school with his son, Pedro, who is to join the class. Shortly thereafter, the women of the village come to collect their children, fearing contact with Pedro. Feeling upset, Pedro runs back home. Determined to speak again with Belforte in order to better integrate Pedro into the school, Lídia goes to Casal de Lobos, Paulo's mansion on the top of the hill (her arrival will be described in more detail below, corresponding to scene six).

In the second act, after Lídia has spent the night at Casal de Lobos due to inclement weather, she returns to the village with Pedro. The villagers do not speak to her on her way to the school, and when she arrives there, she finds her classroom empty. She then returns to Casal de Lobos for fear of remaining in the village, given the superstitions of the townspeople. Belforte accedes to her request to stay another night and confesses that his wife, Isabel, used to be a great artist, but that since an accident she has never been the same; she no longer speaks but only plays the piano, screaming and hallucinating. At night, when Lídia hears the screaming from another of Isabel's attacks, she meets an old servant who whispers, 'This time he will finish her'. When Lídia enquires about Isabel's accident, a maid answers: 'Accident!? He did it with malice.'

The third and final act begins the following morning when Lídia decides to visit the cliff where Isabel's alleged accident took place. When she arrives, and while looking at the bottom of the moat, she is surprised by Belforte, who is not pleased to discover her there. Lídia tries to escape, but Belforte stops her and forces her to listen to his version of the events that occurred there. Attempting to escape this situation, Lídia gets up and slips, but Belforte catches her by the arm and prevents her from falling. Everything that had happened to Isabel is now happening to Lídia, except Belforte had not been able to catch his wife by the arm as he does with Lídia. The two return to Casal de Lobos and Lídia goes to her room to pack her bag and return to the village. Belforte follows her, and asks her to stay in the house and become Pedro's private teacher. She does not reply and leaves, but when she reaches the village she discovers that Bernarda, the town's healer, is going to apply a harmful remedy to one of her students. To prevent this treatment, Lídia returns to the mansion with the child in her arms. The townsfolk, learning that the child is gone, believe that Lídia has taken the child to Belforte's to 'curse the little one' and soon they 'all came to the street with torches', moving towards Casal de Lobos. In the house's courtyard, the villagers create a huge bonfire 'the flames of which reach the height of the first floor'; Isabel 'sees the flames and her excitement reaches its peak'. Suddenly she rises unaided from her wheelchair, cries and laughs – 'she is healed!'. Outside, the villagers still shout for the abducted child. Belforte refuses to release the child until the doctor arrives. The people force their way into the house and then into a secret room where the home's inhabitants have barricaded themselves. On entering they discover that this 'secret room' is, in fact, the mansion's chapel. And at this moment the priest and the village doctor return and everyone calms down.

The next day the school is filled with people and the children dance and sing. Lídia goes back to the village, smiling, holding Pedro by the hand and accompanied by Belforte and his wife. 'Three long and sad days had finished on that sunny and beautiful morning. And then everything became wonderful and happy. And there was from then on, in that mountain village, peace and joy and love and God!'

The preserved film fragment

A look at the film fragment preserved at ANIM (a positive black-and-white celluloid film copy) shows that it corresponds to a series of consecutive scenes that begin with the arrival of Lídia at Casal de Lobos at the time of her first visit. The sequence of the scenes in the two reels, in their 26 minutes (the first divided into a total of 69 shots and the second, shorter reel, into 34), ends when Lídia, on her second night at Casal de Lobos, witnesses Belforte leaving the secret room with an empty wheelchair after she hears Isabel's outburst. The change of reels occurs after the return of Lídia to Casal de Lobos, after discovering that she has no more students to teach and before Paulo Belforte's first confession about his wife's accident.

Most significant is that almost all the action described in the 'dialogue sequence, storyboard basis' corresponds to the action in the film fragment. However, there are some discrepancies in the action and mood that should be noted:

(a) on her first visit Lídia finds Pedro and supports him during his mother's attack, talks to him and calms him down;
(b) in several scenes, lightning flashes are visible, suddenly illuminating the interiors;
(c) when Lídia first finds herself alone in her bedroom, the door handle turns on its own (which later, turns out to be the maid who came to deliver the bedding);
(d) when Lídia tries to teach her only student, she is interrupted by stones thrown through the window of the classroom by the women of the village, and when Lídia then leaves the building, the women are standing quietly at the door, forming a corridor that Lídia passes through;
(e) the lunch scene, when she returns, was omitted (or included in another portion of the film);
(f) although there is no soundtrack and therefore one cannot discern the dialogue, it seems that the presentation of Lídia's theory about the stained glass being the cause of Isabel's hallucinations happens after Belforte's first confession about his wife's accident.

The two storyboards: Comparing scene six

In addition to the comparison between the 'dialogue sequence, storyboard basis' and the preserved fragment of the film, it is still necessary to compare these two with the storyboards themselves, both the annotated version and the one reviewed by the censors. As the size of these two documents renders an in-depth analysis untenable in the scope of this chapter, by way of example I have chosen to compare filming instructions and the final footage for scene six, which corresponds to the first 27 shots of the preserved film fragment.[6] This scene was storyboarded and then shot as described in Appendix B.[7]

The first obvious conclusion from this comparison is that the storyboarding contemplated by the censors corresponds to the first adaptation written by Raúl Faria da Fonseca, which reproduces almost exactly the action described in the 'dialogue sequence, storyboard basis', whereas the annotated storyboard describes almost exactly the scenes as they were actually shot and has therefore been elaborated at a later period and used as an annotation tool during shooting. Thus, in order to understand the gaps resulting from the insufficient preservation of the film, the document that should be considered as more reliable is that of the annotated storyboard, since it is the one that most closely approximates the film materials that have been preserved.

The second important fact to note is the difference in tone between the first version of scene six by Raúl Faria da Fonseca and the second version, which is, I suppose, by Bárbara Virgínia herself. In this regard, it is important to consider the 'clarification' published by Faria da Fonseca in the newspaper *Diário de Lisboa* on the date of the premiere of *Três dias sem Deus*:

> For those interested it must be made clear that in the publicity concerning the film *Três dias sem Deus* it is necessary to mention the fact that the respective initial storyboard was later changed without the intervention of the author, who was absent, and therefore Raúl Faria da Fonseca should only be credited as a writer (cinematographic sequence), as far as the changes to the storyboard have not had a detrimental effect.
>
> (Fonseca 1946: 5)

Thus, not only does the author of the original storyboard protest against the narrative, tone and aesthetic changes that the film sustained in his absence, he also excludes himself from these variations.

In the case of scene six, there is a noticeable tendency towards melodrama in Faria da Fonseca's version (the constant presence of the piano played by Isabel, the introduction of several shots of the stained-glass window lit by flashes of lightning, and the parallel editing between Paulo and Lídia's conversation and the wife's hallucinations). Conversely, in the preserved version and in the second storyboard, the piano is present only in the soundtrack and Isabel's screen time almost disappears, with the exception of the moment in which she is taken to the secret room in her wheelchair. This also reduces the dramatic confrontation between the two women who surround Paulo Belforte (a confrontation prompted by jealousy and disease, which Faria da Fonseca is not afraid to emphasize, revealing in this same scene Belforte's sexual interest in Lídia). In Virgínia's version it is necessary to take into account the heavily emphasized inclusion of Pedro in the action as evidence of Lídia's maternal side (and professional dedication), which also exalts Belforte's potential interest in Lídia from the carnal to the spiritual, as he is moved by the affection that the teacher gives to her student. In addition, there is also the question of the outcome of the scene: in Faria da Fonseca's version it becomes very clear that Lídia does not want to stay in Casal de Lobos and that only the late hour and the bad weather persuade her to remain. In Virgínia's version, Lídia staying seems natural and expected, an event that does not seem to require much explanation. From the perspective of the *mise en scène*, the change of staging in the conversation sequence (in Faria da Fonseca's storyboard Lídia is sitting on a sofa with her back towards a standing Belforte; in Virgínia's version both are standing and facing each other) appears to suggest a change in the presence and strength of the female character. From the point of view of direction for the actors, Raúl Faria da Fonseca's storyboard explains in detail the action and mood of the characters, while the annotated version summarizes the description of certain shots by simply identifying the characters and their positions in the scene – which also shows a significant difference between the approach of the two filmmakers.

This is the possible understanding that we can gain of Bárbara Virgínia's cinematic view in *Três dias sem Deus*, even if only through an opposition with Faria da Fonseca's own idea of cinema. But what is certain is that it is difficult, if not impossible, to determine a clear perspective on what Virgínia's vision for this film would have been. It should be noted that this is not a unique case but is, in fact, typical for films directed by women. In support of this statement, I submit the following quote from Shelley Cobb's essay 'Film authorship and adaptation': 'Western culture's masculine version of individual authorship as the signifier of originality, authority, and ownership [... is] troubled by adaptation and its threat of multiple authors and fragmented identities' (Cobb 2012: 112).

Not only does the film present itself as a mesh of intentions of diverse origins and authorships, but its incomplete conservation also makes this identification even more difficult. However, it is quite clear from scene six (and a similar exercise could be performed for several other scenes of the storyboard) that Bárbara Virgínia introduced a change in tone in her version of the adaptation of Marques' novel, one which reinforces the position of the Lídia character and reduces the melodramatic texture and the sexual tension between her and Paulo Belforte. This change seems to be made in the sense of affirming the duty of the teacher's role in a small community, as opposed to the particular interests of Lídia as a woman (and other people's interests towards her). Hence, the following section will emphasize this particular aspect: the film's portrayal of a primary schoolteacher in a rural village of the 1940s.

Primary schoolteacher: Another form of representation

The character of the primary schoolteacher comes from Gentil Marques' novel – he had already written a film screenplay about a teacher years earlier (Marques n.d.). I shall conclude this chapter with a brief commentary that will help to circumscribe and better frame the matter of the representation of the new figure of the primary schoolteacher in Portuguese society in the late 1940s.

According to Irene Flunser Pimentel in *História das Organizações Femininas no Estado Novo* (2010), António Augusto Pires de Lima, Porto's Civil Governor, initiated a lawsuit to prevent the 'invasion of high schools by girls' (Pimentel 2010: 84). To this end, there was an increase in complementary female schools in order to prevent the possibility that all female students would become doctors instead of 'good housewives and mothers' (Pimentel 2010: 85). In this regard, the Estado Novo's solution for the lack of female-only high schools was to 'channel many female students into the Escolas do Magistério Primário (EMP, 'Primary Education Schools') and technical – female – education, thus simultaneously solving an ideological issue and the overcrowding of high schools' (Pimentel 2010: 85), and also to try to put an end to the co-educational schools established by the First Republic and which the Estado Novo prohibited in 1949 (with very few exceptions).

These women were then trained for typically poorly paid jobs, which nonetheless provided a certain degree of independence and social mobility to lower-class women who could train, for example, to become primary schoolteachers, nurses and social workers (Pimentel 2010: 86). Another ideological driver for these measures was the need for the Estado Novo to reduce the strength of the large number of republican teachers. To this end, António Carneiro Pacheco, then Minister of Public Instruction, progressively lowered teachers' salaries, created the job of 'school regent' (typically a female worker who was illiterate and chosen according to criteria of moral suitability), opened the aforementioned EMP and 'valued the verification of the moral and civic quality of teachers' (Pimentel 2010: 90), a series of measures which would come to be known as Carneiro Pacheco's Reform.[8]

In these circumstances, Lídia's character in *Três dias sem Deus* is representative of the teaching policies of the time, since in 1945/46 the first two-year courses of the EMP had been completed and the first batch of young primary schoolteachers was dispatched throughout the country to fill the many empty teaching posts at the time.[9]

Lídia represents a new social class built by the Estado Novo which, as Maria Filomena Mónica describes, was meant to be passive and adaptable to political, social and cultural conditions; someone who held the highest social position that a woman could achieve in rural areas, who, more often than not, required sponsorship by the priest or an influential person in the area. Given the moral factor in their selection, the great majority of these women were politically conservative and ideally suited to convey the ideology of the state to the children they taught (Mónica cited in Pimentel 2010: 90).

It is clear that the consecration of the primary schoolteacher as a dramatic, unjustly condemned figure and victim of rural ignorance was one that could simultaneously satisfy the Estado Novo's ideology – by sacralizing this new figure of Portuguese society – but also reveal the mysticism and illiteracy that permeated certain rural Portuguese communities. In this sense, *Três dias sem Deus* is an unusual fictional testimony of a remarkable moment in the emancipation of women in the world of work (albeit in a highly controlled way via the Estado Novo), and Lídia (through Bárbara Virgínia) is one of its first cinematic representations. This portrayal reveals the fragility of the female teacher's position, confirming the need for a male counterpart in the social organization. It is not by chance that the entire plot of the film begins with the absence of the priest and the doctor, and that peace is only regained when those same characters return during the most dramatic conflict (a truly *Deus ex machina* plot device). Coincidently – or perhaps not – all the female characters in the village possess more strength and importance in the rural social fabric than Lídia (with the obvious exception of the deranged Isabel). This is justified, of course, because Lídia is a figure who has just arrived in the mountain village. This figure is external to the social organization of the Portuguese countryside – a female figure with unprecedented power in that same environment and a character ontologically exogenous to the circularity of relationships in a small environment. Lídia represents the disruption that occurred in rural life when the need to integrate the first EMP trainees across the country emerged; and this is symbolic of the start of the changes happening concerning the participation of women in civic matters and labour in Portuguese society – albeit in a manipulated way.

Conclusion

In her last interview, given to Pereira and Pianco, Bárbara Virgínia explained: 'What I wanted to do was to direct. So, a friend of mine at the time said, "Do you want to be a man?" And I replied: "Why are only men allowed to direct movies? Why cannot women direct them too?"' (Virgínia 2016: 6). Bárbara Virgínia was also questioned on this by the newspaper *Diário de Lisboa* at the time of the film's premiere: 'And do you not fear that you will not be forgiven for invading a field occupied only by men?' To this, she replied, '[n]o. I may fear that I have not met the minimum requirements of a work of this magnitude. The rest would be sick thoughts that I want to move away from my modest little corner' (Virgínia 1946: 5). And in a talk Virgínia gave at the Emissora Nacional (National Radio Broadcaster') entitled *A Mulher no Cinema* (1949), transcribed in the *Rádio Nacional* magazine, she says:

> There are diverse opinions about a film being directed by a woman. Of course, it is great that not everyone agrees, that there is a discussion, mainly because in this matter if we were to weigh the opinions, unfortunately the balance would fall to the opposition.
>
> (Virgínia 1949: 3)

As a result of statements such as these, it is tempting to sustain a re-reading of this episode from Portuguese cinema history, identifying in Bárbara Virgínia's discourse and film work a feminist point of view. I do not think this is correct. In fact, her positions are sometimes very much in accordance with the official position of the dictatorship – in this regard, one should note as an example the study of José Barreto, *Misoginia e antifeminismo em Fernando Pessoa*, where similar contradictions are evidenced by one of the greatest names in Portuguese culture, the poet Fernando Pessoa, that 'would certainly lead to the labelling [... of Pessoa] as a supremacist or "male chauvinist"' (Barreto 2011: 10).

What is certain is that Virgínia defended, above all else, equal access to the film industry for both men and women.[10] Years later, Bárbara Virgínia described her own film in the introduction of her etiquette manual *Etiquetas sem etiqueta* (1989):

> Very young I even directed a feature film... the subject? A newly trained teacher who went to a distant place with unknown people, struggling to enlighten the young, without forbidding anything, telling them of the importance of the freedom that everyone has, since one is born with it, but with the reminder that it is necessary to know how to use it and for this you must respect to be respected. (Virgínia 1989: 4)

Despite the pedagogical context of this etiquette book, it is nevertheless clear that Bárbara Virgínia's interest in her 1946 film focused particularly on the portrayal of primary education in a poor, rural and essentially illiterate community. This was its thematic core; its purpose. I believe it has become clear, through the comparative analysis of the two film storyboards, as well as of the historical contextualization and discourse of the filmmaker, that although it is difficult to find a properly feminist point of view in *Três dias sem Deus*, it is possible to identify a change in the adaptation of the story by the female director that centralizes the prominence of Lídia's character, thus reducing the melodramatic and sexual tension that Raúl Faria da Fonseca's version constantly insinuated. This change seems to be related to affirming Lídia's role as a primary schoolteacher always devoted to her students, as opposed to Lídia's private interests as a woman – that is, as a sexual being. In a way, this change in adaptation by Virgínia coincides with the study – in spite of its very different scope in terms of the period and origin of the works – by Shelley Cobb in *Adaptation, Authorship, and Contemporary Women Filmmakers*, where she states that her interest is in filmmakers who 'use adaptation to foreground authorship; [and] how these adaptations are places from which the female voice [...] "can speak and be heard"' (Cobb 2015: 2). But it should be noted that this change in adaptation, although made according to a schematic drawing of the characters, describes a possible professional emancipation in Portuguese society of the 1940s, an emancipation of which Lídia is a reflection and Bárbara Virgínia an icon.

REFERENCES

Barreto, José (2011), 'Introdução', in *Misoginia e antifeminismo em Fernando Pessoa*, Lisbon: Ática, pp. 9–34.

Cobb, Shelley (2012), 'Film authorship and adaptation', in D. Cartmell (ed.), *A Companion to Literature, Film, and Adaptation*, West Sussex: Wiley-Blackwell, pp. 105–21.

——— (2015), *Adaptation, Authorship, and Contemporary Women Filmmakers*, Basingstoke: Palgrave Macmillan.

Fonseca, Raúl Faria da (1945), *Três dias sem Deus, Sequência dialogada, base de planificação*, Lisbon: Invicta Filmes – Produtora Independente/Cinemateca Portuguesa – Museu do Cinema.

——— (1946), 'Esclarecimento', *Diário de Lisboa*, 30 August, p. 5.

França, José-Augusto (2014), *O 'Ano XX' Lisboa 1946: Estudos de Factos Socioculturais*, Lisbon: INCM – Imprensa Nacional Casa da Moeda.

Grande Enciclopédia Portuguesa e Brasileira (GEPeB) (1982), vol. 36, Lisbon: Página Editora.

Invicta Filmes – Produtora Independente (IFPI) (1945), *Três dias sem Deus, Planificação visada pela censura em 30 de Outubro de 1945*, Lisbon: IFPI/ Cinemateca Portuguesa – Museu do Cinema.

——— (1946), *Três dias sem Deus, Planificação com anotações*, Lisbon: IFPI/Cinemateca Portuguesa – Museu do Cinema.

Lisboa, Ricardo Vieira (2016), 'O restauro cinematográfico e a Teoria dos Cineastas: O caso de Bárbara Virgínia', in M. Penafria, E. T. Baggio, A. R. Graça and D. C. Araújo (eds), *Propostas para a Teoria do Cinema – Teoria dos Cineastas*, vol. 2, Covilhã: LabCom.IPF, pp. 39–72.

——— (2017), 'A recepção crítica de *Três dias sem Deus* de Bárbara Virgínia', in F. Lopes, P. Cunha and M. Penafria (eds), *Cinema em Português – X Jornadas*, Covilhã: LabCom. IPF, pp. 93–118.

Lourenço, António (1946), '"Três dias sem Deus" realização de Bárbara Virgínia estreou-se no Ginásio com agrado', *O Século*, 30 August, p. 8.

Marques, Gentil (n.d.), 'Ali onde tudo era silêncio', Fundo Geral de Monografias do Fundo Geral da Biblioteca Nacional, quota: B.A. 3297 V.

Matos-Cruz, José de (1999), *O cais do olhar: O cinema português de longa metragem e a ficção muda*, Lisbon: Cinemateca Portuguesa.

Pimentel, Irene Flunser (2010), *História das Organizações Femininas no Estado Novo*, Rio de Mouro: Temas e Debates.

Ramos, Jorge Leitão (2012), *Dicionário do Cinema Português 1895–1961*, Lisbon: Editorial Caminho.

Ribeiro, Manuel Félix (1983), '"Três Dias Sem Deus", de Bárbara Virgínia', in *Filmes, Figuras e Factos da História do Cinema Português – 1896–1949*, Lisbon: Cinemateca Portuguesa, pp. 542–48.

Virgínia, Bárbara (1946), *Três dias sem Deus*, Portugal: Invicta Filmes – Produtora Independente.

——— (1949), 'Mulher no cinema', *Rádio Nacional*, 18 June, pp. 3, 6.

——— (1989), *Etiquetas sem etiqueta – só para 'teen agers', dicas de relacionamento pessoal*, São Paulo: Editora Vozes.

——— (2016), interview with Ana Catarina Pereira and William Pianco, 'Bárbara Virgínia – A primeira realizadora de cinema, em Portugal', *International Journal of Cinema*, 2, pp. 18–29.

Appendix A: Chronology compiled from newspaper and magazine excerpts

3 May 1945: 'Raúl Faria da Fonseca has finished the storyboard for the film *Três dias sem Deus* [...] The shooting of this film, of which the production director will be Felismino Felisberto, should start as soon as Armando Miranda completes the shooting of his current film *José do Telhado* at Cinelândia studios.' In *Filmagem* (1945), 19:3, 3 May, p. 9.

14 June 1945: 'The studio has to be assigned to a new director, Raúl Faria da Fonseca, who will soon start shooting his first film, *Três dias sem Deus*.' In *Filmagem* (1945), 24:3, 14 June, p. 5.

28 June 1945: 'As for Portuguese film productions, the terrifying spectre of the absolute lack of new [35mm] film now looms, a problem that the end of the war, instead of solving, has worsened considerably. It is anticipated that there will be plenty of film again when they reopen the French factories. Until then Portuguese cinema will have to struggle on with serious difficulties.' In *Filmagem* (1945), 26:3, 28 June, p. 5.

28 July 1945: 'The work on Cinelândia's new film, *Três dias sem Deus*, with Felisberto Felismino as producer, has started. The main female interpreter is Bárbara Virgínia and the camera operator will be the well-known cinematographer, Toni.' In *Filmagem* (1945), 30:3, 28 July, p. 9.

28 July 1945: 'We have heard [...] that Raúl Faria da Fonseca will no longer direct *Três dias sem Deus* [...] and that the same filmmaker will become the director of the dubbing section at Cinelândia studios.' In *Filmagem* (1945), 30:3, 28 July, p. 5.

27 September 1945: 'As it has been widely announced, the filming of *Três dias sem Deus* will begin, the first production of Invicta Filmes Independente, Limitada. Adaption of the Gentil Marques novel, *Mundo Perdido* [...] Direction: Bárbara Virgínia.' In *Filmagem* (1945), 39:3, 27 September, p. 10.

4 October 1945: 'One of the most widely talked about issues in our small film scene was that Bárbara Virgínia took on her shoulders the responsibility for the acting and directing of *Três dias sem Deus*. Having not yet had the opportunity to appreciate Bárbara Virgínia's acting work, since Cinelândia's *Sonho de Amor* has still not premiered, we have faith that her fine sensibility and the artistic gifts that we are told she possess are enough for her to untangle this responsibility. These are our hopes.' In *Filmagem* (1945), 40:3, 4 October, p. 9.

27 December 1945: 'And here comes "sympathy" [Bárbara Virgínia] to say goodbye. In haste I ask: "How is this *Três dias sem Deus* going?" "Soon I will begin ... As soon as the new

film arrives ...".' Báptista Rosa, 'Quinentos quilómetros à procura de *Sonho de Amor*!' In *Filmagem* (1946), 53:3, 10 January, p. 9.

5 January 1946: 'At Cinelândia, Lda. studios a new film is about to start shooting and some of its interiors have already been built: it is the film *Três dias sem Deus*, produced by Invicta Produtora Independente, Lda.' In *7.ª Arte: revista mundial de cinema* (1946), 5 January, p. 16.

10 January 1946: 'Our dear comrade, Raúl Faria da Fonseca, went to the United States to visit the best American film studios on a study trip and to solve various issues related to 16mm production.' In *Filmagem* (1946), 53:3, 10 January, p. 10.

31 January 1946: 'Next week, in the studios of Lisboa Filmes and Cinelândia, two new films, *Homem do Ribatejo* and *Três dias sem Deus*, directed by Henrique Campos and Bárbara Virgínia, respectively, begin shooting.' In *Filmagem* (1946), 56:3, 31 January, p. 10.

February 1946: 'Raúl Faria da Fonseca left on 2 January for North America where he will deal with matters that relate to MGM.' In *O.K.* (1946), 1 February, p. 5.

March 1946: 'There is a group of naysayers who bark at the fact that Bárbara Virgínia is going to direct *Três dias sem Deus*. Either it is envy, or it is too much professional pride [...] What it is not is definitely wanting the girl to make the film.' In *Eva* (1946), March, p. 22.

15 March 1946: 'On 18 February the film *Três dias sem Deus* finally started rolling, produced by Invicta Filmes Independente, Lda. The exteriors of this new Portuguese film are already finished, and the shooting is continuing at Cinelândia studios [...] The shooting is running smoothly and if they continue like this, the film should be ready within two months.' In *7.ª Arte: revista mundial de cinema* (1946), 15 March, p. 6.

5 April 1946: 'The finish line for the shooting of *Três dias sem Deus* that Bárbara Virgínia directed is close, after making satisfactory progress.' In *Filmagem* (1946), 63:3, 1 April, p. 10.

10 April 1946: '[*Três dias sem Deus* is] a new Portuguese film that has just entered the laboratories of the Lisboa-Filme for its finishing touches.' In *Filmagem* (1946), 64:3, 10 April, p. 5.

8 August 1946: '[I]t [*Três dias sem Deus*] will have its premiere in the last days of September.' In *Filmagem* (1946), 74:3, 8 August, p. 8.

30 August 1946: *Três dias sem Deus* premieres at Cinema Ginásio.

30 August 1946: 'The directors Leitão de Barros and Bárbara Virgínia will be going to that French town [Cannes]'. In *O Século* (1946), 29 August, p. 9.

5 October 1946: The film is shown in Cannes in the final days of the festival. In Matos-Cruz (1999), p. 80.

19 December 1946: 'Bárbara Virgínia: "It was not my fault that they insisted on taking my film to Cannes!"' In *Cinema* (1946), 6, 19 December, p. 3.

Appendix B: Scene 6: comparison of the two storyboards and the film fragment

No.	Scene 6 from the annotated storyboard	Scene 6 from the censor-reviewed storyboard	Scene 6 from the film fragment
0	'Medium shot: Scene played in the dark, only dimly lit by the light coming from a window on the right. Lídia enters the frame with a lantern. She hesitates, knocks on the door and waits. She starts knocking harder. Silence. Tereza's dragging footsteps begin to sound. She opens the door and looks suspiciously at Lídia. Lídia speaks. Tereza looks her up and down. Lídia speaks to her again. Tereza softly opens the door just a little and walks away. Lídia understands the gesture and enters, in fear. Goes to the entrance hall sofa. Tereza accompanies her with her gaze, and looks at her sideways, closing the door on the camera.'	'Medium shot: Scene played in the dark, only dimly lit by the light coming from a window on the right. Lídia enters the frame with a lantern and a handbag. She hesitates, knocks on the door and waits. She starts knocking harder. The piano stops playing, abruptly. Silence. Tereza's dragging footsteps begin to sound, she opens the door and looks suspiciously at Lídia. Lídia speaks. Tereza looks her up and down. Lídia speaks to her again. Tereza softly opens the door just a little and walks away. Lídia understands the gesture and enters, in fear. Goes to the entrance hall sofa. Tereza accompanies her with her gaze, and looks at her sideways, closing the door on the camera.'	
1	'Wide shot: Lídia standing by the sofa turns off her lantern, puts it down. Tereza, without losing sight of Lídia, goes to the adjoining room and then disappears. Panning shot. Lídia gazes over the room.'	'Wide shot: Lídia standing by the sofa turns off her lantern puts it down. Tereza, without losing sight of Lídia, goes to the adjoining room and then disappears. Panning shot. Lídia gazes over the room. Lídia puts her handbag down, next to the lantern.'	Wide shot: Lídia and Teresa are inside the house next to a bench. Teresa leaves Lídia alone with a lantern in her hand, which she then turns off.
2	'Wide shot: slow panning over the room, until it frames Lídia, on her back, who is looking around.'	'Wide shot: slow panning over the room, until it frames Lídia, on her back, who is looking around. She turns around upon hearing Tereza's footsteps.'	Medium shot: Lídia, on a black background, looks around.

3	'Wide shot: Lídia, facing the camera, looks at the hall. Paulo comes to her, from behind, without her noticing.'	'Wide shot: Tereza is waiting in the piano room and signals Lídia to join her. Lídia grabs her handbag and starts walking.'	Wide shot: a panning shot that frames the stairs, a corridor with columns and the walls in the room.
4	'Medium shot: Lídia turns rapidly when she hears Paulo coming. She turns her back to the camera.'	'Medium shot: Lídia advances, apprehensively, accompanied by a travelling shot. She passes by Tereza, who walks away, and stops looking around the room, to see someone. When she hears Paulo, she looks to her right, surprised (almost frightened). Quick panning shot that frames Paulo, backlit by the lantern behind him. We hear Lídia. Paulo speaks. Lídia enters the frame and sits with her back to Paulo. Lídia speaks. After sitting down, Lídia is not sure of herself because she has Paulo behind her. He hesitates a moment and advances behind the bench to the right side of the frame, finding Isabel, static at the piano.'	Medium shot: Lídia is looking around, Paulo appears from a gothic arch door that is behind her, without her noticing him.
5	'Medium shot: Paulo and Lídia (both standing).'	'Medium shot: Isabel by the piano, only lit by the lantern. She has a frozen expression and is pale. She looks in Paulo and Lídia's direction. She starts getting emotional, albeit discreetly.'	Medium shot: Paulo approaches from the left of the frame without her noticing him. He talks to her, she turns around surprised.
6	'Medium shot: Lídia and Paulo.'	'Medium shot: Lídia is seated. Paulo is standing. Both in profile. She speaks. Paulo, while paying attention to Lídia, whose beauty seems to interest him, also does not lose sight of Isabel, to whom he looks especially at the end of the shot, worried about her.'	Medium shot: the two speak.

(Continued)

7	'Medium shot: Lídia and Paulo.'	'Medium shot: Isabel by the piano, same as in shot 6 [5], but even more emotional.'	Medium shot: both speak in profile, black background, dimly lit, only their profiles are visible.
8	'Medium shot: Lídia and Paulo.'	'Medium shot: Paulo facing the camera; Lídia is in 3/4 position (almost over her shoulder). Paulo listens to Lídia, almost without paying attention, because he is worried about Isabel's attitude.'	Over-the-shoulder shot: Paulo talks to Lídia.
9	'Wide shot: Lídia (facing the camera).'	'Medium shot: Isabel by the piano, getting more excited as she listens to their conversation.'	Reverse shot over the waist, no light continuity: Lídia speaks.
10	'Medium shot: Paulo and Lídia (over her shoulder).'	'Medium shot: Paulo and Lídia as before, he speaks to Lídia. Gets even more worried about Isabel.'	Close-up high-angle shot: Lídia's face; she is speaking.
11	'Medium shot: Lídia, surprised, grabs her things in order to leave.'	'Medium shot: Isabel is very disturbed, looks down over the piano, almost hallucinating.'	Over-the-shoulder shot, facing Lídia: something catches Paulo's attention that makes him leave via the same door through which he entered.
12	'Wide shot: when Lídia is about to leave, Pedro appears and gets close to her.'	'Medium shot: Paulo has just watched Isabel and speaks to Lídia intensely, as if trying to compel her not to stay there any longer. The piano stops Paulo, he looks at Isabel, furious, and Lídia gets up, surprised, and also looks at her, trying to make sense of what is going on.'	Medium shot: Lídia is alone, turns around to another door that is closed.
13	'Medium shot: Lídia and Pedro.'	'Medium shot: Isabel plays the piano, visibly disturbed.'	Medium shot: Lídia is with her back to the camera, facing that closed door, expressionistic lightning, her hair and shoulders backlit. Pedro appears, and she turns around.

14	'Medium shot: Lídia looks surprised.'	'Medium shot: Paulo and Lídia look at Isabel […] Paulo, still furious, leaves the frame, suddenly […], leaving Lídia surprised by all this commotion.'	Closer medium shot: Lídia and Pedro.
15	'Medium shot: Teresa rolls Isabel's wheelchair away, followed by Paulo. They pass through Lídia, on whom the camera stays. Lídia looks surprised.'	'Medium shot: Isabel by the piano; as Paulo reaches her he suddenly takes her hand from the keys and closes the piano with a bang.'	Close-up shot: Lídia looking suspiciously.
16	'Wide shot: Lídia looks at Pedro. He speaks. After he finishes, Lídia hugs him and kisses him.'	'Medium shot: Lídia looks surprised; when she hears Tereza's footsteps, she reacts. Tereza comes from the back and stands behind Isabel. Tereza is obviously disturbed, wringing her hand in worry.'	Wide shot: Paulo goes back through the gothic arch door with Teresa and Isabel in her wheelchair, Following are Lídia and Pedro. In the foreground there is a circular bench that Paulo, Teresa and Isabel circle around.
17	'Medium shot: Paulo approaches, touched [by the previous shot].'	'Medium shot: Paulo rolls Isabel's chair, together with a panning movement. Passes behind Lídia, on whom the camera stays. Tereza, who also fits in the frame, follows the action with her gaze, worried. Lídia also looks.'	Medium shot: Lídia and Pedro, she holds his face and kisses him.
18	'Wide shot: Lídia and Pedro. Paulo is a little behind, listening to their conversation.'	'Wide shot: Paulo, taking Isabel in her wheelchair, disappears in the background.'	Medium shot: Paulo comes from the left with a piece of paper in his hands; he stops under the gothic arch and gazes. He places the piece of paper in his jacket pocket and, holding his gaze, he smiles.
19	'Wide shot: Lídia, Paulo and Pedro'	'Medium shot: Lídia and Tereza stop looking at Paulo. Tereza looks at Lídia, as she blames her for what just happened, and leaves the	Wide shot: in the foreground are Lídia and Pedro, in the background is Paulo, next to the

(Continued)

		frame, still worried, Lídia stays, also looking worried. She is going to take Pedro's hand when the room is suddenly filled with light and thunder is heard. Lídia looks towards the stained-glass window.'	arch. Lídia speaks to Pedro, she is sideways, and he has his back to the camera. A lightning flash illuminates the room. Paulo gets closer, only there they notice him.
20	'Medium shot: Lídia, Pedro and Paulo. Paulo seems to be expecting something. Lídia is hesitant. Pedro speaks.'	'Wide shot: the stained-glass window is illuminated again due to a lightning flash in the sky. New and stronger thunder boom is heard.'	Wide shot: same as the previous, but better lit.
21	'Medium shot: Lídia smiles (at 3/4).'	'Wide shot: […] exterior shot, at night. Rain starts to fall.'	Over-the-shoulder shot facing Lídia: she looks at Pedro.
22	'Medium shot: Tereza by the door with a lantern.'	'Wide shot: […] shot of the sky. Lightning crosses the sky and illuminates it.'	Medium shot: Teresa with a lantern, in the dark.
23	'Medium shot: Lídia and Paulo. Paulo speaks. Tereza approaches and takes a key. They speak. Pedro is also present.'	'Medium shot: Lídia is illuminated by lightning. Looks worried. She reacts. She moves towards the door, accompanied by a panning movement; at that same moment Paulo joins her. Lídia stops. Paulo also stops, undecided on what to do next. Lídia speaks. Paulo stops her. He is also stopped by lightning and the sound of thunder.'	Wide shot: Teresa enters the frame with her back to the camera, she approaches Paulo and receives something from him (keys?). The four are in the frame and they speak. Teresa turns around showing her face, illuminated by the lantern. Paulo and Pedro leave from the left. Small panning shot to the right framing Lídia and Teresa in the centre.
24	'Medium shot: Tereza, with the lantern, approaches Lídia (with a panning shot) that also stays in the frame looking towards the place that Paulo had left.'	'Medium shot: Lídia is facing the camera. the shot is over Paulo's right shoulder. Lídia listens to Paulo, incredulous. She looks towards Tereza entering, Paulo stops speaking, he is surprised by Tereza's return (Tereza is out of frame).'	Medium shot: Paulo approaches a door, stops and looks around.

25	'Medium shot: Paulo is next to door A. Feeling observed, he stops and looks behind him.'	'Medium shot: Tereza is at the door, as if is she has just arrived, looks with irony. After, she becomes perplexed, intimidated.'	Wide shot: Lídia and Teresa in profile, they leave from the right. In the background stands Paulo, next to the door.
26	'Wide shot: Lídia gazes together with Tereza. She follows her (panning shot), the camera stays with Paulo observing Lídia while she climbs the stairs.'	'Medium shot: Lídia and Paulo. Paulo speaks. Tereza approaches, receives some keys and leaves. (Lightning). They speak. Paulo gazes at Lídia with interest. Lídia seems intrigued by his gaze.'	Wide high-angle shot: stairs, Lídia climbs up to the middle, stops and turns around, looks, climbs again.
27	'Wide high-angle shot: Lídia climbs the stairs with Tereza, before disappearing round the corner. Looks behind her discreetly.'	'Wide shot: stained-glass window is lit by lightning.'	Medium high-angle shot: Paulo next to the door follows with his eyes, waits, opens the door and enters.
28	'Wide high-angle shot: Paulo stops observing Lídia. He reflects and enters door A.'	'Medium shot: Lídia and Paulo talk. Tereza comes from the back and into the frame. She then leaves the frame from the left.'	
29		'Medium shot: Tereza holds the lantern, listening ironically to the conversation. She approaches Lídia, (panning shot) that is framed as well, looking towards the place from where Paulo had left. Lídia hesitates. Afterwards, she follows Tereza through the door (panning shot). Arriving at the door she stops, as if she has seen something.'	
30		'Medium shot: Paulo reaches door A, but, feeling observed, he stops and looks behind him.'	
31		'Medium shot: Lídia, next to the door (with Tereza) looks at Tereza, and lowers her eyes. She follows Tereza (panning shot). The camera stays with Paulo as he gazes at Lídia, in the hallway before the stairs.'	

(Continued)

32		'Wide high-angle shot: Lídia climbs the stairs with Tereza, before disappearing over the corner. Looks behind her discreetly.'	
33		'Wide high-angle shot: Paulo stops observing Lídia. He reflects and enters door A.'	

NOTES

1. All translations from the Portuguese by the author.
2. Born on 15 November 1923, Virgínia studied acting at the National Conservatory of Lisbon. She began her artistic career at the *Emissora Nacional* (National Radio Broadcaster) reciting poetry and as a lyrical singer, and also was part of the São Carlos Theatre Ballet Group. On 25 October 1946, she had her acting debut at Teatro Maria Vitória in a popular Portuguese theatre production. In 1947 she starred in the operetta *Flor da Murta (Sua Majestade o Amor)* by Silva Tavares and it was not until 1948 that she acted in a 'serious theatre' production, starring in the *The Thief* by Henri Bernstein, at the Sá da Bandeira Theatre in Porto. From 1949 on, she reduced her career to *diseuse* with a poetry recital at the São Luís Theatre, following that with a tour that took her to Spain, France and the Netherlands. She wrote for publications such as the newspapers *A Voz* and *Diário de Lisboa*, and the magazines *Modas e Bordados* and *Rádio Nacional*, mainly producing theatre criticism, travel chronicles and other types of journalistic writing, including an essay on women filmmakers (Ramos 2012: 453). In cinema, her debut as an actress was in Carlos Porfírio's *Sonho de amor* (1945) and, in that same year, she was responsible for the narration of the documentary *Neve em Lisboa* (1945) by Raúl Faria da Fonseca. After *Três dias sem Deus*, she also acted in *Aqui Portugal* (1947) by Amando Miranda. In 1952 she travelled to Brazil to pursue a career with the television and radio broadcaster Tupi, continuing her work on stage as *diseuse*. She retired from the stage on 15 October 1963 in a show at the Municipal Theatre of São Paulo; eleven days later, she married a Brazilian businessman, and later dedicated herself to writing manners and etiquette manuals, continuing still for some years as an radio announcer for Tupi (GEPeB 1982: 134).
3. This statement needs more careful evaluation, however. Stating that *Três dias sem Deus* was her first film may not be entirely accurate: in a review of *Três dias sem Deus* in the newspaper *O Século*, António Lourenço refers to two short documentary films directed by Bárbara Virgínia: *Aldeia dos rapazes – Orfanato Sta. Isabel de Albarraque* and *Jogo da sardinha* (Lourenço 1946). In the Arquivo Nacional da Imagem em Movimento (National Archives of Moving Image – ANIM) the first of these films is archived as directed by Bárbara Virgínia (although the preserved copy of the film does not include credits), while the second is archived as being directed by José de Oliveira Cosme. The two films premiered together

with *Três dias sem Deus*. It should be noted, however, that there are two films, dating from 1947, that were directed by Adolfo Coelho with similar titles as the first: *A Aldeia dos rapazes da rua* and *A Aldeia dos rapazes do sul,* which may indicate that the first title attributed to Virgínia actually belongs to Coelho's filmography.

4. A 'mediocre' writer (França 2014: 272) who wrote romanticized biographies of well-known national personalities, translations of English novels and literary adaptations of successful films.
5. For an extensive analysis of the reception of the film by the Portuguese press, see (in Portuguese) Lisboa (2017).
6. In both storyboards of this scene a first introductory shot is described, but the preserved fragment does not include any trace of it. This shot, the absence of which could be seen as a gap or as an alteration to the storyboard, is of the mansion's exterior, which may justify its absence since all the interiors were shot in a studio.
7. All the action descriptions I present in Appendix B are direct quotes from the documents concerned, bearing in mind that in these documents there are references to dialogue and the rest of the soundtrack which I did not include, both due to the risk of inundating the reader with unnecessary information, and because in the comparison exercise with the fragment preserved, the absence of soundtrack makes this information superfluous. I also considered superfluous the information regarding the duration of each shot, the types of framing and the lens indicated to film each shot.
8. In Mário de Figueiredo's ministry, given the lack of teachers, measures such as considering school regents and primary schoolteachers to be on an equal footing were adopted (Pimentel 2010, 88–89). In addition to the devaluation of the professional status of teachers, the interference of the Ministry of National Education was also evident in the requirement that female teachers request permission to marry, which was precisely aimed at preventing the social mobility of these women (Pimentel 2010: 89–90). The ministry of Fernando Andrade Pires de Lima also imposed quotas of 1:3 on the integration of women in high schools and, later, a differentiation of salaries between male and female schoolteachers (Pimentel 2010: 89–90).
9. In 1941 there were 337 primary schools without a teacher (Pimentel 2010: 89).
10. For an extensive analysis of Bárbara Virgínia's published discourse (interviews and penned articles), see (in Portuguese) Lisboa (2016).

PART II

Killing the muse: Women as creator

Gender violence and historical memory in Margarida Cardoso and Isabel Coixet

Estela Vieira

Historically, violence against women has been perpetuated repeatedly during periods of political strife or armed conflict; use of rape of women and girls during wartime as a weapon of war, for example, has a long history. This is not to imply gender violence, whether direct or structural, does not happen in non-violent cultures or in times of peace. On the contrary, as much research by sociologists, political scientists, cultural historians and others has shown, misogynistic violence remains shockingly common across societies (Bart and Moran 1993). Thus it is particularly striking to note how often societies that grapple with reconstructing a historical memory of a period of conflict discover how intertwined these events are with violence against women.[1] This chapter explores connections between gender violence and historical memory, in particular how these links surface in fictional films made by women. It asks how visual narratives that both reflect on past conflicts and narrate women's suffering are constructed. There seems to be a disturbing synchrony between women's experiences and an ethnic group's or a nation's collective traumatic memory. In this way, understanding how women survive traumatic pasts or not, how they witness them, or how women artists represent this survival or struggle, is ultimately imperative for a broader understanding of the ways in which societies confront or fail to face their violent histories.

To explore these complexities, this chapter focuses on two quite different films in terms of historical context and style: *La vida secreta de las palabras* (2005) by the Catalan filmmaker Isabel Coixet (1960–present) and *A costa dos murmúrios* (2004) by the Portuguese director Margarida Cardoso (1963–present). Both Cardoso and Coixet work diligently to avoid the clichés inherent in narratives of trauma and violence involving women, and their visual narratives search for alternative forms of telling stories of historical memory and gender violence. While dealing with women as victims of violence, the films also empower the female protagonists to tell or not to tell their personal narrative and that of others, because, as we shall see, their individual story is never quite their own, but part of a wider, collective female-centred account. One could argue Coixet and Cardoso are revisionary historians besides being filmmakers, both in the form and in terms of the content of their work, because they question the ways in which history is construed and how those stories are told visually to others. Their work interrogates how societies approach and figure historical memory, while they challenge themselves to create a film that serves as a rewriting of how women's vulnerability, and stories of women as victims of rape or abuse, are recounted, composed aesthetically and, more importantly, viewed, watched and remembered by audiences. The leitmotif of vision (the spectator's, the character's, the filmmaker's), the representative image of violence, the act of seeing or not seeing suffering, juxtaposing silence or images to words, all fundamentally coalesce as narrative strategies and structure the plot and form of both films. The films' intricate reflections on the visual, and their use of what I call 'visual silences' or 'silent visuals' as formal methods of doing this, is what is analysed and highlighted in this chapter. I hope to show how, through these visual forms, the directors aim to create a complex, multidimensional construction that contests the traditional ways of representing historical narratives of violence against women.

While pondering how one can retell stories of conflicts, narrate histories and remember violence involving women, the films also make important meta-commentaries about the relationship between cinematic violence and gender. Coixet's and Cardoso's films are critiques of the classical gendered narratives and the usual visual structures or generic norms that repeat or reinforce women's problematic relationship with the media, which is comprehensively explored by Byerly and Ross in *Women in Media: A Critical Introduction* (2006). These films do what Lisa Coulthard argues that popular films that portray contradictory postmodern representations of feminist empowerment do not: that is, they interrogate and investigate 'the ways in which violence is understood, defined, represented, and made visible', asking how are violence's 'various forms, tropes, modes, enactments, and representations linked to visibility, politics, community, gender, the body, ideology, and constructions of injury, trauma, evil, or subjectivity' (Coulthard 2007: 158). Both films consciously avoid direct representations of violence, and instead carefully imply the violent scene in their silences, both visual and narrative, thus obliging spectators to question the stakes in viewing this violence and the relationship between our desire to see the violent act and gender. Violence in these films is represented abstractly as a trans-historical notion that crosses time and space. In other words, violence and trauma are ubiquitous, continuous, everlasting, and not some kind of symbol of the breakdown of the social order. Violence against women is not historically isolated, but instead is a sign of a power struggle marked by gender – a power struggle for the maintenance of a certain kind of social order. When the social and power orders are dismantled through political and military strife or aggression, then gender violence might at least be remembered partially, even if never forgotten completely.

The visual logic used by Coixet and Cardoso to explore these difficult connections between gender and historical violence in their films has meaningful implications, especially if we consider some important theoretical approaches. Susan Martin-Márquez (2015: 544–50) explores the ways in which Coixet's work engages with trends in feminist film theory, reminding us also of how deeply influenced Coixet was by British essayist and author John Berger. The filmmaker has spoken enthusiastically of her encounter with Berger's *Ways of Seeing* (1972), referring to her reading of the text as transformative. Berger's groundbreaking descriptions of viewing practices in artistic works showed how profoundly tied up these dynamics are with gender constructions. Laura Mulvey's famous essay *Visual Pleasure and Narrative Cinema*, first published in 1975, extends Berger's ideas into the cinematic context as she theorizes the objectifying gaze while engaging with psychoanalysis (Mulvey 1989). Coixet and Cardoso echo these theoretical concerns throughout their work and have been profoundly troubled with the role, construction and stakes of the gaze not only relative to gender but also in relation to historical or past atrocities. *Mira y verás*, Coixet's 1984 short film and directorial debut, begins with a close-up of an eye, just as Cardoso's *A costa dos murmúrios* is obsessed with her protagonist's eyes and gaze, and zooms in on Evita opening her eyes at the beginning of the film.

As I hope to show, Coixet's and Cardoso's work is ethically concerned with viewing practices both relative to a determined social-historical context as well as to its gender specificity. The female protagonists in both films are the characters who have the power over seeing – they witness and see things denied to spectators – while their male counterparts remain in the dark, metaphorically and/or literally blinded. This is only one of the ways in which the films theoretically break down and question the traditional structure of the male viewer or the dominant, objectifying male gaze. The gaze is transformed into a figure, a form that is reflected and interrogated in the films. Viewers have to critically distance themselves from the female protagonists, as the women can never be objects to be possessed. Viewing or not seeing is portrayed in the films as associated not only with sexual pleasure and gender constructions, but also with power dynamics as the visual is politicized and historicized. In reflecting or silencing the image or the visual representation of what it is possible to see or not see, the directors are also pointing out the limits of reconstructing historical memory and questioning the possibility and/or desirability of making historic or war films that romanticize the past or glorify violence. Reliving or representing former conflicts will not make history go away. Nor should it. But unearthing and questioning power structures at play then and now might at least begin to disrupt patterns of injustice.

Isabel Coixet's visual silences

Isabel Coixet's *La vida secreta de las palabras* (2005) is the director's fifth feature-length film. A Catalan *auteur* who controls her story from different perspectives – she writes, directs and films all of her features – Coixet is one of Spain's most esteemed contemporary film directors, having directed dozens of films – feature-length, shorts and documentaries – since beginning her career in 1988. A number of her films are international, English-language co-productions, and her work untangles films from their national context, reconceptualizing evolving notions of national cinema. She has won several important awards including a handful of Goyas – the Spanish equivalent to the Oscars (*La vida secreta de las palabras* won Goyas for best picture, director, producer and script) – and has a loyal if discreet following. While her work, which Raphael Minder (2011) classified as 'unclassifiable', is diverse in nature, she has repeatedly blurred lines between drama and documentary and has dealt with sensitive social issues, including domestic abuse and violence against women during periods of war. *La vida secreta de las palabras* results from work Coixet did with battered women in Tamaia, Spain, which in turn helped her with a documentary on victims of torture, including survivors of the Balkans war, released in 2003: *Viaje al corazón de la tortura*.

In her feature films, Coixet is not interested in drawing clear lines between documentary and fictional modes of representation, and continuities between her previous work on this topic and *La vida secreta de las palabras* are evident. Most of the characters in the film are fictional, but she also uses actual figures, such as Julie Christie, who plays Inge Genefke and who was the real-life head of the non-governmental organization that Coixet worked with: the International Rehabilitation Council for Torture Victims. The indeterminacy between what is real and what is fictional highlights the challenges of recovering historical memory. In addition, *La vida secreta de las palabras* is filmed with a handheld camera, giving the film, the frame of which is constantly moving, a sort of visual instability. Besides the ambiguous relationship between fiction and documentary, this unsteadiness of visual style reinforces not only the tenuousness of the characters' situation and their communication, but also the uncertainty that characterizes the viewing experience and the difficulties of capturing or representing an unrepresentable violent trauma.

The movie tells the story of Hanna (played by actress Sarah Polley), a Yugoslavian survivor of the Balkans War (1991–2002), employed and living in Ireland. Forced by the manager of the factory where she works to take a holiday, Hanna ends up in a coastal town and is hired, by chance and for a short time, as a nurse to care for an offshore oil rig worker named Josef (played by Tim Robbins), who is recovering from severe burns after an explosion on the rig and is, as a result, temporarily blind and bedridden. Hanna, also a victim and physically impaired – she is partially deaf, not from an accident, but from the trauma she experienced during the civil war – is taciturn, isolates herself from others and wears a hearing aid. As she gets to know the few other men still left on the rig, and as she grows closer and possibly romantically attached to Josef, her painful history is partly uncovered, as are the details of Josef's tragic accident.

In her insightful essay 'Women and violence in contemporary Spanish cinema', María José Gámez Fuentes analyses three contemporary Spanish films – *La vida secreta de las palabras*, *Mataharis* (Bollaín, 2007) and *Elisa K.* (Colell and Cadena, 2010), and the ways in which these films undermine 'the cultural violence inscribed in the representational legacy when portraying violence against women' (Gámez Fuentes 2015: 3). She argues that in *La vida secreta de las palabras* Coixet never unravels or visually represents the atrocities Hanna and countless other women suffered during the war. The film is a formal attempt at reconfiguring narratives of violence, tragedy and trauma. While it seems to tell a story of historical memory, and of individual traumatic experiences, juxtaposing rape and physical abuse of women during war with the fire and explosion on the oil rig by bringing together the two wounded characters, who then seem to connect through their trauma, it is ultimately pointing out the limits of visual narratives, asking what, if any, are the possibilities of narrating, filming and archiving such stories. As Gámez Fuentes writes, the film 'plays with the spectator's desire to explore beyond the symptoms articulated by the narrative' (Gámez Fuentes 2015: 10), and one could argue that, more than the masochistic wishes of audiences to see representations of violence and torture, the film is in fact engaging with questions of what is at stake when viewing and visually representing violent narratives, particularly those involving women. Gámez Fuentes sees in the three films she analyses a similar question to the one I pose in this chapter. She writes:

> by relating contextualized processes of violence to the attempt to undermine the representational legacy of symbolic violence, these films successfully explore the problematic relationship between technologies of representation, femininity and violence in the construction of a historical memory. This, in turn, contributes a further layer to the debate: how to write cultural memory without having to resort to symbolic violence in the representation of the feminine.
>
> (Gámez Fuentes 2015: 8)

The film seems to suggest that Hanna's trauma will never be erased. Coixet portrays a woman who can endure hardships but also one who will perhaps never forget. The protagonist is figuratively and physically scarred for life – this is confirmed by her deafness and the wounds and scars on her body. In fact, it seems undesirable to overcome, transcend or erase the trauma through some visualizing or narrative process. The scene where Hanna tells her story to Josef is emblematic and illustrative of Coixet's significant visual dynamics and of the complex relation established between image and word. In this scene we see the director visually silencing the violent narrative while at the same time asking about the implications of viewing gender violence. Ironically, this takes places exactly at the moment when the atrocities are revealed and partly spoken. When Hanna feels that she can finally tell Josef something of her past, she sits in front of him and speaks; he lies in his sickbed as they are still on the offshore oil rig. The room is dark, and the light mostly shines on him. Josef does not see Hanna, of course, as he is still blind at this point; he only hears her words. Her words, or her narrative, incidentally, tell a story of words. She first remembers the lyrics of an Italian song she and her friend were listening to on their drive back home from school minutes before they were kidnapped and taken to a hotel that was used as a rape camp during the war. She recalls the voices of the soldiers who abused the women: 'they spoke like me, they spoke my own language', and 'voices like yours Josef, talking like you'. She speaks of whispers and screams, repeating the voices, words and phrases spoken by the perpetuators of the rape and abuse. The shot places her constantly in the dark, sometimes only half of her (her upper body) occupies the screen, and at other points she is completely blurred (see Figure 1).

The chiaroscuro work of the camera in this scene is of utmost importance as it juxtaposes light and dark in meaningful ways. As viewers, we are led by the light

FIGURE 1: Hanna (Sarah Polley) sits by Josef's (Tim Robbins) sickbed. Isabel Coixet, *La vida secreta de las palabras*, 2005. Spain. El Deseo.

and camera to see and focus on Josef's face and opened eyes, which we know do not see anything; while the shot of Hanna is dark, Josef has a bright light on his face. The light on Josef's face reminds us of his seeing and ironically of his inability to see, and thus of our own viewing of Hanna's body relative to the horrific events she narrates, which we do not see as they are not visually represented. The light does not simply represent Josef's seeing of the truth behind Hanna's story or mysterious dark character; instead, the interplay between the two characters and the light and darkness suggests that while some consciousness or knowledge-gaining takes place at this pivotal and confessional moment in the film, much of the traumatic experience remains secretive or in the dark. Her story is not straightforward, chronological or logical; the individual aggressions she suffered are not specified. Instead she talks about what happened to other women, although some of the narratives could be her own.

This bringing together of words with the emphasis on the darkness and blurriness of images, and the visual references to seeing and blindness, creates a complex interplay that seems to be more than anything a formal reflection on both visual representation and on the role of the viewer, a questioning of how verbal and visual narratives emerge as well as an interrogation of our failure to remember and/or our desire to see. If words seem to have a secret enigmatic life, as the title of the film would suggest, then it is especially commendable that a film, which speaks in images, is able to echo or speak those intertwined stories of gender violence and historical memory so effectively, and yet so secretively. The visual silencing is a form of communication as well. A voice-over opens the film by saying that there are very few things: silence and words.

Film, then, is more than light, shadow, image. It is also silence and sound. Hanna, who rarely speaks (as opposed to Josef who clearly compensates for his blindness by talking too much), communicates in a similar way to the film with marked and framed silences. For example, she occasionally calls her counsellor, only to not say a word on the phone; but as we learn later in the film, this silence is a way in which the two communicate. The visual silences are an important communicative strategy, articulating the ethical stakes involved not only in our attempts to figure past tragedies, but also in viewing violence, particularly when it is sexual and perpetuated against women. The silences exist in opposition to important words and sounds, as Patricia Hart (2012) shows in an article analysing the design soundscape of the film, and demonstrating how the interplay between silence and sound in the film is crucial for the creation of meaning.

Like Josef who can only hear Hanna's story of words and whispers, as viewers we are also left without visual representations and instead hear voices throughout the film. The mysterious voice-over accompanying the storyline corresponds, according to the script, to the voice of a young child whose gender is unspecified

(Rivera-Cordero 2013: 232). Critics have interpreted this uncanny voice emanating from outside the frame differently. Victoria Rivera-Cordero, who reads the film within the context of disability studies showing how Coixet connects trauma with disability and questions how to rebuild or accept a wounded self, argues convincingly that the voice ought to be associated with Hanna's inner consciousness. In other words, it may be 'viewed as a kind of meta-consciousness, one which in its repetitious return figures the mental trauma itself' (Rivera-Cordero 2013: 241). Rafael Cerrato and others point to the fact that the voice Hanna hears is possibly the voice of the baby she was presumably pregnant with and who was killed by her torturers (Cerrato 2008: 149). In the final scene the voice refers to the two young children – who we assume are the children of Hanna and Josef – as brothers, suggesting that the voice represents Hanna's own child, but whose circumstances of conception, birth and death remain unknown. María Donapetry, who reads in the film's silences an affective narrative strategy that exemplifies Coixet's ethical attitudes and concerns, argues that the voice is the protagonist's 'memory and its transformation', leaving Hanna at the end of the film when the protagonist finds 'the will to live beyond her victimization' (Donapetry 2012: 92–93). Hart notes the importance for the sound director in creating 'just the right eerily calm tones' for this voice, which she describes as 'high-pitched, and greatly manipulated' (Hart 2012: 56–57). The voice is most important in the final scene, showing and confirming the fact that Hanna will always remain fundamentally alone, or at least will always engage with her consciousness, her memory, her trauma. The voice can also be interpreted as an unseen character, creating with it not only a plot secret but also a strategy that connects words, silence and sound to the visual, the seen and the unseen.

In the final scene, a Sunday morning, Josef is out getting a newspaper and their two children – it is suggested that time has passed, and that they now have two children – are outside playing. We see Hanna alone in the kitchen; the shot isolates her inside the house, framing her with the closed opaque glass windows. We hear the children laughing outside and see only a blurred image of the two running and skipping boys behind a closed window or screen. Their blurriness and red-coloured cloaks make them even more enigmatic, as if they were melancholic wounds that begin to fade away visually and are slowly replaced with a resonance or the sound of laughter.

The visual finale or, in other words, the film itself, is only for the protagonist; it is made in dedication to Hanna's experience, just like the video cassette of Hanna's recorded therapy sessions with Inge, Hanna's counsellor, who claims during her conversation with Josef that it contains all of Hanna. The cassette can serve as a metonym for Coixet's film. Suffering and hope coexist in this mournful happy ending that is purposely left unresolved as trauma's wound remains open. But the craft of filmmaking, documenting, archiving, is vital not because it can help that

FIGURE 2: Blurry image of Hanna's two children outside in the garden. Isabel Coixet, *La vida secreta de las palabras*, 2005. Spain. El Deseo.

wound heal, but because it can, like Hanna, endure and choose to share or not share with others. And most importantly, because it can provoke spectators to question the role and the significance of our viewing violence, particularly sexual violence against women, ultimately making what we do not see or hear, in fact, more difficult to forget, and making us, as spectators, aware that most films that represent violence ultimately erase the significance of suffering.

Margarida Cardoso's silent visuals

Margarida Cardoso, one of Portugal's most respected contemporary filmmakers, has also made documentaries that influence her fictional work. Having lived in Mozambique until the age of twelve, Cardoso's fictional films and documentaries often turn thematically to Portuguese-speaking African countries and to Portuguese colonial and post-colonial tensions. Faulkner and Martins (2016: 39) describe *A costa dos murmúrios* as 'a critical intervention in feminist filmmaking about Portuguese decolonization'. One can identify formal concerns in her adaptation of award-winning Portuguese author Lídia Jorge's well-known novel *A costa dos murmúrios* (2004) that were already present in Cardoso's admirable *Kuxa Kanema: Nascimento do Cinema* (2003), where she documents the intense but short-lived history of the post-independent Mozambican film industry (see Vieira 2013). In *Kuxa Kanema*, the forgotten reels of film left abandoned on the

National Institute of Cinema's shelves, and filmed like living presences in close-up shots, remind us of the archive of video cassettes of trauma and torture victims in *La vida secreta de las palabras*. Both signal the potential and limitations of filming and of the image to capture or create new or alternative narratives. Like Coixet, Cardoso explores the role of the visual and of words – hence her interest in adapting the novel in her film – in creating historical memory, while ethically and being formally committed to questioning film's own role or limits as image-maker.

On the one hand, *A costa dos murmúrios* tells the story of Eva Lobo, a young woman who travels to Mozambique to marry her fiancé who is fighting there in the Portuguese army against the guerrilla liberation forces striving for independence. It follows Eva's personal experience as she discovers Beira, the Mozambican city where the story is set, realizes how fraught her husband is and confronts their ideological incompatibilities. On another level, the film uncovers and unravels the intrinsic and structural violence in Portuguese colonial society before and during the time of the armed conflict. With time and exploration, Evita will discover Portugal's war crimes during the colonial wars and her husband's role in the military fighting. The double private/collective narrative suggests that historical context is inseparable from the experiences of women who observe and suffer violence. While Evita (played by Portuguese actress Beatriz Batarda) is not subjected to the same level of trauma, aggression or physical abuse as Hanna is in *La vida secreta de las palabras*, she is, nonetheless, a key witness to a violent reality, observing gender violence against other women, both native and Portuguese, and is herself a victim of aggression.

Paulo de Medeiros who has written about the way the film contrasts a dominant male gaze with a female one (Medeiros 2008), confirms in an earlier article how the intertwined narratives bringing the stories of women and of war together suggest the ways in which political conflict 'unfolds and reaches all civil or domestic activities', revealing the existence of a 'a kind of war between individuals, between men and women, between a past and present time' (Medeiros 1999: 65–67).[2] Mariana Cepeda (2016: 127) seconds Medeiros' readings, adding her interpretation of how this double story seems to imply 'a kind of war between the sexes'.[3]

Despite the difference in intensity in their individual experiences, the two women have a lot in common. Evita and Hanna are both independent-minded and portrayed as loners and women of few words. Both filmmakers focus on creating female protagonists who have strong personalities, with uncompromising natures that conveys a sense of authenticity and power over their personal identity, which they do not easily surrender. Both women control their stories and those of others; they are protected from the penetrating, overbearing attempt to understand them and thus to be possessed by their viewers. Instead, they themselves have a penetrating gaze that functions to witness and see for others. They are not objects of pity, but seem distant from their viewers, intelligent, even stubborn –

qualities that allow them to survive and persevere. They embody endurance and remembering, and are exceedingly mindful of their realities as well as consciously in tune with the experiences of others, especially those of other women. In addition, they are keenly self-aware, even if they discover more about themselves as the stories progress. Both women keep their identity well guarded and do not relinquish their subjectivity.

In a 2004 interview with journalist Ana Sousa Dias, included in the extras section of the film's DVD, author Lídia Jorge explained how, despite her tremendous admiration for Margarida Cardoso's film, in her view, the film downplayed the violence that was in the novel. In her response, Cardoso admits that she indeed shies away from representations of violence, claiming that when she sees many dead bodies on screen, she feels that they are there to make audiences forget death. For Cardoso, explicit representations of violence and trauma are not effective, or in her words 'the most direct expression of violence is not the one that shocks me most'. She adds:

> I did not see the same thing that Lídia saw [...] as a witness [...] I did not see the same thing, what I know, what stayed with me forever was that contained violence [...] in ricochet, that comes to us from others [...] it came from my mother's eyes [...] that violence cannot be expressed [...] it is part of a fiction [...] a mask.[4]

Besides not being effective, for Cardoso representing violence might not be possible. Violence is thus something unseen but omnipresent, and the director prefers to theorize its diverse forms in her film. As she explains, what was fundamental for her to do in her work was to try to identify violence in itself and its form.[5]

Hence, her visual narrative, besides being a reading of words, an adaptation of a novel, is primarily a visual inquiry epitomized by Evita's gaze and the opening of the protagonist's eyes at the beginning of the film, about the implications and meanings of seeing and not seeing, and its relation to historical memory and political and gender violence. *A costa dos murmúrios* intertwines the female experience and a woman's perspective with a semantics of seeing that points both to consciousness-gaining and to our limited access to historical truth. Like Coixet's film, Cardoso's film makes references to documenting via images, questions how narratives, visual or otherwise, help or fail to reconstruct historical memory, and interrogates the role of spectators in the process, also giving audiences only partial access to the story. The leitmotif of the visual, which permeates the entire visually beautiful feature, is also a self-reflective device on how to create, interpret and identify the stakes of visual narratives of violence. The first scene exemplifies this central preoccupation in the film. The camera transitions from the written word to Evita opening her eyes. While the photographer captures the bride and groom

FIGURE 3: Guests at Evita's (Beatriz Betarda) wedding. Margarida Cardoso, *A costa dos murmúrios*, 2004. Portugal. Filmes do Tejo.

kissing in bright light, the wedding party looking on is mostly in dark sunglasses as if partially blinded (and at least one of the guests/soldiers has a bandaged eye) (see Figure 3).

Besides the interplay between light and dark, which Coixet's camera also uses to strategically underpin relations between image or absence of the visual with the word and silence, Cardoso also uses the visual both metaphorically and as a formal strategy. For example, towards the end of the film, a blind army general giving a speech with its misguided propagandistic and nationalistic discourse epitomizes the regime's ignorance and obstinacy, while Evita's powerful gaze throughout the story underscores her growing self-awareness and her increasing political and social consciousness as she sees and becomes more in tune with the community around her. The ways in which Evita persistently stares into the camera and looks back at the viewer, as well as the repeated aesthetic images of reflections of light, mirrors, glass and different bodies of water, are all visual motifs that function self-reflectively throughout the film (see Figure 4).

While images can serve to question versions of histories, they also hide and keep secrets. Cardoso's priority is to represent a pervasive, structural and inscribed violence that is not only witnessed but felt, the one she claims – in the interview with Lídia Jorge quoted above – to have seen in her mother and father's eyes when she lived as a child in Mozambique. She makes a conscious choice to keep war atrocities and violence against women off screen. This complex, displaced representation of violence echoes Coixet's attempt to safeguard Hanna's narrative

FIGURE 4: Evita (Beatriz Betarda) looks directly into the camera. Margarida Cardoso, *A costa dos murmúrios*, 2004. Portugal. Filmes do Tejo.

and the film she has made about her. Like Coixet's film, Cardoso's film is hesitant; it struggles to reveal and to hold on to riddles at the same time. These connections between violence and what is invisible is exemplified in the memorable scene when Evita is on the floor of her hotel room with her husband Luís (played by Portuguese actor Filipe Duarte). After a struggle between the newlyweds, there is a violent cut echoing the implied violent aggression that seems to take place off screen and which is reinforced in the sound of Luís's closing of his army bag (see Figure 5).

Other examples of resonances of sounds pointing to domestic violence include the screams of a married couple fighting that are heard coming from the hotel room next door to Evita and Luís's room. Furthermore, as in Coixet's film, there is also an important voice-over at the start and end of the film. Mark Sabine's insightful feminist interpretation of *A costa dos murmúrios* stresses the crucial role of this extra-diegetic simultaneously absent and present voice, reading it as a meta-narrative and comparing it to Evita's 'mind's eye' as it 'conjures for us her younger self, gazing on past events as they happen' (Sabine 2014: 90). Thus, silence and voice combine to question our understanding or incomprehension of historical and traumatic memory and its association with gender violence.

The leitmotif used in Cardoso's film that best signifies the visual strategies that I argue are adopted in the filmography of both directors is the complex incorporation of photography as a crucial intertext. Faulkner and Martins reread the connections between the novel, the film and the medium of photography, showing how

FIGURE 5: Evita (Beatriz Betarda) on the floor of the hotel room. Margarida Cardoso, *A costa dos murmúrios*, 2004. Portugal. Filmes do Tejo.

'photography, like trauma, also instigates narrative impulses' and explaining that 'photographs hold a unique potential to destabilize the very act of narration, due to their similarities with the structure of trauma' (Faulkner and Martins 2016: 43). The authors argue that and analyse how Cardoso's feminist critique of colonial Mozambique and its cinematic investigation of Portugal's post-colonial trauma lies in the director's juxtaposition of movement with stillness: Cardoso's formal recreation in the film of slow-moving images implying the actual genre or medium of photography, and the story's plotline, which includes having Evita discover in a closed/dark room the classified photos that document the atrocities committed by the Portuguese military during the colonial wars, and which implies several stories of gender violence, including the abuse of an African woman who stood up to the Portuguese soldiers. The photographs, like many other shots in the film, can be understood or read as silent visuals, a way in which Cardoso questions and problematizes the violence present but hidden from view, thus more effectively and poignantly revealing through stillness, silence and absence the past violent and traumatic memories experienced by women in these socio-political contexts of conflict and war.

Violence, memory, gender

Connections between war, memory and gender violence motivate these filmmakers to re-examine the ways in which reliving collective traumatic memory and uncovering historical truth overlaps with women's experiences. The two directors see their filmmaking largely as attempts not to document or historicize events, but instead to reflect on words and images and re-conceptualize the ways in which one can or cannot give visibility, or visual coherence, to trauma and violence. At the same time, the self-reflective processes in the films speak to a questioning of their own medium's purpose and possibilities in recovering, living and surviving violent pasts. Both films suggest that showing violence, and especially violence perpetuated on women, will result in viewers more likely forgetting these past atrocities. Violence has conventionally been represented on screen – primarily by male filmmakers or in mainstream movies and television programmes – as an exercise in the erotization of violence. These women director's conscious choice not to show the violence and torture of women's bodies is a rejection of conventions and of the role of the viewer as a passive consumer of stimulating and sensual images, both of which only reinforce internalized perceptions of objectified desire. Instead the films demand audiences to hear, to feel, to open their eyes, experience the aftermath, the ambiguity, the blurred, partial, complex images that speak critically of narrative, historical and visual traditions. The violence perpetuated is clearly known, even if not seen or described by the protagonists in detail. Viewers witness horror and trauma intertwined with beauty and hope, and they are reminded of their role and complicity in these processes. The films build on affective and aesthetic modes and leave spectators emotionally involved and ethically mobilized.

REFERENCES

Bart, Pauline B. and Moran, Eileen Geil (eds) (1993), *Violence Against Women: The Bloody Footprints*, Newbury Park: Sage Publications.

Berger, John (1972), *Ways of Seeing*, London: Penguin.

Byerly, Carolyn M. and Ross, Karen (2006), *Women in Media: A Critical Introduction*, Malden: Blackwell.

Cardoso, Margarida (2003), *Kuxa Kanema: Nascimento do Cinema*, Portugal: Filmes do Tejo.

——— (2004), *A costa dos murmúrios*, Portugal: Atalanta Filmes.

Cepeda, Mariana (2016), 'De olhos bem abertos: uma leitura do livro e do filme *A costa dos murmúrios* em diálogo com os estudos feministas', *Cadernos de Literatura Comparada*, 35, pp. 119–45.

Cerrato, Rafael (2008), *Isabel Coixet*, Madrid: Ediciones JC.

Coixet, Isabel (1984), *Mira y verás*, Spain: Cameo Media.

——— (2003), *Viaje al corazón de la tortura*, Spain: Canal+.

——— (2005), *La vida secreta de las palabras*, Spain: El Deseo.

Coulthard, Lisa (2007), 'Killing Bill: Rethinking feminism and film violence', in Y. Tasker and D. Negra (eds), *Interrogating Postfeminism: Gender and the Politics of Popular Culture*, Durham, NC: Duke University Press, pp. 153–75.

Donapetry, María (2012), 'Ethics, silence and the gaze in two films by Isabel Coixet', *Studies in Hispanic Cinemas*, 8:1, pp. 87–100.

Faulkner, Sally and Martins, Ana (2016), 'Intermedial dialogue in *A costa dos murmúrios/The Murmuring Coast* (Lídia Jorge 1988/Margarida Cardoso 2004): Novel, photography, film', *Journal of Romance Studies*, 16:2, pp. 36–57.

Gámez Fuentes, María José (2015), 'Women and violence in contemporary Spanish cinema: *La vida secreta de las palabras* (2005), *Mataharis* (2007) and *Elisa K.* (2010)', *International Journal of Iberian Studies*, 28:1, pp. 63–82.

Hart, Patricia (2012), 'Sea breezes, synesthesia and the subtle soundscape design in Isabel Coixet's *The Secret Life of Words*', *Studies in Hispanic Cinemas*, 9:1, pp. 49–62.

Martin-Márquez, Susan (2015), 'Isabel Coixet's engagement with feminist film theory: From the G (the gaze) to the H (the haptic)', in J. Labanyi and T. Pavolvic (eds), *A Companion to Spanish Cinema*, Hoboken: John Wiley & Sons, Incorporated, pp. 544–62.

Medeiros, Paulo de (1999), 'Memória infinita', in C. Pazos Alonso (ed.), *Lídia Jorge in Other Words*, Dartmouth: Tagus Press, pp. 61–77.

——— (2008) 'Double takes: violence, representation and the border gaze', lecture delivered at the University of Leeds, Centre for World Cinema, Leeds, 23 April. Unpublished.

Minder, Raphael (2011), 'Isabel Coixet, an "unclassifiable" director', *New York Times*, 28 September, https://www.nytimes.com/2011/09/29/arts/29iht-coixet29.html. Accessed 13 June 2018.

Mulvey, Laura (1989), *Visual and Other Pleasures*, Bloomington: Indiana University Press.

Rivera-Cordero, Victoria (2013), 'Rebuilding the wounded self: Impairment and trauma in Isabel Coixet's *The Secret Life of Words* and Pedro Almodóvar's *Los abrazos rotos*', *Arizona Journal of Hispanic Cultural Studies*, 17, pp. 227–44.

Sabine, Mark (2014), 'Colonial masculinities under a woman's gaze in Margarida Cardoso's *A costa dos murmúrios*', in H. Owen and A. M. Klobucka (eds), *Gender, Empire and Postcolony: Luso-Afro-Brazilian Intersections*, New York: Palgrave Macmillan, pp. 87–109.

Skjelsbæk, Inger (2001), 'Sexual violence and war: Mapping out a complex relationship', *European Journal of International Relations*, 7:2, pp. 211–37.

Vieira, Estela (2013), 'Politics and the aesthetics of absence in Margarida Cardoso's cinematic work', *Hispanic Research Journal*, 14:1, pp. 67–85.

NOTES

1. For an assessment of the diverse conceptualizations of the interrelation between sexual violence and war, see Skjelsbæk (2001).
2. My translation from the original Portuguese: 'se desdobra e atinge todas as actividades civis ou domésticas'; 'espécie de guerra entre indivíduos, entre homens e mulheres, entre um tempo passado e um tempo presente'.
3. My translation from the original Portuguese: 'uma espécie de guerra entre os gêneros'.

4. My translation from the original Portuguese: 'a expressão mais direta da violência não é a que me choca mais' and 'Eu não via a mesma coisa que a Lídia viu [...] como testemunha [...] eu não vi a mesma coisa, o que eu sei, o que me ficou para sempre era essa violência contida [...] em ricochete, que vêm-nos dos outros [...] vinha dos olhos da minha mãe [...] ela não tem expressão [...] ela faz parte de uma ficção [...] uma máscara.'
5. My translation from the original Portuguese: 'identificação da violência em si, da forma'.

'People don't understand [the] world': The limits of transnational authorship in the cinema of Isabel Coixet

Katarzyna Paszkiewicz

Isabel Coixet is one of the few women filmmakers in Iberian cinema who have been granted an elevated degree of visibility and critical, as well as industrial, recognition. Her films, the majority of which were shot in English and have been consumed transnationally, have been framed in critical discourses by the individualist models of auteurism, closely interrelated with values such as autonomy, originality and singularity. By way of stark contrast with these readings, in this chapter I will argue that Coixet engages with, but also questions such auteurist discourses of exceptionality, self-consciously positioning herself as a white female auteur and foregrounding the limits of her own perspective.

Exactly what constitutes female authorship is, of course, a much discussed and contested topic. As Deborah Jermyn astutely observes, many feminist scholars refuse 'to play ball with the concept of the auteur per se'. She explains that 'there remains something enduringly attractive about [...] the idea(l) of the talented and singular artist able to stand apart from others and record something exceptional that speaks to us in uncommon ways', but 'the conditions of culture through much of history have been ones which conspired, first, against women's creative production and participation in recognized modes and spaces and, second, against recognizing women's creative production outside of these structures as being "art"' (Jermyn 2017: 124).

The difficulties involved in contemplating a female author are numerous and cannot be addressed in detail here. As I have argued elsewhere (2018: 36), both the celebration of the auteur by the *Cahiers du Cinéma* critics, as well as the author's supposed death – which can ultimately be viewed as two sides of the same coin with regard to the exclusion of women from both empirical histories and authorial pantheons – created several obstacles for the conceptualization of women's film authorship. It is not my intention to offer a lengthy overview of the history of authorship in film studies, as such an overview lies beyond the scope of this chapter and has already been provided in several collections (see, for example, Caughie 1981). Instead, I want to draw on Jane Gaines' useful summary of key challenges in early feminist scholarship on authorship and/or auteurism:

> Feminism has been in a somewhat awkward position in relation to these historical developments. Some have lamented the coincidence of the death of authorship and the discovery of new works by women. A case could also be made that the male auteur director as a figure has eclipsed the contributions of women who worked as screenwriters and editors and even actresses. Since 1950s and 1960s auteurism in France as well as the United States overlooked women directors, it could be argued that these women should now receive their due, but no major initiative has been mounted within the academy to achieve this – although the women's film festivals of the 1970s must now be appreciated for their initiative on behalf of so many 'lost' pioneers. Some efforts were made by feminists, beginning in the 1970s, to restore to critical importance the work of such silent-film directors as Alice Guy-Blaché and Germaine Dulac and such sound-era pioneers as Ida Lupino and Dorothy Arzner. Then the pipeline of discoveries seemed to dry up.
>
> (Gaines 2002: 62–63)

It would seem that the benefits for feminist theory of raising the question of female authorship in relation to the contribution of women to cinema were even less evident than in the case of literary authorship (Grant 2001: 114), which translates into a surprising lack of theoretical works on female directors, at least in the first decades of feminist film criticism. Making reference to this issue, Judith Mayne speaks of the spectre of essentialism, which she claims has haunted feminist criticism since its beginnings:

> While virtually all feminist critics would agree that the works of Germaine Dulac, Maya Deren, and Dorothy Arzner (to name the most frequently invoked 'historical figures') are important, there has been considerable reluctance to use any of them as privileged examples to theorize female authorship in the cinema, unless, that is, such theorizing affirms the difficulty of women's relationship to the cinematic apparatus. This reluctance reflects the current association of 'theory' with 'antiessentialism'.
>
> (Mayne 1990: 90)

While recognizing this difficulty, Mayne (1990: 97) defends authorship as a viable method for thinking about the cinematic practices of women, and several feminist scholars – at least in the anglophone studies – have more recently followed this path. For example, in 'Secret agents: Feminist theories of women's film authorship', Catherine Grant poses a thought-provoking question: maybe, in their approach to women's film authorship, feminist film theorists have been 'overly anxious about the wrong kind of "essentialism"'. In situating the author as a fictional figure within the text, this text has been constructed as an ideal essence, removing whatever ties it to the 'social and historical outside' (Grant 2001: 121). Grant proposes, thus, that we consider various aspects of female directorial 'authors' as agents: '[f]emale subjects who have direct and reflexive, if obviously not completely "intentional" or determining relationships to the cultural products they help to produce, as well as to their reception' (Grant 2001: 124). In order to think about the interventions of women as cultural producers and their sociocultural reception in wider terms, Grant and other scholars – such as Susan Martin-Márquez (1999) and, more recently, Barbara Zecchi (2014), both in the context of Spanish cinema – consider agency through the optic of Judith Butler's positing of gender, as a 'reiterative or re-articulatory practice, immanent to power, and not a relation of external opposition to power' (Butler 1993: 15). Examining not only films or 'facts' of the director's life, but also interviews, film reviews, academic studies, photographs and press materials, can enable the much more complex understanding of the multiple mediations operating in the creation and imagining of the authorial figures of female directors.

This turn to context, which opens up a way to reconsider authorial perspectives and methodologies in relation to films directed by women, is particularly evident in the scholarly writings on Isabel Coixet. Núria Triana Toribio (2006), Valeria Camporesi (2007) and Belén Vidal (2008) have all demonstrated that Coixet carefully negotiates with the repertoire of cultural narratives in order to construct her image as an auteur. Drawing on the concept of the auteur as a 'commercial dramatization of self [and] as the motivating agent of textuality', developed by Timothy Corrigan (1991: 108), Triana Toribio analyses how Coixet has turned herself into a commercial brand, an intertextual sign to be read through diverse sources, including advertising, press articles, interviews, her official website[1] and frequent appearances on television and in a wide variety of cultural fora (Triana Toribio 2006: 50–51). Perfectly aware of her positioning in the constantly transforming globalization of cultures and her status as an *autora mediática* ('a media-savvy director': Triana Toribio 2008), Coixet constructs herself, and is also constructed through, a set of marketing strategies which regulate the reception of her authorial image and her work.[2]

The existing scholarship on Coixet shows that close examination of promotional and critical discourses surrounding her films can be extremely useful for uncovering a series of underlying narratives that circulate around her public persona and her performance as an auteur. The significant prevailing discourse in the construction of her brand authorship is possibly the one that focuses on the global range of her 'authorial signature' and her attempts to detach herself from the label of 'national filmmaker'. Much has been written about her choices in terms of filming locations (she has made most of her films outside Spain), her devotion to international cast and crews, co-productions with North American partners and the adoption of English as a lingua franca. Her aesthetic and marketing strategies have been identified as following the models of both European art cinema and American independent film (Triana Toribio 2006; Camporesi 2007; Vidal 2008), instead of the most prevalent models in Spanish cinema: 'genre films *a la Hollywood* or cultural films/social realism or well-rooted comedies like *Torrente* (*a la traditionally Spanish*)' (Triana Toribio 2006: 59).

The difficulty in classifying Coixet's work is often paired with her ambiguous relationship with national identity. As Vidal (2008: 222) argues in reference to Coixet's marketing expertise and her public appearances, 'through such carefully staged interventions, the director inserts herself into a preferred lineage of cinephile filmmakers, bypassing other more contested categories such as "Spanish director" or even "Spanish woman director"'. Not only has Coixet's commercial strategy not veered towards Spain, she has also avoided being associated with Catalonia; she has declared on many occasions that she is not particularly keen on shooting in her home city, Barcelona (Camporesi 2007: 63). As Triana Toribio (2006: 52) puts it, 'this adds to the mix a difficult history of locality, power and identity'. Coixet's open disregard for any type of nationalism – she stated that she does not believe herself to be a citizen from anywhere[3] – has often been the spark of backlash from institutions and, to some extent, the public. What might be considered a postmodern suspicion of ideologies or of the *grands récits* has been more often than not interpreted as treason (Triana Toribio 2006: 58). Perhaps somewhat paradoxically, Coixet 'cannot [...] escape the label Catalan, whether she likes it or not – and on her website she writes about still receiving threats for and accusations of being a "bad Catalan"' (Triana Toribio 2006: 52). As a number of scholars have shown, this discourse has negatively affected institutional support for her films and Coixet's validation as an auteur throughout her career, and it has loomed particularly large in the socio-political context following the Catalan declaration of independence on 27 October 2017.[4]

In a nutshell, Coixet fashions herself – and is read by critics and scholars – as a filmmaker who resists 'the trends of the "nation" in whatever form' and who wishes 'to work on "universal" themes, with a transnational cast and as part of "world cinema"' (Triana Toribio 2006: 59). While these considerations of Coixet's commercial identity and film aesthetics capture her crucial resistance to totalizing narratives of the nation state, I also take as a pressing research question the ways in which the framework of 'transnational authorship' risks reinforcing the discourse of exceptionality that has plagued the studies on film authorship from its inception. As with auteur theory, I contend that the concept of the transnational is a complex one for the (white) woman filmmaker and by extension for the feminist film scholar.

As Gerard Dapena, Marvin D'Lugo and Alberto Elena remind us, in the Spanish context the term 'transnational cinema' has been commonly associated with co-production strategies and broadly applied to 'Spanish films that have involved production with one or more international partners or have included the presence of non-Spanish actors' (Dapena et al. 2013: 15). However, what is also at stake here is 'a cultural dynamic that goes well beyond typologies of transnational collaboration based on percentage formulas' (Dapena et al. 2013: 15). The scholars argue that 'since its beginnings, standard histories of film have tended to foreground the idea of national cinema, a strategy that has enabled their authors to bestow a certain coherence and common identity on a heterogeneous array of movies', but more recently 'the concept of the transnational has gained ascendancy among film historians as a means to interrogate and problematize this very process of homogenization', seeking 'to illuminate processes of exchange and interpenetration that are given short shrift and often obscured under the national paradigm, and to remind us that films are far more hybrid, protean texts than this paradigm, with its emphasis on authenticity and purity, is willing to entertain' (Dapena et al. 2013: 16).

In *Transnational Feminism in Film and Media*, Katarzyna Marciniak, Anikó Imre and Áine O'Healy have shown that the category of gender necessarily cuts through this understanding of transnational cinema, if sometimes unpredictably. They highlight the need to acknowledge that 'transnational processes are inherently gendered, sexualized, and racialized' (Marciniak et al. 2007: 4)[5] and they argue for the adoption of 'transnational feminist cultural studies' that have 'a potential to transform traditional methodological approaches by engaging complex accounts of gender in the national, global, and diasporic contexts situated within histories of imperialism and decolonization' (Marciniak et al. 2007: 10). If, following these scholars, we understand 'transnational cinema' as a film practice that 'focuses on the intricate connection between the local and the global, the domestic and the foreign, questioning the legitimacy of national borders while critiquing the easy rhetoric of connectivity and progress' (Ponzanesi 2017: 29), then we might ask if, and to what extent, Coixet's cinema might be inscribed within this trend.

Drawing on this approach, then, my aim is to expand the interpretative framework of Coixet's 'transnational authorship' to interrogate the questions of exceptionality, gender, ethnicity and nation. My purpose is to unpack the ways in which the filmmaker is restricted by, but at the same time manages to question, her own status as a transnational auteur, often read as exceptional among contemporary women directors in Spain (Lázaro-Reboll et al. 2013: 184). Coixet is a good example of a woman filmmaker who dexterously navigates institutional politics and makes films 'that have a chance to travel and be seen' (White 2015: 5). In looking at the conditions that enable as well as limit her recognition as an auteur, I will turn to Patricia White's analysis of twenty-first-century transnational women's film practice *Women's Cinema, World Cinema*, in which she observes that 'though still drastically underrepresented, women directors are increasingly coming into view within the current circulation of world cinema' (White 2015: 4).[6] In reference to Deleuze and Guattari's concept of the minor, White argues that too often women's films are 'reterritorialized' through prevalent discourses of authorship and nation. While 'the first decade of the twenty-first century showed the contours of women's cinema being redrawn by shifts in global production, circulation, and evaluation of films as well as by changing perceptions and practices of feminism', women directors tend to be 'ambivalently recruited to this corrective project' (White 2015: 6). White contends that 'the category of Woman is a powerful representation to decenter, and the idea of the minor risks minimizing the way diverse women's visions can be recuperated within it' (White 2015: 13).

In her close reading of a number of films and directorial personae, White finds that women directors often deploy critical figures of authorship in order to deconstruct art cinema's myths of femininity, as well as other discourses of taste, authenticity or victimhood. Building on this premise, I will argue that Coixet offers a recalibration of film practice, resisting and inhabiting two paradigms that define her public image: that of transnational cinema and that of film authorship understood through notions of exceptionality and autonomy. In order to address these issues, I will centre on *Nadie quiere la noche* (2015), a Spanish–French–Bulgarian co-production with international stars – Oscar-winner Juliette Binoche (*The English Patient*: Minghella, 1997), Gabriel Byrne (*The Usual Suspects*: Singer, 1995) and Rinko Kikuchi (*Pacific Rim*: del Toro, 2013) – set in the Arctic seclusion of Greenland, and which speaks volumes about Coixet's resistance to the narrowly prescribed ideas of transnationality, exceptionality and authorship. While my focus in the second part of this chapter is mainly on textual analysis, I will trace correspondences between the film itself and Coixet's authorial persona as discussed in the first part. Thinking back to Grant (2001), what is at stake in new studies of female authorship is not so much moving away from close textual readings, but rather expanding definitions of textuality towards a more complex understanding of women's film practice. In this sense, my method builds on Grant's (2001) and White's (2015) consideration of 'the figure – or more accurately, figures, in a rhetorical sense – of the woman director as a way to index questions central to contemporary feminism such as visibility, agency [...] and power' (White 2015: 19).

Nadie quiere la noche: *The white woman's burden*

Analysing the male-centredness of auteurism, Angela Martin (2008) argues that the critics writing for *Cahiers du Cinéma*, for example Jacques Rivette, infused the term 'auteur' with a set of notions such as 'self-expression', 'youth', 'violence', 'virility' and 'rage'. However, these were often incompatible with the practice of many women filmmakers and with the feminist tenet that the personal is political, which is very different from the *Nouvelle Vague*'s call for personal self-expression (Martin 2008: 129). In what follows, I would like to suggest that Coixet revisits precisely this traditional view of auteurism while, at the same time, she does not necessarily offer what might be considered its feminist equivalent based on ideals of female solidarity.

Nadie quiere la noche premiered in 2015 during the 65th Berlinale International Film Festival, but following poor reviews (the film was dismissed by Peter Bradshaw (2015), writing for *The Guardian*, for its 'blandly humanistic flavours, new-agey gestures and quaint stereotypes, self-consciously performed by an international cast'),[7] it was later recut by Coixet and released under the new title *Endless Night*. Inspired by true events, the story is set in 1908 and focuses on Josephine Peary and her trek to join her celebrated adventurer husband, Robert E. Peary, as he comes closer to achieving his dream of placing himself at the centre of the Northern Hemisphere.[8] Coixet dramatizes an intercultural encounter in the bleak Arctic[9] between two female protagonists: an upper-class American, Josephine (Binoche) and a young Inuit woman, Allaka (Kikuchi). Allaka lives in an igloo she has built next to Robert Peary's base camp and, as it turns out, she is also there to wait for him, because she is expecting his baby.

Robert Peary, whose claims to have reached the geographic North Pole have been widely disputed by historians, is actually never seen in the film. However, his epic adventure, and his dream to be *the first man* to succeed, play an important role in the narrative. This (absent) protagonist might be read as the epitome of a white male Western explorer conquering the virgin land, evincing the symbolic connection between hyper-manhood and the wilderness thoroughly explored by ecofeminism.[10] His loyal wife, Josephine, not only supports and encourages his grand ambitions – despite the fact that it means spending most of her marriage apart from her husband – but she also mimics the type of masculinity he presumably stands for. When she finally reaches the base camp, Josephine meets a man who has participated in her spouse's expedition. Gangrenous, exhausted and almost dead, the man complains bitterly about Robert Peary's methods: 'He abandoned me. Like one of his filthy dogs [...] I was of no use to him', to which Josephine responds: 'The Lieutenant did what he had to do.' In the same sequence we see her standing in front of the cabin, US flag clearly visible in the shot. Earlier in the

FIGURE 1: Fantasies of imperial domination (Juliette Binoche). Isabel Coixet, *Nadie quiere la noche*, 2015. Spain/France/Bulgaria. Ariane & Garoé, Canal+ España, Institut del Cinema Català (ICC), Instituto de la Cinematografía y de las Artes Audiovisuales (ICAA), Neo Art, Noodles Production, One More Movie, Radio Televisión Española (RTVE), Televisió de Catalunya (TV3), Televisión Española (TVE).

film, she 'marks' the land by leaving a sign that reads 'Josephine Peary slept here on September 9th 1908' – yet another example of how she is inscribed within the narrative of exceptionality, discovery and conquest, which dominated in the masculinized realm of Arctic exploration and, at the same time, complemented American imperial aspirations (see Pierce Erikson 2009: 102).

Josephine is represented as an impetuous, headstrong woman with steely determination, who constantly tries to prove that she is as brave and as resourceful as her spouse. This is immediately clear in the startling moment at the beginning of the film when Mrs Peary shoots a polar bear and is extremely pleased with herself. 'I got my first bear!' she calls out happily. There is no space for empathy or ecological sensitivity that would make her question killing animals; most importantly, at no point does she question her privileged, dominant position towards nature and the people that live in this land, nor does she seem to feel part of it.

Unsurprisingly, it is the Inuit woman who gives Josephine a lesson on ecology. 'People don't understand world, only understand people [*sic*]', says Allaka after Josephine states exasperatedly that Allaka 'doesn't understand a lot of things'. Josephine's subsequent transition from a self-contained to a relational, porous subject – a recurrent trope in Coixet's oeuvre (Sabadell-Nieto 2014, 2017) – is made possible precisely through her encounter with Allaka. Gradually, as Josephine gets close to the dangerous onset of winter, her relationship with Allaka begins to change. The two women are forced to cooperate in order to survive the harsh weather, and this 'getting closer' becomes very literal in the second part of the film, in which

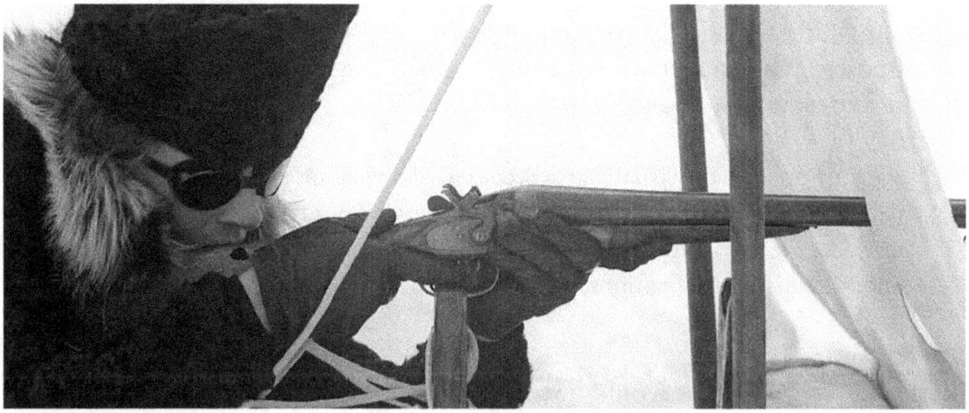

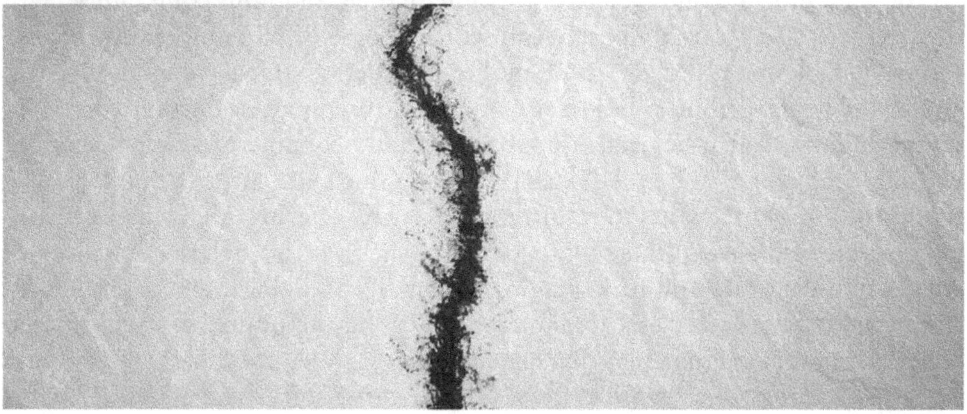

FIGURES 2 and 3: Mrs Peary (Juliette Binoche) shoots a polar bear. Isabel Coixet, *Nadie quiere la noche*, 2015. Spain/France/Bulgaria. Ariane & Garoé, Canal+ España, Institut del Cinema Català (ICC), Instituto de la Cinematografía y de las Artes Audiovisuales (ICAA), Neo Art, Noodles Production, One More Movie, Radio Televisión Española (RTVE), Televisió de Catalunya (TV3), Televisión Española (TVE).

we are offered a number of shots of the two women embracing each other, skin to skin, in the claustrophobic igloo.

Making reference to the use of space in Coixet's and Lucrecia Martel's films, Jennifer Slobodian observes:

> Though the directors are conscious of their negotiations of the borders between culture, class, and even social acceptance, the physical space and community formation of both directors' films tend to be rigidly defined [...] while also representing the liminal through the settings' respective isolation and transitory nature.
>
> (Slobodian 2012: 165)

Drawing on these remarks, we could think of *Nadie quiere la noche* as an example of postcolonial/transnational cinema which negotiates the borders between culture and class or as Coixet's

> engagement with the visual that is decolonized and de-orientalized, becoming a relational mode of representation, breaking down the *grands récits* and opening the space for specificities that refract larger, often repressed, omitted or deleted, unofficial histories of nations, communities, genders and subaltern groups.
> (Ponzanesi 2017: 30)

Nevertheless, I believe it would be reductionist to read Coixet's film as a utopian tale of intercultural bonding and non-conflictual, harmonious community, with the Arctic as a neutral, blank space in which people of different cultural backgrounds can come together. The film does not depict an easy communication and idyllic being-with between the two women. Josephine is constantly irritated by the smiling, warm-hearted Allaka and would probably prefer to spend her waiting time alone. When Allaka saves Josephine's life after she collapses in the snow, Josephine wants to return the favour by offering Allaka a gift (probably inspired by the capitalist logics of debt): she tries to teach the 'uncultured' Allaka to use a knife and fork, staging a formal, candlelit dinner in the shack. 'From me to you', stresses Josephine, establishing the limits between the two subjects, at the same time marking her superiority. 'Very good' – she encourages

FIGURE 4: Josephine's lessons on 'civilization' (Juliette Binoche and Rinko Kikuchi). Isabel Coixet, *Nadie quiere la noche*, 2015. Spain/France/Bulgaria. Ariane & Garoé, Canal+ España, Institut del Cinema Català (ICC), Instituto de la Cinematografía y de las Artes Audiovisuales (ICAA), Neo Art, Noodles Production, One More Movie, Radio Televisión Española (RTVE), Televisió de Catalunya (TV3), Televisión Española (TVE).

and praises her new friend in a patronizing tone, while giving her a few lessons on 'civilization'.

Coixet's film seems to evoke, then, the well-known 'colonial images of gender, race and class [which] carried ideological connotations that confirmed imperial epistemologies and racial taxonomies, depicting natives – in documentary or fiction films – as savages, primitive, and outside modernity' (Ponzanesi 2017: 25–26). The filmmaker clearly revisits a number of dichotomies such as humans/infrahumans, explorers/servants, science/nature, white/native or American (national)/ Inuit (transnational) (Sabadell-Nieto 2017), as well as the iconic figure of 'the homesteading white woman common to fictions of empire', whose ideological function has been precisely a 'civilizing' one (White 2017: 219). This is emphasized by Josephine's ridiculously elegant dress and pompous hat, unsuitable for the extreme weather conditions, as well as her vigorous speech about the importance of *owning* things in the moment in which both women are facing death. 'Where we come from things have [...] owners. They belong to somebody. Like that pretty hair belongs to you.' The protagonist embodies, thus, as a colonial mistress, a mix of traditional views on the civilizing mission of white women (the white wo/man's burden) and feminist ideals of independence. As Patricia Pierce Erikson suggests, this was also the case for the real-life Josephine Peary:

> On one hand, she rejected the growing movement to achieve broader rights for women and embraced the ideology that a woman's duty was devotion to her husband and children. Yet on the other hand, she advocated the intellectual cultivation of women, including the pursuit of first-hand knowledge of a wider world [...] Like other colonial women in places considered as 'wilderness' or 'frontier', Josephine significantly bolstered the expedition's domestic, subsistence economy, [assuming] food preparation and cleaning responsibilities.
>
> (Pierce Erikson 2009: 102)

According to Patricia White (2017: 219), 'historically and hegemonically, the colonial mistress is portrayed as the tamer of both Western masculinity and the childlike natives, imperial patriarchy's moral compass'. The scholar analyses *White Material* (2009, Claire Denis), a contemporary film about the legacy of colonialism, and *Meek's Cutoff*, directed by Kelly Reichardt, a 2010 Western that revisits a foundational myth of the USA, showing how both films take on the question of white female power and literal 'direction' as their heroines make decisive choices. Similar to these films, *Nadie quiere la noche* also acknowledges the symbolic function of a white settler woman implicated in imperial and expansionist projects; 'the limitation of – and to – the white women's point of view is the ethical challenge' (White 2017: 221) posed in all of these films.

FIGURES 5 and 6: White female power and literal 'direction' in transnational contexts (Juliette Binoche). Isabel Coixet, *Nadie quiere la noche*, 2015. Spain/France/Bulgaria. Ariane & Garoé, Canal+ España, Institut del Cinema Català (ICC), Instituto de la Cinematografía y de las Artes Audiovisuales (ICAA), Neo Art, Noodles Production, One More Movie, Radio Televisión Española (RTVE), Televisió de Catalunya (TV3), Televisión Española (TVE).

We could extend this observation towards Coixet's authorial inscription: the heroine represented in *Nadie quiere la noche* figures Coixet's own 'exceptional' and privileged status within world cinema circuits. Coming from Europe, Coixet seems to fit the model of a First World director and, similarly to Denis and Reichardt, she is among the few women filmmakers who have been considered auteurs by important film festivals and other tastemakers. Coixet's work and reputation have been likewise framed by the understanding of authorship as expressive genius – as measured by festival invitations, award recognition and critical reception; for example, she was the first Spanish woman filmmaker to be invited to screen a film at the Cannes Film Festival. While it could be argued that Coixet is a director who works on the margins of the global film industry, she is in fact one of the most *visible* representatives of transnational cinema, both in Spain and abroad.

In her important contribution to the issue of female authorship in transnational contexts, White looks at the increasing recognition of women directors from and outside the USA and Europe, showing how 'gender asymmetries are disguised either by emphasizing individual "genius" (privatizing) or by appropriating women directors' personae and work to stand in for concepts of "culture", in the sense of both "nation" and "taste" (domesticating)' (White 2017: 216). Building on this eloquent formulation, I want to suggest that *Nadie quiere la noche* poses ethical questions associated with world cinema authorship, 'culture' and the prestige accorded to films from dominant countries as they circulate in a globalized art cinema context. As a white woman filmmaker, Coixet critiques the concept of the transnational auteur through her singular relationship to aesthetics, to ownership and to privilege, and positions herself reflexively 'by mapping discourses of exceptionalism onto gendered and racialized national and imperial narratives' (White 2017: 216) in her work.

Conclusion: Looking beyond the exception

In her article 'Anyplace North America: On the transnational road with Isabel Coixet', Núria Triana Toribio usefully observes that:

> both Coixet and her oeuvre engage with the demands and strategies of globalization and the attendant issues of space and place, but they can also be read as forms of resistance to narrowly prescribed ideas of national cinemas and to labels such as 'Spanish'/'Catalan'/'European'/'woman' filmmaker.
>
> (Triana Toribio 2006: 47)

As I have tried to show, drawing on Patricia White (2017), they also self-consciously critique gendered, racialized and imperial narratives that underpin Coixet's privileged status as a transnational auteur, offering an allegory of white female authorship inscribed within the colonial imaginary. *Nadie quiere la noche* stages the limitation of – and to – the white woman's point of view and, following White (2017), I take this portrayal of the white woman's partial point of view as an inscription of Coixet's authorship. Coixet's film and her public persona both enact and subtly critique the power (white) women have attained in current world cinema. The filmmaker makes the limits of her own perspective part of her political project in a film that depicts intersections of colonialism and gender and 'allegorize[s] authorship as a dilemma of cultural authority' (White 2017: 225).

If we consider *Nadie quiere la noche* within the current context of women's cinema as world cinema, as studied by White (2015), Coixet is *not* an exception in this respect. The limited perspective of the (post)colonial heroine,[11] which poses ethical questions about cultural authority, exceptionality and white female authorship, can be found in other recent films by women filmmakers. As previously mentioned, Coixet's work resonates strikingly with small-scale dramas and unhurried paces in Kelly Reichardt's films. They all displace white male heroes (in *Nadie quiere la noche* the male hero is absent), but they foreground women's ambivalent relationship to power. Similar to Reichardt's revisions of the road movie or the Western, Coixet's adventure/survival film is far from epic in tone: her narrative is quotidian, her setting almost domestic and her heroine's actions conceivably pointless. The formal and thematic connections among these women's films may be to a great extent accidental or, as White suggests, 'consistent with more general trends' (White 2009: 156–57). White (2015: 17) contends that 'thinking through relations of alliance and exchange among women (rather than assuming their sameness) is crucial to both the future of feminism and any picture of the world'. Therefore, I want to conclude, echoing Kathleen McHugh (2009) (also quoted in White's book), that we should move beyond paradigms that marginalize women's film production as an 'exceptional anomaly (the female *auteur*)', and instead 'articulate a more intertextual sense of women's and feminisms' productive relations to the cinema' (White 2009: 115) – and, we could add, to the world.

REFERENCES

Bradshaw, Peter (2015), 'Berlin 2015 review: *Nobody Wants the Night* – Juliette Binoche's arctic role requires more defrosting', *The Guardian*, 5 February, https://www.theguardian.com/film/2015/feb/06/berlin-2015-review-nobody-wants-the-night-juliette-binoches-arctic-role-requires-more-defrosting. Accessed 15 May 2018.

Butler, Judith (1993), *Bodies that Matter: On the Discursive Limits of 'Sex'*, New York: Routledge.

Camporesi, Valeria (2007), 'A ambos lados de todas las fronteras: Isabel Coixet y el cine español contemporáneo', in M. Á. Millán Muñío and C. Peña Ardid (eds), *Las mujeres y los espacios fronterizos*, Zaragoza: Prensas Universitarias de Zaragoza, pp. 55–69.

Caughie, John (ed.) (1981), *Theories of Authorship*, London: Routledge.

Coixet, Isabel (2015), *Nadie quiere la noche*, Spain, France and Bulgaria: Mer Film, New Art Productions, Noodles Production, One More Movie.

Corrigan, Timothy (1991), *A Cinema without Walls: Movies and Culture after Vietnam*, New Brunswick: Rutgers University Press.

Dapena, Gerard, D'Lugo, Marvin and Elena, Alberto (2013), 'Transnational Frameworks', in J. Labanyi and T. Pavlović (eds), *A Companion to Spanish Cinema*, Malden: Wiley-Blackwell, pp. 15–49.

Gaines, Jane M. (2002), 'Of cabbages and authorship', in J. Bean and D. Negra (eds), *A Feminist Reader in Early Cinema*, Durham, NC: Duke University Press.

Grant, Catherine (2001), 'Secret agents: Feminist theories of women's film authorship', *Feminist Theory*, 2:1, pp. 113–30.

Jermyn, Deborah (2017), *Nancy Meyers*, New York: Bloomsbury Academic.

Lázaro-Reboll, Antonio, Marsh, Steven, Martin-Márquez, Susan and Zunzunegui, Santos (2013), 'Strategic auteurism', in J. Labanyi and T. Pavlović (eds), *A Companion to Spanish Cinema*, Malden: Wiley-Blackwell, pp. 152–89.

Marciniak, Katarzyna, Imre, Anikó and O'Healy, Áine (2007), 'Introduction: Mapping transnational feminist media studies', in K. Marciniak, A. Imre and Á. O'Healy (eds), *Transnational Feminism in Film and Media*, New York: Palgrave Macmillan, pp. 1–20.

Martin, Angela (2008), 'Refocusing authorship in women's filmmaking', in B. K. Grant (ed.), *Auteurs and Authorship: A Film Reader*, Malden: Blackwell Publishing, pp. 127–34.

Martin-Márquez, Susan (1999), *Feminist Discourse and Spanish Cinema: Sight Unseen*, Oxford: Oxford University Press.

Mayne, Judith (1990), *The Woman at the Keyhole: Feminism and Women's Cinema*, Bloomington: Indiana University Press.

McHugh, Kathleen (2009), 'The world and the soup: Historicising media feminisms in transnational contexts', *Camera Obscura*, 72, pp. 110–51.

Paszkiewicz, Katarzyna (2018), *Genre, Authorship and Contemporary Women Filmmakers*, Edinburgh: Edinburgh University Press.

Pérez, Jorge (2013), 'La "road movie". Directoras españolas al volante. La "road movie" como viaje de concienciación ética', in B. Zecchi (ed.), *Gynocine: Teoría de género, filmología y praxis cinematográfica*, Zaragoza: Prensas de la Universidad de Zaragoza, pp. 129–60.

Pierce Erikson, Patricia (2009), 'Josephine Diebitsch Peary (1863–1955)', *Arctic*, 62:1, pp. 102–4.

Ponzanesi, Sandra (2017), 'Postcolonial and transnational approaches to film and feminism', in K. Lené Hole, D. Jelača, E. A. Kaplan and P. Petro (eds), *The Routledge Companion to Cinema & Gender*, New York: Routledge, pp. 25–35.

Sabadell-Nieto, Joana (2014), 'Passionately losing oneself', in J. Sabadell-Nieto and M. Segarra (eds), *Differences in Common: Gender, Vulnerability and Community*, Amsterdam: Rodopi, pp. 143–60.

——— (2017), 'Ese hermoso deshielo y su olor a podrido. Isabel Coixet lo ha vuelto a hacer', *International Symposium 'Memoria encarnada: Emociones, cuerpos y migraciones en la producción cultural hispánica del siglo XXI'*, University of Warsaw, Warsaw, 1–3 June.

Shohat, Ella (1991), 'Gender and culture of empire: Towards a feminist ethnography of the cinema', *Quarterly Review of Film and Video*, 13:1–3, pp. 45–84.

Slobodian, Jennifer (2012), 'Analyzing the woman auteur: The female/feminist gazes of Isabel Coixet and Lucrecia Martel', *The Comparatist*, 36, pp. 160–77.

Triana Toribio, Núria (2006), 'Anyplace in North America: On the transnational road with Isabel Coixet', *Studies in Hispanic Cinema*, 3:1, pp. 47–64.

——— (2008), 'Auteurism and commerce in contemporary Spanish cinema: *Directores mediáticos*', *Screen*, 49:3, pp. 259–76.

Vidal, Belén (2008), 'Love, loneliness and laundromats: Affect and artifice in the melodramas of Isabel Coixet', in J. Beck and V. Rodríguez Ortega (eds), *Contemporary Spanish Cinema and Genre*, Manchester: Manchester University Press, pp. 219–38.

White, Patricia (2009), 'Watching women's films', *Camera Obscura*, 72, pp. 152–62.

——— (2015), *Women's Cinema, World Cinema*, Durham, NC and London: Duke University Press.

——— (2017), 'Pink material: White womanhood and the colonial imaginary in world cinema authorship', in K. Lené Hole, D. Jelača, E. A. Kaplan and P. Petro (eds), *The Routledge Companion to Cinema & Gender*, New York: Routledge, pp. 215–26.

Zecchi, Barbara (2014), *Desenfocadas: Cineastas españolas y discursos de género*, Barcelona: Icaria.

NOTES

1. http://misswasabi.com. Accessed 6 September 2018.
2. In her article on auteurism and commerce, Triana Toribio (2008: 270) analyses the ways in which Spanish directors such as Isabel Coixet, Pedro Almodóvar and Álex de la Iglesia use online media 'to create and perpetuate a cult of personality' and to construct a unique public persona through the assertion of individual taste. For Triana Toribio, such strategies of 'e-auteurism' play a significant role in crafting a recognizable 'image' of the director, which helps critics and fans to identify the filmmaker's primary obsessions and thematic preoccupations as the product of individual expression.
3. 'At all events I would like to be a citizen of a country where nobody stopped you in the street to reproach you about nonsense' (Coixet cited in Slobodian 2012: 164).
4. See Triana Toribio (2006). Coixet's recent declarations, for example when she spoke out against the independence referendum held on 1 October 2017, have led to heavy criticism.
5. Advancing an argument about transnational methodology, the authors argue that the issues of borders, belonging, otherness and displacement cannot be analysed without taking into consideration gender, sexuality or racialization: 'The borders that [transnational processes] erase and erect affect different groups differently' (Marciniak et al. 2007: 4).
6. Building on Lúcia Nagib, White prompts us to move away from thinking of world cinema in opposition to Hollywood and to see it instead as 'simply the cinema of the world' (Nagib cited in White 2015: 4). As White explains (2015: 4), 'this approach pulls notions of core and periphery out of orbit'. From the beginning of the twenty-first century, we have witnessed a proliferation of other labels applied in the context of transnational cinema, which in different ways question the notions of belonging, identity and borders: exile cinema, accented cinema, haptic cinema, diasporic cinema, intercultural cinema or border cinema. All of these labels attempt 'to indicate the porous character of a cinema that is

no longer linked to national schools and traditions, and signalling the diasporic nature of its subject matter and of new global apparatuses, showing the disaffection with and overcoming of dominant paradigms such as Hollywood, Art Cinema, and Third Cinema' (Ponzanesi 2017: 29).

7. In this sense, one could consider Coixet's film *una película-ONG* ('an NGO film'), following the term proposed by Jorge Pérez (2013: 155), which makes reference to films which 'se articulan con un explícito afán de potenciar una ética de solidaridad, de generar conciencia social y abrir espacios de diálogo intercultural'. These comments point to another, perhaps less common, narrative that defines Coixet as an auteur: that of the *artista comprometida* (engaged artist).
8. As Patricia Pierce Erikson (2009: 102) shows in her article on real-life Josephine Diebitsch Peary, she was 'one of the first non-Inuit women to establish, somewhat reluctantly, a high profile as a female Arctic explorer'. This is a huge achievement considering that 'the genre of Arctic literature is heavily populated with male adventure-hero protagonists'.
9. According to Triana Toribio (2006: 59), 'markers of a particular location are generally not sought after' in Coixet's films. The white landscape can be considered, therefore, as an example of the deliberate use of the 'anywhere, anyplace' strategy discussed by this scholar.
10. Multicultural, postcolonial, and transnational feminist scholars, such as Ella Shohat, Trinh T. Minh-ha and others, have written extensively on the crucial role of sexual difference in this colonization of the imagination. In her 1991 article 'Gender and the culture of empire', Shohat examines how imperial narratives are often organized around metaphors of sexual domination or rape, fantasies of rescue and eroticized geographies.
11. According to Joana Sabadell (2017), the film's narrative is colonial in terms of the time in which the story is set, but also postcolonial if we think of it as a critique of the colonial binaries that underpin Josephine's conquest.

Murmuring colonial ghosts in Margarida Cardoso's filmography

Adriana Martins[1]

Margarida Cardoso represents a singular filmmaker within the framework of contemporary Portuguese film. The uniqueness of her work derives, to a great extent, from the controversial topics her films address, and that mostly focus either on the experiences of the Portuguese in Africa during the Colonial War (1961–74) or on life in Mozambique after independence. Her work compares and contrasts colonial and postcolonial times and memories, thereby constituting relevant examples through which the dynamics of cultural memory and the tensions between hegemonic and marginalized memories are thrown into relief through various processes of remediation.

Having grown up in Mozambique while her father, a former Portuguese Air Force pilot, was fighting in the Colonial War, Cardoso always encountered difficulties in coping with the culture of silence that characterized Salazar's regime (Gil 2004, 2011). This silence prevented people from talking openly about the conflict and other issues as this might disrupt the image of harmony and unity cultivated by the Estado Novo. The culture of silence interlinked with the atmosphere of fear and repression that pervaded the decades-long rule of this authoritarian regime and that bore long-lasting effects. A good example of the latter is the silence on the Colonial War that continued to be observed in the wake of the 1974 Revolution. Medeiros (2000) and Ribeiro (2004) associate this silence with the fact that the men who initiated the revolution were the same men who fought in Africa during thirteen long and violent years. In other words, just as it was necessary to celebrate the April Revolution, so was there the need to silence the war's violence. This tension between that which was to be remembered and that which was to be obliterated reveals how the politics of national memory have been contentious, a fact which, in turn, explains why the meandering end of the Colonial War, the April Revolution, post-revolutionary Portugal and the relations between Portugal and its former colonies within a postcolonial framework have mostly been addressed by literary and filmic texts.[2] The processes of literary and filmic mediation through which the past is revisited illustrates the importance that Assmann (2008 cited in Brunow 2015: 15) attributes to the circulation of images and narratives that cease to be viewed as 'storage memory' to become elements of 'functional memory', with new meanings through their dissemination in different contexts of enunciation.

Interested in archival materials, Cardoso began challenging the culture of silence by digging into private memories and asking her father about the years her family had lived in Mozambique, which then led to her questioning the politics of national memory in Portugal before and after the 1974 Revolution. At the same time, in searching for her personal identity, Cardoso remained connected to Africa and curious about the construction of Mozambique as an independent nation, especially from a filmic perspective. This personal background has shaped her filmography, and in particular four of her films: *Natal 71* (1999), *Kuxa Kanema: O nascimento do cinema* (2003), *A costa dos murmúrios* (2004) and *Yvone Kane* (2014). Even though in diverse ways (*Natal 71* and *Kuxa Kanema: O nascimento do cinema* are documentaries, while the latter two are fictional feature films) and across different levels, all these films problematize the construction of national memory in Portugal and in Mozambique, and all of them revolve around wars: the Colonial War (1961–74) and the post-independence war in Mozambique (1977–92). In other words, Cardoso depicts nations whose pasts were interconnected for a long time and that were then trapped and torn by war at key moments in their histories, and have therefore had to cope with traumatic memories; memories that still continue to haunt the present and that have conditioned the national narratives built upon the dialectics between, on the one hand, what to inscribe and remember and, on the other hand, what to erase and forget. In sum, by unveiling how societies imagine themselves, Cardoso's films discuss how the past has conditioned the present in the visual construction of the nation.

This chapter aims to establish a dialogue between *A costa dos murmúrios* and *Yvone Kane*, taking into account the semantic and aesthetic complementarity between these films so that the ambiguities and contradictions derived from power relations established in colonial times can best be understood and handled in a postcolonial period. This might seem a peculiar approach to Cardoso's work if one considers that, on the one hand, *A costa dos murmúrios* discusses the demise of Portugal's empire in Mozambique during the final years of the Colonial War, while, on the other hand, *Yvone Kane* revisits the mysterious murder of a fictional female political hero and guerrilla fighter about a decade after the independence of the former Portuguese colony (even if Cardoso's film does not make any explicit reference to a specific country). However, the parallels between the films are significant, as this chapter will argue below.

Both narratives attempt to break the silences surrounding the deaths of young people: the suggested suicide of a young Portuguese officer in *A costa dos murmúrios* and the death of Yvone Kane in *Yvone Kane*. What interconnects these deaths stems from how their lives became trapped by the regimes they defended and for which they sacrificed themselves. The fact that both characters were young when they died is also relevant. Their youth is the 'hook' that relates the past (behind the reasons leading to their death) to a problematic present. This also provides a strategy for paving the way for a reflection, not only on the future of those with whom they had bonds and who would outlive them, but also of their generation in broader terms. Moreover, both films address the national past and their ghosts from a female-gendered perspective that deserves our attention. While cinematic discussions of the Colonial War are mostly depicted from a male perspective that often focuses on male heroes or the lives of combatants, representations of national heroes following the Portuguese colonial wars of independence tend to portray the experiences of male leaders from an ideologically biased point of view that translates the dominant party's official interpretation of the national past.[3] The few representations of female revolutionaries that do exist depict women as perfect beings devoid of either sexuality or any personal life: in sum, as myths whose lives were consecrated to the party's ideals.[4]

The semantic complementarity between these movies is primarily thematic. Both films discuss how different generations of Portuguese and African people relate to the experience of colonialism and of its associated conflicts. It does not matter that *A costa dos murmúrios* addresses the Colonial War and *Yvone Kane* discusses the complexities of building up a nation independent of imperial power while having to cope with the constraints imposed by the hegemonic ideology. Despite the diversity in terms of historical conditions, class and age divisions, the characters in both films are affected by war, having experienced losses of various kinds. Cardoso uses the losses of her characters as a base for the discussion of national losses in allegorical terms: (1) the imminent loss of Portugal's empire in *A costa dos murmúrios*; and (2) the loss of the initial national dream of creating an equal and fair society in Mozambique in *Yvone Kane*. Therefore, both films set out works of mourning at individual and collective levels that allow spectators to reflect on the rhetoric underlying colonial and postcolonial politics of memory and their respective underlying fallacies.

Even though this chapter does not claim that Cardoso attempted to rewrite *A costa dos murmúrios* in *Yvone Kane*, which would be impossible since the 2004 film was based on Lídia Jorge's novel, it does argue that *Yvone Kane* may to some extent be considered a sequel to *A costa dos murmúrios* given its setting in a former colony in a postcolonial time.[5] This hypothesis gains consistency when the aforementioned semantic parallelism is reinforced by the aesthetic parallelism that exists between the films. The aesthetic parallelism rests on the following aspects: (1) the characterization of female characters and the relevance attributed to them; (2) the characterization of spaces in both narratives; and (3) the appropriation and role of archival material in both films.

It is similarly not a coincidence that Beatriz Batarda is the actress chosen to incarnate both Evita in *A costa dos murmúrios* and Rita in *Yvone Kane*. The filmmaker's choice immediately creates in viewers knowledgeable about Cardoso's work a sort of continuity between the plots, which is reinforced by Batarda's enquiring and penetrating gaze in both films.[6] At the level of fictional character composition, both protagonists are young women seeking their identities and striving to endow their existence with meaning. Evita experiences the loss of her husband, a loss here understood not only as his physical death but particularly as the loss of his former self, considered distorted by his experiences of war. In other words, the man with whom Evita shared the dream of building a life together in Portugal was definitely not the man she met when she arrived in Africa to get married. Moreover, it is in Africa that Evita understands the fallacy of the regime, the imperial lie and the effect that both were able to generate on women's lives within the framework of a rigid patriarchal society, a condition that she firmly rejects. Evita's experience in Africa represents the loss of her innocence and her transition to maturity. Her husband's death symbolically anticipates the end of the war and of the regime, as well as the loss of empire. In *Yvone Kane*, following the death of her young daughter and her suggested subsequent attempt at suicide, Rita encounters a process for coping with her pain and continuing to live in the search for the truth about Yvone Kane's death. It is the need to dig into the events related to Kane's death that leads her to Africa, where the journalist meets her mother, Sara, a white Portuguese doctor who embraced the revolutionary ideal and who remained in Africa after decolonization to help build an independent nation. In *Yvone Kane*, Rita's experience in Africa allows the filmmaker to once more examine, following *Kuxa Kanema*, the construction of an independent nation, bringing to the forefront the stereotypes, prejudices and cultural tensions inherited from colonial times as well as the constraints imposed by the party's ideologically biased view on the construction of national memory. However, in *Yvone Kane* Cardoso's perspective of analysis remains the same as that adopted in *A costa dos murmúrios*, that is the perspective of white Europeans.

The encounter between daughter (Rita) and mother (Sara), even more than anticipating another loss in Rita's life (Sara's death), sends the viewer back to the interaction between Evita and Helena, the captain's wife in *A costa dos murmúrios*. Even if it is not possible to draw parallels between Helena and Sara in terms of character composition,[7] it is undeniable that the character of Helena in *A costa dos murmúrios* was crucial to making Evita understand the other side of the Colonial

War in terms of its effects on the domestic life of women and the evils of the patriarchal system underpinned by the authoritarian regime. In *Yvone Kane*, Rita and Sara's coexistence, when both know that Sara has a terminal illness, allows them to reconcile after years of separation. With a view to protecting her children, and to dedicating herself fully to the ideological mission of contributing to building the independent nation, Sara, the white doctor, had sent her children to Portugal, but had neither later brought them back nor established any relationship of proximity with them. The distant relationship between mother and daughter is best illustrated by Sara's silence over the death of her granddaughter whom she had never met. By not addressing the issue, it seems as though the little girl never existed. The scene when she asks Rita if she has a photo of the girl is particularly poignant. This is the only time when mother and daughter are seen physically close to each other, lying on Sara's bed. At the same time as Sara asks to see the photo, she hesitates, as she believes that if she never sees the photo it would be as if the girl had never existed, which would spare her the experience of a painful loss.

Sara's hesitant attitude, resulting from a debate between her curiosity about her granddaughter and the need to preserve herself in emotional terms, raises an interesting reflection on Assmann's opposition between storage and functional memory, and pre-empts the discussion that Cardoso's film fosters about the importance of the archive, its statute and potentialities. The child's photo is evidence, a trace of the child's existence, and could thus be considered a component of storage memory. The willingness to contemplate the photo after the child's death and, in a moment of proximity with Rita, creates in Sara an effect that also reveals an affect she does not know how to cope with as she had placed her allegiance to the political cause before her allegiance to her family. This episode deserves particular attention as it anticipates and somehow announces a reflection both on the ways in which individual and collective memories can be dealt with through diverse processes of remediation, and on the potentialities of the archive when Rita enquires about Yvone Kane's death.[8]

Just as Helena proves to be a fundamental character in *A costa dos murmúrios* through her revelation of the other side of the Colonial War, the same can be said of Sara in *Yvone Kane*. Rita's attempt to reconstitute the guerrilla fighter's life allows Sara to look back over the first years of the independent nation, and to reveal the resentment of its people towards Europeans, even when the latter were fighting for the formerly colonized people's cause. Besides having known and befriended Yvone Kane, Sara is the character who directly experiences the inequalities resulting from the ideological tenets of the new regime. Despite having abandoned everything out of her dedication to her political beliefs, Sara is removed from her position as a hospital doctor due to being white and has to work in a religious mission in order to secure employment, thus experiencing racial discrimination in a postcolonial context.[9] The proximity of death makes her reflect on her relationships with people, and particularly with those whom she loved, even if she had not expressed her feelings to them. It is for this reason that she is not able to recognize her son performing when watching a DVD Rita brings for her. She also realizes that, despite knowing and trusting Gabriel, her faithful employee, for 30 years, she has never been to his house. Similarly, despite having adopted Jaime, she is still unable to establish a close relationship with the young man. Jaime is, along with the two girls raped in the mission where Sara works, the representative of the youngest generation who had experienced the evils of colonialism. Besides being 'children of the empire'[10] (as Rita and her brother also were), they are also children of the war that took place following independence and, as such, direct victims of violence, which leads them to experience a problematic sense of belonging; in a nutshell, they are people adrift who mourn their condition as social outcasts.

It is interesting to observe how Cardoso shoots all these characters caught by history's traps. They are portrayed as observing one another from afar in silence, which serves to reinforce the impression of distance and the lack of communication. People are not represented patting or touching one another; indeed, there is no physical connection between them, only distance and a disturbing gaze that translates fear, mistrust, resentment, suffering and solitude. This physical and affective distance (often translated as indifference towards the Other because the ideological context demanded this) is skilfully stressed by the ways in which Cardoso visually brings these characters together. The filmmaker makes the best of mirrors, reflections, filters, windows and ruins in a puzzle of frames that intensifies the effects deriving from the lack of communication among the characters and their melancholy. Cardoso had already used this aesthetic expedient in the shooting of *A costa dos murmúrios*, and resorts to it again widely in *Yvone Kane* in order to stress the impact of war(s) and of ideologies on people's lives. Through the characters' disturbing gaze, what is not verbalized is stressed, drawing the viewer's attention to how the independent nation was also haunted by a culture of silence similar to that which had existed during colonialism.[11]

When considering the aesthetic parallelisms between these films in terms of the characterization of spaces, it is worth paying particular attention to: (1) domestic spaces (Helena's house in *A costa dos murmúrios* and Sara's place in *Yvone Kane*); and (2) the hotels in both narratives. In *A costa dos murmúrios*, Helena's house is simultaneously a space of confinement and liberation: confinement since it is a kind of prison where Helena lives while the captain is at the battlefront, and which she is not supposed to leave during his absence. It is also the domestic space in which, besides the tense relations between husband and wife, the hierarchical relationships with servants are also evident. However, Helena's house could also be considered a space of liberation as it is the setting where she shows Evita the photographic archive that proves the atrocities committed by the Portuguese army against the colonized people.[12] In *Yvone Kane*, Sara's house reveals the domestic side of her life as a solitary woman whose most loyal friend is her dog. Despite the fact that Sara is sometimes portrayed in her bed, or in the living room comfortably reading, the house cannot be considered hospitable, which might explain why Jaime wants to live in one of the annexes. From the depiction of Sara's house and her domestic life, viewers realize that Sara does not maintain close relationships with the people who work for her, which suggests how the distance between Europeans and Africans continued to exist after the former colony's independence.

In *A costa dos murmúrios*, the Stella Maris hotel, once a symbol of the glorious times of colonialism when it hosted guests from higher social classes visiting the colony or doing business there, is converted into lodgings for military officers and their families. It is a space of learning for Evita as regards both her relationship with her husband and the subaltern condition of women who followed their husbands into scenarios of war. Due to its new function, the hotel somehow has a feeling of decay too. In fact, it is the decay being experienced by the colonial enterprise. In *Yvone Kane*, the hotel where Rita stays while trying to obtain further details on Kane's death is under refurbishment. Having been used by the rebels during the war, the hotel witnessed executions and is viewed by the locals as a haunted place. The hotel swimming pool gains relevance as it is empty and unused. According to the hotel's new owner, the swimming pool was used as a venue for torture sessions and executions during the war. In other words, what might usually be understood as a major attraction represents memories of pain and violence. It is in this same space that Rita, after receiving proof of the party's corruption that Yvone Kane's lover had uncovered, begins writing a non-official version of Yvone Kane's murder. In this sense, and contrary to what happens in the Stella Maris, the hotel in *Yvone Kane* can be considered a space of regeneration in a post-war period. It represents Rita's regeneration after her daughter's (and also her mother's) death and a new direction for her life. But it also represents a new beginning when, in one of the film's last scenes, the swimming pool appears filled with sand as an attempt to cope with past horror. The filled pool symbolically represents a new beginning for that particular space and for a nation having to find ways of handling its ghosts on its path to reconciliation and stability.

The appropriation and role of archival material is the last aspect of the aesthetic parallelism between the films that this chapter discusses. In *A costa dos murmúrios*, the photographic archive stored in Helena's house contains evidence that atrocities have taken place, and this explains why Captain Jaime Forza Leal, Helena's husband, starts burning everything when he realizes the Portuguese will not win the conflict. Through the photos found in Helena and Jaime's house, the violence of the war against Africans, so far invisible in the film except for the rumours of 'natives' being poisoned, becomes clear. In *Yvone Kane*, the spectator first learns about Yvone Kane's life through the archive, which configures a myth around the guerrilla leader, omitting her criticism of the party as well as aspects of her personal life.[13] In Cardoso's fiction, Yvone Kane's existence is literally 'arrested' by the regime's archive to serve its own interests. This idea arises from the twofold meaning of the verb 'to arrest', since, as Agostinho (2014) suggests, after analysing Derrida's premise in *Archive Fever: A Freudian Impression* (1995), the archive represents a site of authority and, as such, 'arrests' knowledge. Through creating a fictional archive about Yvone Kane (that could have been produced by any official historiography), Cardoso discusses how the archive is subject to manipulation. Moreover, she demonstrates that a '[r]epresentation is not neutral and is pervaded by power relations' (Brunow 2015: 8), and points out the corresponding need to pay attention to the archive's inconsistencies, to its epistemological gaps, or, in other words, to what it excludes.[14]

The point made here is that both in *A costa dos murmúrios* and *Yvone Kane* (as the filmmaker also did in *Natal 71* and *Kuxa Kanema*), Cardoso's films constitute exercises of mediation and self-reflexivity that, by placing archival footage into new contexts of enunciation, 'free' the archive and confer new meanings upon it. This belief leads back to the aforementioned scene from *Yvone Kane* in which Sara asks whether Rita has a photo of her daughter. When Sara hesitates over looking at the photo that the spectator never sees (metonymically understood as the archive as a whole), Cardoso is inviting the viewer to acknowledge the potential for manipulating archives and, ultimately, the power of the image in either creating or erasing/excluding certain realities, certain orders of things. Should one consider that *Kuxa Kanema* was a weekly 10-minute documentary that aimed at filming the people with a view to both returning the image to the people and documenting the birth of a new nation, it becomes easier to understand how Cardoso's films result from the filmmaker's need to 'free' the archive. Such a need explains why the viewer, when watching her films, hears the murmuring colonial ghosts reverberating loudly through the same narrative: that which attempts to demystify the intricate relationships between the power of the image and the image of power.

REFERENCES

Agostinho, Daniela (2014), 'Arresting images: Inhabiting the Nazi archive in Yael Hersonski's *A Film Unfinished*', *Diffractions*, 3, https://www.academia.edu/9622857/Arresting_Images_Inhabiting_the_Nazi_Archive_in_Yael_Hersonskis_A_Film_Unfinished. Accessed 7 August 2019.

Antunes, António Lobo (1979), *Memória de elefante*, Lisbon: Vega.

——— (1979), *Os cus de Judas*, Lisbon: Vega.

——— (1980), *Conhecimento do inferno*, Lisbon: Vega.

——— (1997), *O esplendor de Portugal*, Lisbon: Dom Quixote.

Botelho, João (1985), *Um adeus português*, Portugal: Madragoa Filmes.

Brunow, Dagmar (2015), *Remediating Transcultural Memory: Documentary Filmmaking as Archival Intervention*, Berlin and Boston, MA: De Gruyter.

Cardoso, Margarida (1999), *Natal 71*, Portugal: Filmes do Tejo and IPACA.

——— (2003), *Kuxa Kanema: O nascimento do cinema*, Portugal: Arte France Cinéma, Filmes do Tejo, RTBF, RTP.

——— (2004), *A costa dos murmúrios*, Portugal: Lisboa Filme.

——— (2014), *Yvone Kane*, Portugal: Filmes do Tejo II, MPC Filmes.

Derrida, Jacques (1995), *The Archive Fever: A Freudian Impression* (trans. E. Prenowitz), Chicago: Chicago University Press.

Faulkner, Sally and Liz, Mariana (2016), 'Introduction: Portuguese film: Colony, postcolony, memory', *Journal of Romance Studies*, 16:2, pp. 1–11.

Faulkner, Sally and Martins, Ana (2016), 'Intermedial dialogue in *A Costa dos Murmúrios/The Murmuring Coast* (Lídia Jorge 1988/Margarida Cardoso 2004): Novel, photography, film', *Journal of Romance Studies*, 16:2, pp. 36–57.

Foucault, Michel (1972), *The Archaeology of Knowledge and The Discourse on Language* (trans. A. M. Smith), New York: Pantheon Books.

Gil, José (2004), *Portugal Hoje: O Medo de Existir*, Lisbon: Relógio d'Água.

——— (2011), 'A psicanálise e o poder', in I. Gil and A. Martins (eds), *A Cultura Portuguesa no Divã*, Lisbon: Universidade Católica Editora, pp. 19–35.

Jess-Cooke, Carolyn and Verevis, Constantine (eds) (2010), *Second Takes: Critical Approaches to the Film Sequel*, Albany: State University of New York Press.

Jorge, Lídia (1988), *A costa dos murmúrios*, Lisbon: Dom Quixote.

Lança, Marta (2015), 'Entrevista à Margarida Cardoso, a partir de *Yvone Kane*', Buala, http://www.buala.org/pt/cara-a-cara/entrevista-a-margarida-cardoso-a-partir-de-yvone-kane. Accessed 12 June 2018.

Leitão, Joaquim (1999), *Inferno*, Portugal: Lusomundo Audiovisuais.

——— (2006), *20, 13*, Portugal: MGN Filmes.

Lisboa, Ricardo Vieira (2015), '*Yvone Kane* (2014) de Margarida Cardoso', À Pala de Walsh, http://www.apaladewalsh.com/2015/02/yvone-kane-2014-de-margarida-cardoso/. Accessed 12 June 2018.

Martins, Adriana (2012), 'Writing the nation beyond resistance: Portuguese film and the colonial war', *Revue LISA/LISA e-journal*, 10:1, http://lisa.revues.org/5028. Accessed 15 June 2018.

Medeiros, Paulo de (2000). 'Hauntings: Memory, narrative, and the Portuguese Colonial wars', *Cadernos de Literatura Comparada*, 1, pp. 47–76, http://ilc-cadernos.com/index.php/cadernos/article/view/41/28. Accessed 13 June 2018.

Oliveira, Manoel de (1990), *Non, ou a vã glória de mandar*, Portugal: Madragoa Filmes.

Pepetela (1992), *A geração da utopia*, Lisbon: Dom Quixote.

Ribeiro, Margarida (2004), *Uma História de Regressos: Império, Guerra Colonial e Pós-Colonialismo*, Porto: Afrontamento.

Ribeiro de Menezes, Alison (2011), 'Introduction: Cultural memory and the legacies of war and dictatorship in contemporary Portugal and Spain', in A. Ribeiro de Menezes and C. O'Leary (eds), *Legacies of War and Dictatorship in Contemporary Portugal and Spain*, Oxford and New York: Peter Lang, pp. 1–34.

Sabine, Mark (2014), 'Colonial masculinities under a woman's gaze in Margarida Cardoso's *A Costa dos Murmúrios*', in H. Owen and A. Klobucka (eds), *Gender, Empire and Postcolony: Luso-Afro-Brazilian Intersections*, New York: Palgrave Macmillan, pp. 87–109.

Silva, Antônio M. (2016), 'Archives, memory and colonial resistance in the work of Portuguese filmmakers Margarida Cardoso and Filipa César', *Journal of Romance Studies*, 16:2, pp. 96–111.

Vasconcelos, António-Pedro (1974), *Adeus até ao meu Regresso*, Portugal: RTP.

——— (2003), *Os Imortais*, Portugal: Animatógrafo.

Vieira, Estela (2013), 'Politics and the aesthetics of absence in Margarida Cardoso's cinematic work', *Hispanic Research Journal*, 14:1, pp. 67–85.

Villaverde, Teresa (1990), *A idade maior*, Portugal: Invicta Filmes.

NOTES

1. The author of this chapter is grateful to Paulo de Medeiros (University of Warwick) for sharing some of the bibliographical items included in this chapter.
2. On how the end of empire remains a traumatic issue for contemporary Portuguese culture, see Ribeiro de Menezes (2011). Among other literary and filmic remediations of the Colonial War, consider the following examples: (1) Lobo Antunes's novels, here referred to by the year of their publication: *Memória de elefante* (1979, not available in English), *Os cus de Judas* (South of Nowhere, 1979), *Conhecimento do inferno* (Knowledge of Hell, 1980), and O *esplendor de Portugal* (The Splendour of Portugal, 1997); (2) Lídia Jorge's novel *A costa dos murmúrios* (The Murmuring Coast, 1988); and (3) diverse films on the Colonial War, such as *Adeus até ao meu regresso* (Vasconcelos, 1974); *Um adeus português* (Botelho, 1985); *A Idade Maior* (Villaverde, 1990); *Non, ou a vã glória de mandar* (Oliveira, 1990); *Natal 71* (Cardoso, 1999); *Os imortais* (Vasconcelos, 2003); *A costa dos murmúrios* (Cardoso, 2004); and *20, 13* (Leitão, 2006).
3. The male-gendered perspective by which heroes tend to be portrayed in literary and filmic texts that address the Colonial War or the civil wars that followed can be illustrated by, among other examples, the novels by Antunes cited in note 2 and by Pepetela's novel *A geração da utopia* (1992). Within the framework of Portuguese film, consider, for instance, *Um adeus português* (Botelho, 1985), *Non, ou a vã glória de mandar* (Oliveira, 1990) and *Inferno* (Leitão, 1999).

4. Cardoso makes reference to this characterization of female revolutionaries in an interview she gave to the site Buala (Lança 2015). On the gendered representation of heroism in *Yvone Kane*, see Silva (2016).
5. As far as the author of this chapter knows, no one has thus far characterized *Yvone Kane* as a sequel to *A costa dos murmúrios*. The term 'sequel' applies here in a broad sense and is inspired by the Jess-Cooke and Verevis (2010: 5) understanding of what a sequel is: that is, 'primarily a site within which communal spectatorship and paratextual discourses may be circulated, and by which the experience of an "original" may be extended, revisited and heightened'. Despite having never suggested that *Yvone Kane* may be a sequel to *A costa dos murmúrios*, Faulkner and Liz (2016: 2) refer to the closeness between both of these Cardoso films in terms of 'the cinematic questioning of the interconnections between gender, power and memory in the postcolonial era'.
6. Sabine (2014) analyses in detail Evita's gaze in *A costa dos murmúrios*, reflecting on how the conventional scopic regime of patriarchy is thrown into jeopardy. Evita's gaze is also examined in Chapter 4 of this volume by Estela Vieira.
7. Helena epitomizes the ideal of the subaltern woman who is cherished by patriarchal society, and represented as a sexual object. Sara, on the contrary, is an independent woman who has a professional life, who is never portrayed as being dependent on her husband, and who did not hesitate to remain in Africa far from her children to contribute to the dream of transforming a former colony into an independent nation, thus accomplishing an ideological goal. Right up until the end of her life, she is depicted as a strong-willed person, despite her solitude.
8. Although approaching the work from a different perspective and focusing on the intermedial dialogue between Cardoso's film and Lídia Jorge's novel *A costa dos murmúrios*, Faulkner and Martins (2016) set out an interesting approach to the role of photography in the structure of Jorge's novel and on the performance of doubleness by the female protagonist in Cardoso's film. It would be fruitful to expand on the authors' reflection on photography in Cardoso's intervention in the archive, taking into account *Yvone Kane*, which can only be done within the scope of another essay.
9. Sara was not the only white character in the film subject to racial inequality. Amelia Zuri's photo is not in the military museum despite being present in the female detachment that helped to transform the revolution into a reality in Cardoso's creation of a fictional archive. Silva (2016: 103) discusses this specific case also as an example of gender inequality, as Zuri was a lesbian.
10. I borrow this expression from Ribeiro, who coordinates the research project 'MEMOIRS – Children of Empires and European Postmemories'. The child of the empire is defined as 'someone for whom the empire, the colonial wars and decolonisation are only a representation, because s/he has no first-hand knowledge of the events nor is s/he the author of first-hand testimony. Rather, the child is the symbolical inheritor of an open wound from which he or she draws up a narrative constructed from fragments of family narratives made up of

discourses, snapshots, maps, letters, aerograms and other objects taken from the private domain and also from fragments drawn from public narratives'. See http://memoirs.ces.uc.pt/index.php?id=14991&id_lingua=2&pag=14997). Accessed 28 July 2019.

11. The sense of distance and indifference is intensified by the disruption caused by the camera's stillness on viewer modes of perception, an expedient already adopted by Cardoso in *A costa dos murmúrios*. On this issue, see Martins (2012), Vieira (2015) and Faulkner and Martins (2016).
12. Sabine claims that '[t]he dystopian nature of [these] domestic spaces is a crucial indicator of the colonizer's failure to establish a home in Africa, wherein the installation of a loyal wife signals the completion of the "civilizing" land grab' (2014: 100).
13. In the interview given to Buala, Cardoso acknowledged that she had created the archive about Yvone Kane in line with the mythical representation of other female fighters in official archives (Lança 2015).
14. When analysing the ambiguities, inconsistencies and potentialities of the archive, Foucault (1972) and Derrida (1995) constitute mandatory references. On the archives' epistemological gaps and inconsistencies, see also Agostinho (2014).

PART III

Beyond the author: Recognizing other cinematographic professions

Weaving a cinematographic culture and writing about film, or how to reconstruct the subject of women in Spanish silent cinema

Begoña Soto-Vázquez

Starting point

In May 1928 María Luz Morales Godoy (A Coruña 1895–Barcelona 1990[1]) delivered the opening lecture in a series of cultural talks on cinematography, organized by the Asociación de Empresarios de Espectáculos Públicos de Cataluña (Catalan Society of Public Entertainment Businesses). A summary of this lecture, as she herself described it, in seven sections was published over eight consecutive Sundays between May and July 1928 in 'Comentario', her weekly column in the 'Vida Cinematográfica' section in the Barcelona daily newspaper *La Vanguardia*. The seven instalments were published under the common heading *¿Una cultura cinematográfica?* (A Cinematographic Culture?). Morales contributed to this section of the paper from 17 November 1923 until 30 July 1933 under the pseudonym Felipe Centeno (Centeno 1928a, 1928b, 1928c, 1928d, 1928e, 1928f, 1928g, 1928h, 1928i, 1928j). The section was devoted exclusively to cinema, and was founded on 27 October 1923 with the following declaration of intent:

> Our resolution to devote a weekly section to cinema demonstrates *La Vanguardia*'s commitment to meet the needs of the public and is clear proof that we are not against cinema, even if at times there have been articles published in these pages that could lead readers who are easily deceived by first impressions to believe this. *La Vanguardia* is not, and could not possibly be against the cinema.
>
> (Cid 1923: 13)

This film section was first published on Saturdays and later on Sundays. The title was changed some months before Morales left from 'Vida cinematográfica' to just

'Cinematografía'. Her weekly column was always headed 'Comentario' with a subheading introducing the subject. She signed all her film articles Felipe Centeno while writing other articles for the same newspaper on different subjects such as literature, theatre and fashion as María Luz Morales. The last article by Morales in *La Vanguardia* was a long article titled 'La historia del peinado' (the history of hairstyles) on 22 September 1972.

The cinematographic culture that was the subject of the lecture, and hence of Morales/Centeno's columns, is where this work begins. She outlines her series of articles on this subject by saying:

> The initiative shown by the Catalan Society of Public Entertainment Businesses, Cinema Section in organizing the first series of Lectures on Cinematographic Culture, will be warmly welcomed by all real film lovers [...] The initiative itself is already a victory [...] And also, almost in the linking of those two words, which still sound distant and distinct [...] 'Cinema culture'.
>
> (Centeno 1928a: 18)

She ended the last paragraph of the same piece with:

> Language, words, are the essential medium of every culture. And it is getting to the point where we must create, weave,[2] at least, a culture of film [...] And now is exactly the right moment [...] There is a desire, a great interest in film. Film is beginning to be studied as an abstract concept, we are beginning to look far into the future of the potential of film. A Cinema Culture will emerge from all of this.
>
> (Centeno 1928a: 18)

This inaugural point of cinema culture – that tacking, threading, weaving – is our starting point.

Morales, using the pen name Centeno, was not the only female film journalist writing in the Spanish press during the first decades of the twentieth century. However, she did have the most consistent career, writing more than 400 articles over nearly ten years. Carmen Prada Mantrana was writing about film in the Spanish press before Morales, starting in 1918 and stopping in 1921. She wrote for the newspapers *El Día*, *El Fígaro* and *La Correspondencia de España*, the magazine *Mundo Gráfico* and two magazines specializing in cinema: *Cine-Mundial* and *Cinema* (Rivas Morente 2017). Prada used the pen name Duquesa de Borelli and ended her career as a film journalist just as Morales began hers. But there were other women writing about film in the press who have been even less of a focus of scholarship. For some we have little more than a name: Cecilia Alonso i Bozzo, María Álvarez de Burgos, Carlota O'Neill de Lamos, Encarnación Osés and Angelita Pla. We are interested here in those women writing about film in that period that Centeno/Morales identifies as a time when cinematographic culture was still being sketched out and woven together.

Chronologically we are exactly at that time between 1918 and 1933, suggested by Prada/Borelli's and Morales/Centeno's writing, 1918 being the year Prada begins to write about cinema and 1933 being the year when Morales stops writing about film to start writing about theatre. This is a time that encompasses the age of silent cinema, when the era of the cinema of attractions was already over, and right in the middle of the establishment of the history of film, ending at the incipient introduction of sound. Rarely has the pairing of women and film been seen in this way before the 1970s when a generation of filmmakers such as Pilar Miró, Cecilia Bartolomé and Josefina Molina began to achieve recognition (García López 2019). In the era of silent cinema and early sound films the contribution of women to the making of Spanish cinema, as well as the research on this contribution, is uncharted territory.

Background: Subject and sources

Lauren Rabinovitz (2005: 22–23) notes that what is interesting about the convergence of feminist film studies and the social history of cinema is that it poses major questions about methodology, such as who should be the subject of history and what constitutes appropriate sources to be analysed for that historical research. Let us look at the first question, who should be the subject of that history, as posed by Jane M. Gaines (2010: 32).

Since our research is a part of the significant progress being made in the development of feminist film studies and the review of methodology in the history of cinema itself,[3] our contribution must be critical and inclusive. We must ask ourselves who the subject of history should be while questioning the history we want to narrate. Following on from Monica Dall'Asta (2010: 43) and Karen Ward Mahar (2008), new feminist history has the potential to question the paradigm of the central position of Classical Hollywood Cinema. The unchallengeable status of the leading discourse on classical cinema has meant that it is not only the role of women in different national cinemas (silent or otherwise) that has been rendered invisible. In fact, every national cinema has been eclipsed by the Classical Hollywood Cinema paradigm. Women's history has the potential to drag the re-reading of these marginal or peripheral cinemas into this discourse, which has been established as the central axis. We must break away from the hegemonic and patriarchal view in which it is mainly men who make cinema, just as we must avoid film discourse that presumes that there is only one line where everything else is inserted as an addendum or as a note in the margin. It is easy to be swept along by this dynamic where women are viewed as lost items in some forgotten corner, as an enterprise of lost and found (Rabinovitz 2005: 26). In other words, we must always be on the lookout for opportunities to add our discoveries and missing links to the established canon, taking responsibility for completing the picture without questioning the appropriateness of the frame.[4] This will involve texts, film seasons or research, the objective of which is to discover or highlight 'the first woman who ...' or 'the female film pioneers who first ...', and those firsts will almost certainly be producers or directors of cinematographic work.

Let us now consider the second question: what are appropriate sources for research into the history of women's relationship with (Spanish silent) cinema? Spanish silent film is a research subject where it is difficult to access the most important primary source: films. In addition, those of us who work on the history of Spanish film have not had many opportunities to conduct fieldwork, and very little basic documentation exists. Catalogues, inventories, directories, press research and screenings, among other valuable resources, are still in production and therefore not accessible. Due to the lack of films and the difficulty of finding reliable reference works, it is not at all surprising that scholarship on women's contribution to Spanish silent cinema is left to one side in all previously written work, as women simply do not exist and it stands to reason that this vacuum is not questioned. The problem of the subject of history and the sources of that history are locked into an immutable vicious circle. The simplistic but generally accepted logic that, without films, there is no possible object of research will unquestionably lead us to the view that indeed there are no films made by women in the early decades of the twentieth century. Therefore, in those decades there are no women working in film.

Dall'Asta (2010: 43–45) notes that, more often than not, it is not possible to tackle a study of women's cinema from the perspective that the only possible cinema history is constructed from the cinephile pairing of author/oeuvre as the only subject of historiographic research, as the most difficult thing is finding a continuous body of work attributed to a woman filmmaker[5] that can be analysed from this cinephile authorship perspective. The women who write, direct or produce cinema do not achieve continuity in these professions. They produce a small amount of work and, for the most part, produce a single title. This situation where women write, direct and produce only one piece of work is exemplified in Spanish cinema. From the silent era we have evidence that three women were able to direct and (self)produce: Elena Jordi, Helena Cortesina and Carmen Velacoracho.[6] Each of these women made just one film: Jordi *Thais* (1918), Cortesina *Flor de España* (1921) and Velacoracho *El descubrimiento de América* (1928). Of these three titles there is only one single frame of *Flor de España* left at the Filmoteca Española. Absolutely nothing else.

For the most part, women did not work in the professions established as having the status of cinematographic authorship. That is, they did not direct (or at least they did not write or produce), but were involved in filmmaking in other ways. Telling their story is inevitably complicated by the fact that they were limited to working as assistants, collaborators or partners of another person (a man). A serious obstacle to historical research is that women's involvement in Spanish films is as an anonymous mass of cutters, film splicers, laboratory workers, title writers or adapters, publicity writers or translators. If we use the cinephile model to examine Spanish silent cinema, we will come to the irrefutable conclusion that there were no female filmmakers. The works we can refer to and read with this formalist authorial analysis are so scarce that they cannot even be considered anecdotal. Moreover, if these works did in fact exist at one time, they have not survived and have permanently disappeared. It is indisputable that no Spanish films attributable to women filmmakers have been preserved to allow us to analyse them. This reductive model of authorial cinephile analysis is the superstructure that prevails in Spanish cinema culture, and a part of this is the historiographical logic (determining the subject) and the work of the film archives (providing the sources and methodology). This now well-established cinema culture, which Morales/Centeno herself helped to define in 1928, conspires 90 years later to make her invisible.

However, if we go beyond this concept of cinephile authorship, other sources, other subjects must be viable. This is what we are proposing to do through the analysis of the general interest and specialized film press. From this analysis, women do exist in Spanish silent cinema. There are not many references to and about women in the film press, but those that do exist appeared without interruption during the silent cinema period. Of course, there are no big news items, but rather a continuous scattered trail of clues. Women (except for actresses) are not in the headlines, but their presence in Spanish cinema cannot be questioned. The press shows us that women are present (obviously) as spectators (Soto Vázquez 2001), and also shows that women became involved in Spanish cinema in writing roles, not only as reporters or columnists, but also as scriptwriters, intertitles translators and adapters, or as essayists and teachers. Both Prada (Camarero Rioja 2013: 108) and Morales had considerable interest in the didactic possibilities of cinema, and Morales also gave lectures and taught courses on cinema. The importance of this cinematographic writing stems not from its quantity, which is in itself striking, but from its relevance to what Morales/Centeno was beginning to call the weaving (*hilvanando*) of cinema culture.

Writing culture

Our main focus is on women writing about film in the general and specialist press. Morales and Prada stand out among these female film writers because they have more often been the subject of scholarly research, but there are others such as: Cecilia Alonso i Bozzo, critic, contributor to newspapers and to various film magazines (Munsó Cabús y Romaguera i Ramió 2005); and Carlota O'Neill de Lamos, a contributor to at least five issues of *Arte y Cinematografía* (O'Neill 1923a, 1923b, 1923c, 1923d, 1923e). We have just two of Encarnación Osés's pieces, an interview with Max Linder in *El Cine*, dated 24 September 1912 and a profile of Italian actress María Jacobini in *Tras la pantalla* magazine on 3 September 1921 (Osés [1921] 2014). According to *Arte y Cinematografía* (X.X. 1926: 43), Angelita Pla was the Spanish representative in the magazine *La Cinematographie française*. There are also the writings on cinema of Emilia Pardo Bazán (Herrera 2005), Carmen de Burgos (Palomo 2010) and Concha Méndez Cuesta (Utrera Macías 2017), who had prestigious literary and journalistic careers in addition to their cinematographic writings.

A significant number of these women wrote under a pseudonym. María Luz Morales wrote as Felipe Centeno, Carlota O'Neill as Carlota Lionell or Laura de Noves, Carmen de Prada as Duquesa de Borelli, Cecilia Alonso as Travelling. Morales explains how her choice of pen name, which she used only for her contributions on film and not for her literary and theatrical writings, was determined by the sales and publicity systems of the cinema:

> – In 1923 they offered me the running of a film page which was going to be published by the film ads. I accepted and was put on the payroll as a cinema subeditor. And that's where 'Felipe Centeno' was born.
>
> – To hide the fact that you were a woman?
>
> – I can assure you that wasn't the reason. It was just an internal policy at the paper [...] The Felipe Centeno thing just came about because at that time cinema had the same problems as fashion; nobody gave it any weight and they thought that anybody could write about it. The advertising agents themselves wrote the film reviews. Madness! Serious journalists didn't want to author cinema columns, but in *La Vanguardia* they decided to give it to someone writing under a pseudonym to avoid problems and attacks on their independence. They didn't want people to know who it was. It was later that it was in the public domain.
>
> (Comín 1972: 41)

It is not unreasonable to think that Morales and Prada, the other two female film journalists, had similar motives. Furthermore, it was not only women who used pen names to write about film. Three of the film reviewers who are essential to our understanding of the establishment of film criticism in Spain (Rivas Morente 2013) write under a pseudonym. Federico de Onís writes as El espectador and both Martín Luis Guzmán and Alfonso Reyes use the pen name Fósforo. For both men and women to write about cinema under cover is consistent with Morales' explanation. It has nothing to do with women's integration into film journalism but is caused by the need for columnists and critics to avoid the pressure placed on them by film distributors and exhibitors.

Another matter for consideration is the choice of pseudonyms. The pen names used show a connection with a degree of knowledge of cinema in the case of Duquesa de Borelli and Travelling, or with a wider cultural sphere in the case of Felipe Centeno, a character from a series of novels by Benito Pérez Galdós. We will discuss the meanings of these pseudonyms from a different perspective. For these women, writing about film is just one aspect in a much longer and more significant career, within a much wider and lengthier context and interest in culture. Their intellectual careers and concerns go beyond cinema as a main objective. These women are part of a cultural elite that is interested in cinema as a means of understanding and participating in the surrounding cultural context rather than as an end in itself. This is a common feature among women in Spanish silent cinema; participation in cinema is just one more activity within a diverse professional career with more extensive intellectual interests, as is the case for the three women who directed and produced films in this era. Jordi and Cortesina had continuous long-standing careers in the theatre and Velacoracho had a fruitful career in literature and journalism. Their professional careers in the development of culture (theatre, poetry, literature, translation, among other pursuits) were not just a way of making a living, but also a way of life.

The women writing about film, at least those on whom we have enough information to write a biographical sketch, especially Morales and Prada, but also to a certain extent O'Neill and Alonso,[7] did so from a position of privilege for women of their time. They were among the estimated 43 per cent of Spanish women who were not illiterate, and also came from a position that allowed them access to education and training, which was very rare for Spanish women in the early decades of the twentieth century. Morales says in 1972:

> – In those days there were no journalism schools. Where did you train?
>
> – I owe a lot to one woman: Paquita Bonnemaison de Verdaguer Callís, who founded the Institut de Cultura per la Dona (the Institute of Culture for Women) [...] She created her school especially to open the world of culture to women workers; it was also an employment agency, but daughters of the *bourgeoisie* and the liberal professions began to frequent it with great enthusiasm. You paid ten pesetas a month.
>
> (Comín 1972: 41)

We have much less information about Prada, but we do know that she started working as a shorthand and typing teacher (Anon. 1914: 33–39). An article published in *El Mundo taquigráfico* (the world of shorthand) reports:

> Carmen Prada Mantrana: studied shorthand in the year 1900, under the direction of Don Pedro Cerdán, Private Teacher, following the Flores de Pando system, with some modifications and extensions. She spent twelve years at Orenstein and Koppel-Arthur Koppel, a railway materials factory, working as a shorthand typist.
>
> (Anon. 1914: 39)

Working outside the home as well as receiving that very rare education and training, Morales and Prada both started to write about cinema in their thirties, having gathered significant educational and life experience.[8] With these two women, added to the little information we have on a considerable number of female cinema writers, we can put forward a hypothesis about how the emerging cinema culture, and within that, the inception of film criticism, created very favourable conditions for women to work in film. Joan Minguet (2008: 34) analyses the arrival of cinema in the cultural system with the early film criticism of the period between 1913 and 1917, and establishes that an essential moment is the inclusion of a film review section (it was authored under the pseudonym Fósforo) in *España* magazine by a leading cultural figure, Ortega y Gasset. When Prada, and then Morales and the others, became involved in film criticism, it had already passed the first stage of institutionalization. This was a film criticism that, despite still being dependent on advertising and on the retelling of film plots, was beginning to move in different directions. Those new directions point towards what Morales calls cinema culture, a culture which she herself admitted was still in its gestation period.

The subject, once again

Women writing about film, or at least Alonso, Morales, O'Neill and Prada, were part of a culturally and financially privileged group working in the two great urban centres of twentieth-century Spain – Madrid and Barcelona – a social and geographical context that allowed them to write about film in specialist magazines and general newspapers relatively easily and fairly continuously. With this writing they helped to lay the foundations for a cinema culture that was beginning to be constructed, and played a decisive role in sketching it out and laying out its structure. Although we will leave it to future research to determine, it is difficult not to make a connection between the opportunity they had to take part in the writing and culture of cinema and the important presence that women must have had in the cinemas of Madrid and Barcelona at least between 1918 and 1933.

If the number of women linked to cinema by their writing is striking in its quantity, quality and continuity, we must also draw attention to their invisibility. The invisibility of women writing about film in the history of Spanish cinema can be explained from two equally perverse positions: first, the lack of interest in the history of something as fundamental as the significance of the female public in the configuration and establishment of Spanish cinema in the early decades of the twentieth century. Women writers can be but the tip of the iceberg of this hidden historiographical subject. The second is the cinephile attachment Spanish historians have to the idea there is nothing else apart from the oeuvre and the author (usually masculine singular), and this does not allow us to discern that there is another possible, if as yet invisible, cinema culture.

REFERENCES

Anon. (1914), 'Oposiciones a plazas de profesoras de taquigrafía y mecanografía/las profesoras de taquigrafía y mecanografía', *El Mundo taquigráfico*, XV, 167, 15 February, pp. 31–39.

Camarero Rioja, Fernando (2013), 'Teoría y práctica del cine educativo en España (1895–1923)', *Cahiers de civilisation espagnole contemporaine. Dossier: Cinéma éducatif en Espagne*, 11, https://journals.openedition.org/ccec/4843#tocto1n1. Accessed 6 May 2018.

Centeno, Felipe (María Luz Morales Godoy) (1928a), '¿Cultura cinematográfica? I. Silencio y charla', *La Vanguardia*, 20 May, p. 18a.

——— (1928b), '¿Cultura cinematográfica? II. El cine – sorpresa', *La Vanguardia*, 27 May, p. 22a.

——— (1928c), '¿Cultura cinematográfica? III. Prehistoria e historia', *La Vanguardia*, 27 May, p. 22a.

——— (1928d), '¿Cultura cinematográfica? IV. Los pecados del cine', *La Vanguardia*, 3 June, p. 20a.

——— (1928e), '¿Cultura cinematográfica? IV. Los pecados del cine', *La Vanguardia*, 10 June, p. 15a.

——— (1928f), '¿Cultura cinematográfica? V. Valores del cine', *La Vanguardia*, 17 June, p. 21a.

——— (1928g), '¿Cultura cinematográfica? V. Valores del cine', *La Vanguardia*, 24 June, p. 15a.

——— (1928h), '¿Cultura cinematográfica? VI. Significado del cine', *La Vanguardia*, 1 July, p. 19a.

——— (1928i), '¿Cultura cinematográfica? VII. Porvenir del cine', *La Vanguardia*, 8 July, p. 25a.

Cid (1923), 'Una aclaración', *La Vanguardia*, 27 October, p. 15.

Comín, María Pilar (1972), 'Mirando hacia tras sin ira. Una mujer en la aventura política', *La Vanguardia Española*, 26 January, p. 41.

Cordero Hoyo, Elena (2013), 'El salto del espectáculo de variedades a la dirección cinematográfica en el cine mudo: El caso de Helena Cortesina en España (1904–1936)', MA dissertation, Madrid: Universidad Rey Juan Carlos.

Cunill Canals, Josep (1999), *Elena Jordi: una reina berguedana a la cort del Paral.lel: el teatre de vodevil a Barcelona (1908–1920)*, Berga: Ambit de Recerques del Berguedà.

Dall'Asta, Monica (2010), 'What it means to be a woman: Theorizing feminist film history beyond the essentialism/constructionism divide', in S. Bull and A. Widing Söderbergh (eds), *Not So Silent: Women in Cinema before Sound*, Stockholm: Acta Universitatis Stockholmiensis, pp. 39–47.

Gaines, Jane M. (2002), 'Of cabbages and authors', in J. M. Bean and D. Negra (eds), *A Feminist Reader in Early Cinema*, Durham, NC: Duke University Press, pp. 88–118.

——— (2004), 'Film history and the two presents of feminist film theory', *Cinema Journal*, 44:1, pp. 113–19.

——— (2010), 'Women and the cinematification of the world', in S. Bull and A. Widing Söderbergh (eds), *Not So Silent: Women in Cinema before Sound*, Stockholm: Acta Universitatis Stockholmiensis, pp. 20–38.

——— (2013), 'What happened to the philosophy of film history?', *Film History*, 25:1/2, pp. 70–80.

García López, Sonia (2019), 'Miradas invisibles: mujeres en la Escuela Oficial de Cinematografía (1947–1976)', in C. Jareño Gila and A. Sanz-Gavillon (eds), *Espacios de creación feminista: Soportes y discursos alternativos en España (1960–1990)*, Zaragoza: Prensas Universitarias de Zaragoza.

Gran Enciclopèdia Catalana (2018a), 'Gastó A. Màntua', https://www.enciclopedia.cat/EC-GEC-0039879.xml. Accessed 7 July 2018.

——— (2018b), 'Cecília A. Màntua', http://enciclopedia.cat/EC-GEC-0039878.xml. Accessed 7 July 2018.

Herrera, Javier (2005), 'Emilia Pardo Bazán y el cine', *Archivos de la Filmoteca: Carmen en Hollywood*, 51, pp. 141–47.

Julio, Teresa (2017), 'María Luz Morales, traductora: estado de la cuestión y perspectivas de investigación', *Confluenze*, I:2, pp. 55–68.

McMahan, Alison (2013), 'Alice Guy Blaché', Women Film Pioneers Project, https://wfpp.cdrs.columbia.edu/pioneer/ccp-alice-guy-blache/. Accessed 27 September 2018.

Minguet Batllori, Joan M. (2008), *Paisaje(s) del cine mudo en España*, Valencia: ediciones de la Filmoteca.

Moya García, Concepción and Fernández-Pacheco Sánchez-Gil, Carlos (2009), 'Carmen Belacoracho: Una mujer periodista, productora de cine y líder feminista en el primer tercio del siglo XX', in L. Branciforte, C. González Marín, M. Huguet and R. Orsi (eds), *Actas del primer congreso internacional 'Las mujeres en la esfera pública: Filosofía e historia contemporánea'*, Madrid: CERSA, pp. 335–54.

Munsó Cabús, Joan and Romaguera i Ramió, Joaquim (2005), 'Cecília A. Màntua', *Diccionari enciclopèdic del cinema a Catalunya*, https://www.enciclopedia.cat/EC-CINEMA-650.xml. Accessed 7 August 2019.

O'Neill, Carlota (1923a), 'Finalidad cultural del cine I', *Arte y Cinematografía*, 263, 1 p. 11.

——— (1923b), 'Finalidad cultural del cine II', *Arte y Cinematografía*, 264, pp. 15–16.

——— (1923c), 'Finalidad cultural del cine III', *Arte y Cinematografía*, 265, pp. 10–11.

——— (1923d), 'Observaciones desde la butaca', *Arte y Cinematografía*, 266, pp. 26–27.

——— (1923e), 'Observaciones del cine y de la vida', *Arte y Cinematografía*, 267, pp. 15–16.

——— (2006), *Una mujer en la guerra de España*, Madrid: Oberon.

Osés, Encarnación ([1912] 2014), 'Una interviú con Max Linder', Sempre in penombra, 13 September, https://sempreinpenombra.com/2014/09/13/una-interviu-con-max-linder/. Accessed 30 September 2018.

——— (1921), 'La risa de María Jacobini', *Tras la pantalla,* 2:41, pp. 2–4.

Palomo, María del Pilar (2010), 'Colombine y el cine mudo en España (La mejor film)', *Arbor: Carmen de Burgos, Colombine (1867–1932) en el periodismo y la literatura*, 186, pp. 21–30.

Petro, Patrice (1990), 'Feminism and film history', *Camera Obscura* 22, 8:1, pp. 8–27.

Rabinovitz, Lauren (2005), 'Past imperfect: Feminism and social histories of silent film', *Cinémas: Femmes et cinéma muet: Nouvelles problématiques, nouvelles methodologies*, 16:1, pp. 21–34.

——— (2006), 'The future of feminism and film history', *Camera Obscura* 61, 21:1, pp. 38–44.

Rivas Morente, Víctor (2013), 'La construcción cultural del cine: Anomalías, resistencias y desvíos en Madrid en torno a 1913', doctoral thesis, Madrid: Universidad Rey Juan Carlos.

——— (2017), 'Una primera aproximación a la figura de Carmen Prada, periodista cinematográfica y empresaria en el Madrid de los años veinte', *Secuencias: Revista de historia del cine*, 46, pp. 59–82.

Soto-Vázquez, Begoña (2001), 'Las mujeres y los niños primero: Segmentación familiar del primer público cinematográfico', in À. Quintana and J. Pons (ed.), *La construcción del público de los primeros espectáculos cinematográficos*, Girona: Museu del Cinema, pp. 147–53.

Tomadjoglou, Kim (2013), 'Elvira Notari', Women Film Pioneers Project, https://wfpp.cdrs.columbia.edu/pioneer/ccp-elvira-notari/. Accessed 27 September 2018.

Utrera Macías, Rafael (2017), 'Mujeres "cineastas" de la generación del 27 (II) Concha Méndez. Josefina de la Torre', https://criticalia.com/articulo/mujeres-cineastas-de-la-generacion-del-27-ii-concha-mendez-josefina-de-la-torre. Accessed 28 June 2017.

Ward Mahar, Karen (2008), *Women Filmmakers in Early Hollywood*, Baltimore: Johns Hopkins University Press.

Williams, Tami M. (2014), *Germaine Dulac: A Cinema of Sensations*, Champaign: University of Illinois Press.

X.X. [signed as] (1926), 'Madrid', *Arte y Cinematografía*, 299, p. 43.

NOTES

1. For further details on the life of Morales, see Julio (2017).
2. The Spanish verb used is *hilvanar*, which we have translated as weave. *Hilvanar* is exactly the right term, as in Spanish it is a hyponym of needlework, and therefore a task for women: to stitch something together loosely in a provisional way before it is put together more definitively, therefore giving an initial structure, but allowing for errors and their correction.
3. See Gaines (2004, 2013) Rabinovitz (2006) and Petro (1990).
4. The concept of authorship as formulated by cinephilia, and historical research related to that cinephilia, is not a concept favourable to the analysis of women's contributions to cinematographic work. See Gaines (2002: 111), Rabinovitz (2005: 27).
5. Dall'Asta (2010) gives the examples of Alice Guy, of whose work there are 40 titles preserved, just from her time as a director in the USA (McMahan 2013); Germaine Dulac, who directed more than 30 films and where all her earlier works have been lost (Williams 2014); and Elvira Notari, who directed 60 works of which only four survive and one is incomplete (Tomadjoglou 2013).
6. On Elena Jordi, *nom de plume* Montserrat Casals i Baqué (1882–1945 Barcelona), see Cunill Canals (1999). On Helena Cortesina, *nom de plume* Elena Cortés Altabás (1903 Valencia–1984 Buenos Aires), see Cordero Hoyo (2013). On Carmen Velacoracho de Lara (1890s Ciudad Real–1960 Madrid), see Moya García and Fernández-Pacheco (2009).
7. We have very few details about Carlota O'Neill's cinema career, but we have an autobiographical piece about the Civil War years titled *Una mujer en la guerra de España* (O'Neill 2006). On Alonso (Barcelona 1905–1974) her biographical details are easily recovered, as she was the daughter of a dramatist and actor and an actress of some renown in the theatrical world of Barcelona in the twenties and thirties. See entries for father and daughter in the *Gran Enciclopèdia Catalana* (2018a and 2018b).
8. In Prada's case it was probably motivated by the need to have a minimum income as we are assuming that she started to work and study when she was very young. Morales' case is slightly different. Therefore, she would have started her training when she was 20 years old. She herself says that she started working when she was 31 years old.

A woman censor during the Portuguese dictatorship (1968–74)

Ana Bela Morais

This chapter[1] aims to contribute to the study of the female film censor during Marcello Caetano's dictatorship tenure of 1968 to April 1974. The present investigation focuses on the noteworthy role played by the censor Mariana Rita Nova Goa, which is also significant for enabling a broad understanding of the Portuguese Censorship System of the time. As an unpublished study, it emerges from a wider post-doctoral investigation titled 'Cinema and censorship: love and violence in Portugal and Spain (1968–74)'.[2] How was the Film Censorship Commission set up during this period of Portuguese history? Were there fewer women censors than men? Was the part they played ever relevant to the Commission's outcomes? Who were these women? Were any of them able to distinguish themselves in their role as censors? These questions are developed from a focus on mentalities and the history of private life which governs the present chapter, and which seeks to help understanding of the cultural and psychological climate of the time.

The investigation draws largely on the information in the National Secretariat of Information and Tourism (SEIT)'s archives. Since all the materials produced by the Estado Novo's Entertainment Examination and Classification Commission are now also held at the Portuguese National Archives in Lisbon (ANTT, Arquivo Nacional da Torre do Tombo), this study also attempts to articulate the study of cases of film censorship by surveying the Censorship Commission's minutes for the period between late 1968 and April 1974.

The film censorship files reveal the censors' modus operandi, and include appraisals, appeals and reports, whereas the Censorship Commission's minutes summarize what went on during meetings called to deliberate on those films and plays which were perceived as being especially problematic. Banned films, or those which raised classification uncertainties and reservations, were scrutinized during these sessions.

The study of Estado Novo film censorship is still in its early stages, and the dictatorship's concluding period, under the leadership of Marcello Caetano, has received even less attention. This is mainly explained by the fact that most, if not all censorship documents had been kept at the Palácio Foz (the former headquarters of the National Propaganda Secretariat (SPN), the National Secretariat of Information (SNI) and SEIT) until 2006, the year in which they were transferred to the National Archives and made available to researchers. Based upon this premise, the current study sets out to present its results as new and original research.

It was in September 1968 that Marcello Caetano succeeded Salazar as President of the Ministerial Council. With such an important change at the very top, hope rose of political renovation that would lead to greater freedom and the extinguishing of state censorship. During those first few years, more or less between 1969 and 1971, optimism still abounded that change would start to materialize; but soon after, this turned into the realization that any profound reform would remain illusory. In fact, film censorship would stay in force throughout the period of Caetano's leadership: even if the first few years saw a small relaxation in censorship – between 1968 and 1971, during the so-called 'Marcellist Spring' – controls would soon intensify once more. With the unsteady progression of Marcello Caetano's tenure, all allusions to the regime or the colonial war would be banned, the decline of Marcellism ostensibly being accompanied by a strengthening of censorship control.

As Lauro António puts it, commenting on Portuguese cinema but also the foreign films arriving in Portugal at the time:

> on 9th December 1970, a note from the Union of Entertainment Guilds [União de Grémios de Espectáculos] signed by the engineer José Gilera was delivered to Marcello Caetano's office. It was a 'distressing' text, which accounted for a reversal in the progress of censorship criteria: from 157 films censored and to be distributed in the first few months of the 1970/71 season, 34 were banned (21.6%), and 76 (49.7%) were subjected to mutilations!
>
> (António 2001: 49)[3]

With reference to the Censorship Commission's composition and modus operandi, Leonor Areal's study is still the most instructive. After emphasizing the 'democratic' nature of censor meetings (based upon the corresponding minutes) – sessions that addressed films and plays of a more polemic nature, and during which opinions were voiced and a majority vote was passed – Areal proceeds to point out that, throughout the years, the number of members varied between 8 and 18 (excluding the president, vice-president and secretary), but the way in which the body operated remained largely the same. The censors would be grouped into pairs, with each receiving a weekly list of films and plays to review; these would be classified by age and rate of approval (passed without cuts, approved with cuts, rejected) in the course of the following session, with the final decision then ratified by an official report, signed by those present at the meeting. Areal also mentions that, from 1961 onwards, members were grouped into threes, and that in 1971 they started to be distributed into two separate subcommissions, one for theatre and the other for cinema, with an extra third subcommission set up as an Appeals Commission. The need to group censors into pairs was felt early on to mitigate prejudice and suppress hesitation. However, every time a group of censors could not reach a decision, or when this implied outright rejection, the process would be passed to a second group and, if doubts still persisted, to a third, until, if necessary, it reached the Commission's president, who would pass final judgement (Areal in Cabrera and Costa 2014: 35).

The passing of Decree-Law 263/71, on 18 June 1971, is also worthy of mention in relation to the Censorship Commission. This legal framework introduced a new rating regime with the purpose of rearranging existing age groups. From that moment onwards, an A rating determined that any show was suitable for ages 6 and older, a B rating that it was for ages 10 and older, a C rating that it was for ages 14 and older, and a D rating that it was suitable for adults from the age of 18. Decree-Law 263/71 also affected the structure of the Entertainment Examination and Classification Commission, decreeing the redistribution of its members between two subdivisions: one dedicated to cinema, the other to theatre. Finally, this law also confirmed the creation of a new Appeals Commission, to be run independently from the Entertainment Examination and Classification Commission and yet to be made up of its corporate members (Cabrera 2008: 38).

Our study of the Censorship Commission's minutes (from the meetings addressing films or plays which raised additional approval or censoring reservations) has revealed a few unexpected tendencies concerning the ratio of men to women censors.[4] In the Commission's regular sessions, the number of women is always greatly inferior to that of male members; however, in the Appeals Commission's meetings (we have only been able to access records pertaining to 1974) female participation is totally absent.

The minutes record the dates and list the names of attendees:

> On the nineteenth of January of the year nineteen seventy-one, no later than eighteen hours and thirty minutes and in the National Secretariat of Information and Tourism, assembled the Entertainment Examination and Classification Commission. The session was presided over by His Excellency Dr António Caetano de Carvalho, the most honourable Director-General of the Popular Culture and Entertainment General Office and President of the

> Commission, attending, in addition to His Excellency Dr Alfredo António Barbieri Cardoso, the Commission's Vice-President, and His Excellency Dr José Maria Alves, Director of the Entertainment Services, the members, Her Excellency Madam Mafalda de Castro Vaz Pinto, Her Excellency Madam Maria Eugénia Sá da Bandeira and the Gentlemen Dr Alberto Machado, Dr Albino Pinto Fernandes, Dr António Monteiro Fernandes, Dr António Neves Martinha, Dr António Pedroso de Almeida, Dr Fernando de Azevedo Moreira, Dr João de Deus Figueira, Dr José António Guerreiro de Souza Barriga, Dr José Cabral, Dr José Maria Gonçalves Pereira, Reverend Priest José Teodoro Marques da Silva and Dr Manuel Alambre dos Santos.
>
> (ANTT 1968–74)

Typically, an average of two to three women attended these sessions: in addition to the aforementioned Mafalda de Castro Vaz Pinto and Maria Eugénia Sá da Bandeira, the names of Dr Júlia Maury and Mariana Rita Nova Goa also appear. These women were practising Catholics, housekeepers and mothers; few held a degree, but they came from so-called 'respectable families', often closely linked behind the scenes to those in power. Depending on the type of film raising reservations, specialized censors who could deal with such matters were recruited: for instance, when a film alluded to the army and to military issues, the opinion of an army officer would be requested (typically that of Colonel Almeida Nave); and for any matter relating to religion, the counsel of church ministers would be called upon.[5]

The minutes corresponding to the meeting of 19 March 1974 state that His Excellency Dr António Caetano de Carvalho was, on that date, appointed to the high office of State Subsecretary for Information and Tourism, also stepping down in the course of this session from his role as Commission president. However, the most interesting minutes are those relating to the meeting on 19 October 1971, which detail the renovation of the Commission's directorate following the adoption of Decree-Law no. 263/71, and the Commission's division into subcommissions for theatre and cinema. As far as women censors are concerned, the news is that Madam Maria Eugénia Sá da Bandeira had left the Commission, having been replaced by Madam Mariana Nova Goa.

For the purposes of our investigation, it is Mariana Rita Nova Goa who will prove to be the most interesting female case study. The first minutes mentioning her as a censor are those of 26 October 1971. The fact that Mariana Rita Nova Goa is never formally addressed as 'Doctor' leads us to believe that she never completed a university degree. Nevertheless, from what is recorded in the minutes that include her name, she appears to be one of the most demanding censors when passing a verdict. This was the case, for example, in the evaluation of the film *Desculpe, você conhece...* (Caprioli, 1968), which, despite having already received approval by majority vote, was resubmitted on Nova Goa's request, 'given the strong reservations [the film] has incited in her' (Minutes of 14 December 1971). The following year, in Minutes 8/73 (Acta no. 32/73) of 17 October 1972, the president, speaking on behalf of the entire Commission, expressed his deepest sorrow at the death of one of Mariana Rita Nova Goa's sons, and praised her resolve to still attend said session, despite her painful loss.

Minutes 11/73 (Acta no. 11/73) of 27 March 1973 contain her comments on the film *Family Life* (Loach, 1971):

> Her Excellency Madam Mariana Nova Goa has highlighted that, as the mother of twelve children, she is positively sure that this film should be approved, on account of the fine lesson it may teach a few couples. She does not foresee that it will pose any great risk to even the least prepared youngsters, the majority of whom fall victim to that same problem at home and suffer the effects of a deficit of parental common sense, parents who do not know how to love their children and who lack indispensable flexibility. In her own mind, she, who was brought up a certain way and has educated her daughters in another, considers this film to be highly educational and, on that account, approves it.

Our interest in this censor lies above all in the examples she provides of a key feature of the Censorship Commission: the arbitrariness of its criteria. In other words, what was censored, taking into account the censorship reports and the Commission's minutes, suggests a lack of uniform and concrete criteria governing what should and should not be censored – all evidence points to different group morals colouring each Censorship Commission, and to the influence of the personal principles of each individual censor.

From the beginning of the dictatorship to its end, including the years of Marcello Caetano's tenure, film censorship proceedings frequently displayed quite dissimilar criteria. Some of these may be logical, given the cyclical changes at the heart of the Commission (changes in officers, but also of the president) – transitions that were constantly debated in the meetings – and also the transformations brought about by the passage of time, by fluctuating relationships with exhibitors and distributors, and by the evolution of the film industry itself.

Addressing the problem of subjectivity, Marcello Caetano himself remarks:

> This censorship problem is, however, one of the most difficult to resolve satisfactorily. Could the law define what matters are prohibited, which are permitted and what can be released subject to ratification by prior examination: the law is practised by men and they each have their own criteria of interpretation. Some

> will judge one way, others another. Issuing more and more directives has never supressed the existence of a certain free will among censors.
>
> (Caetano 1974: 73)

The statesman then confirms that it has never been his intention to correct this 'free will':

> The law has established the right to appeal and has nominated the institution competent to deal with any appeals submitted. A few people have occasionally approached me protesting against this or that cut: usually, the cabinet would send these protests to the authorities whose legal duty it is to superintend the observance of given instructions. For my part, I have explained to several complainants that I couldn't and shouldn't play the part of chief-censor, meddling with a service which has its own departments, its own staff and its own norms, and which should be held responsible for its own activities.
>
> (Caetano 1974: 73)

In fact, the most obvious examples of the kind of subjectivity characteristic of censor activity are the comments by Mariana Rita Nova Goa in the censorship reports. For example, in the report about the film *El hombre de Río Malo* (1971) directed by Gene Martin, the censor concludes:

> My assessment of this film is that it should be banned. The film is rotten, it lacks interest, it's not well made, it's bereft of any moral sparkle, it's destructive and, above all, it's repulsively violent. To kill and steal is its only idea. I think that one day, we, the censors, who have the obligation to watch over the moral well-being of the public, with that task in mind we were put in [*sic*] here, will have to adopt a more energetic attitude: to say *no* to violence, and maybe that day is today. The majority of the public is tired of pornography, of eroticism, of violence. So many of our youngsters have told me: violence is as bad as pornography. They are right. Why shouldn't we, the censorship officers, in the year 1972, live up to our forward-thinking public, a public tired of paying to relax in the cinema and leaving it feeling even worse? Why don't we remedy this? There are boys, my acquaintances, who leave in the middle of a film as a sign of respect for the girls they're out on a date with.
>
> (ANTT 1971–74: Censorship Process 26245 SNIDGE, 4 August 1972, original emphasis)

The patriarchal family, with its well-defined social and gender roles, was one of the pillars of the corporate world that was the Portuguese Estado Novo. The need to appeal to the moral standards of the audience, which is expressed in this and other comments made by the censor, aimed to maintain this moral control over all cultural production, namely film content. The comment goes on:

> Despite film, theatre, radio and television employing all their efforts to try to poison our young, diminishing love, removing all that in it is spiritual to retain only the animal part, it is amazing [that] there are still some youths who are sane, splendid. Why don't we gather all our strength to educate that other public, of the 2nd balcony,[6] to stop being obsessed with sex and with enjoying all the bloodshed? I have been noticing that the producers of films, having squeezed pornography and eroticism to the last drop, now start to attempt destruction through violence. And here is my opinion, which I admit is not true [in the sense that other censors have different opinions and that she is not the owner of the truth], about this film and all violent cinema.
> (ANTT 1971–74: Censorship Process 26245 SNIDGE, 4 August 1972)

The same degree of subjectivity is evident in the process concerning the film *Au hasard Balthasar* (1966) directed by Robert Bresson. The film generated controversy among the censors; on 16 January 1972, Nova Goa's group reports:

> Undoubtedly, this is a film to veto. Could it have been cut even before it reached us? The girl, surrounded by a gang of out-and-out delinquents, conveys the horrifying impression that she is not normal and that there are abject aberrations. Obviously, maybe because it has suffered cuts – which is beyond doubt – we cannot attest to these aberrations, but they can be felt. Anyhow, this is a horrible film bearing a cynical philosophy. It's sordid, as sordid as it is depressing and dissolute.
> (ANTT 1971–74: Censorship Process 26105 SNIDGE, 3 March 1972)

Another process displaying Nova Goa's opinion also reveals the general views of the Censorship Commission about the average Portuguese spectator. This concerns the film *Pope Joan* (1972) directed by Michael Anderson, a film which generated some controversy. The first group of censors, in the report from 3 January 1973, thought it appropriate that the film be reviewed by the 'Reverend Priests who are part of this Commission'. In the same report, on 18 January 1973, Nova Goa writes:

> My conscience does not allow me to approve this film. At a time when the greatest confusion reigns over spirits, vis-à-vis the crisis that penetrates the Church, letting this film show in a country like ours, with a spectatorship of

> such a low intellectual level, would generate even more confusion. Of course we understand it, but it would be misconstrued by the majority of the public, the blending of the hippies' cross, of their 'God is love' expression (?) – all that casts into even greater confusion those spirits which are little enlightened. *It is not suitable to be shown* here in Portugal. *It is dangerous and we cannot afford the risk.*
>
> (ANTT 1971–74: Censorship Process 26500 SNIDGE, 2 March 1973, original emphasis)

Nevertheless, the film was approved on 1 February 1973.

On 2 February 1973 the film's release was confirmed with a Group D rating, along with its accompanying trailer, also rated D (ANTT 1971–74: Censorship Process 26500 SNIDGE, 2 March 1973).

In the 10 April 1973 process regarding the Chinese film *Tian xia di yi quan* (Five Fingers of Death) (1972) directed by Changhwa Jeong, Nova Goa again delivers a highly subjective view:

> I approve the film for a D rating. It is *extremely* violent, but since it depicts professional Chinese fighting schools, the *cruel* Asiatic details are not surprising. I don't think it should be vetoed, I repeat, *because it's Asian.* For that reason alone. I always denounce great numbers of violent films which are set in the West and are therefore a lot more dangerous and [...] avoidable.
>
> (ANTT 1971–74: Censorship Process 26780 SNIDGE, 23 April 1973, original emphasis)

On 13 April 1973 both the film and its trailer were allowed general release with a D rating and without cuts. However, on 23 April 1973, after review, the Entertainment Examination and Classification Commission deliberated its reclassification to 'Group C, with the following cuts: (a) removing the images of the blinding of a student, between subtitles 435, 436 (8th part); (b) substantial cuts to all fighting scenes (3) between subtitles 495 and the end of the film' (ANTT 1971–74: Censorship Process 26780 SNI-DGE, 23 April 1973).

And yet even films approved with an A rating and without cuts still merit the opinion of Nova Goa. This is what happens with *Tokyo Grand Pageant*, from Japan, which the censor reports on without mentioning the director. This is her comment dated 6 February 1973: 'Deploring the evidence of a lack of personality by the Japanese who [...] to make more money become Americanized, and poorly, because the ballerinas' body shapes are unfit for the genre. Group A' (ANTT 1971–74: Censorship Process 26956 SNI-DGE, 7 February 1973).

Again, the censor's comment about the film *Amsterdam Affair* (1968) directed by Gerry O'Hara, provides instructive evidence. Her statement is dated 26 June 1973 and appears in the 4 July 1973 report approving the film with a D rating:

> I veto the film. It is well made, but being well made is in my opinion no reason to approve it. We are witnessing the moral breakdown of society. I hold no such illusion to think that I can improve it myself, but I have the obligation (this is why I was elected to sit here as a member) to prevent that this society *sees itself in the mirror* (it's the film) and continues to happily deprave itself, or rather 'naturally', which is even worse. I want to be constructive, this is why I offer my opinion. I want to be at peace with my own conscience which is to carry out what 'someone' asked me to do when I came here. I do not censor my colleagues who approve it. I always respect their opinions. Some will say that a lot has been seen which is far worse than this, it is true, I'm sorry, but I will continue trying [...] to improve the world, using my limited strength. Only my generous good will is strong.
>
> (ANTT 1971–74: Censorship Process 22 73 SNI—DGE, 4 July 1973, original emphasis)

This comment reveals that each censor felt that she/he had as her/his mission to watch over the moral standards and other socially accepted values of Portuguese spectators. In this sense, the message of José Carvalheiro and Maria Silveirinha (2015: 748) becomes clear, when they say that censorship should be understood as 'a wider phenomenon than the simple interdiction of ideas, political expression, or artistic items', also including 'an entire system of socially repeated disapprovals and reprimands that exercised social power [...] with the aim of regimenting consciences and attitudes'.

And even when a film is banned, Nova Goa's comments still afford interesting reading. Such is the case with *Homo eroticus* (1971) directed by Marco Vicario. The film was banned on 9 March 1973 and again on 25 April of the same year after an appeal was rejected. Still, Mariana Rita Nova Goa offers the following comment, dated 27 February 1973, in the corresponding censorship report:

> *I reject this film.* Were it allowed to pass, I understand perfectly why so many people would (thankfully) ask the question: what is censorship good for? In fact, approving this film (which no amount of cutting would allow) censorship, at least as far as I'm concerned, should [...] look for another line of business [...] This way, Portugal, which up until now has been known as one of the few countries where public morality is still respected, will no longer merit such a distinction. Soon it will start to go downhill, marching towards the end of

> civilization. I say what the sensibility of my conscience allows me to. I would feel the greatest sadness were I to offend my two colleagues and friends, whom I so greatly admire.
>
> (ANTT 1971–74: Censorship Process 31674 SNI-DGE, 25 April 1973, original emphasis)

On 13 January 1974, on the verge of the revolution, in the process about the film *40 Carats* (1973) directed by Milton Katselas, Nova Goa writes:

> Well, I will add something [to the previous verdict]. This film is, in my opinion, completely amoral. Also in it there isn't a single person of character who is serious, or with a hint of shame. If I approve it, this is solely because, sadly, I am certain that if it is seen by another group it will be immediately passed and [...] without cuts (by the way there is no malicious criticism in this, each to their own, some are more liberal and I ... well, you know) I find it hard to approve. For those lacking in moral education it is a way to get excited and lead a life like these people do: disrespecting morality, ignoring the responsibility that marriage merits etc. The incredible, stupid way the protagonist's mother and daughter act disgusts me, and I won't even mention the fool that is the husband. Accepting an affair between a 40-year-old woman and a 20-year-old boy is horrible, shameful. Lots of evil thoughts can be learned from this double-edged sword that is cinema!
>
> (ANTT 1971–74: Censorship Process 1286 SNI—DGE, 17 January 1974)

On 9 January 1974 the film was classified 'in Group D, with the cutting of the last scenes and respective subtitles, from 1651 or 1655 inclusive, such that the protagonist [...] misses her flight and fails to arrive in Greece. *Trailer* approved for Group D'. However, on 17 January 1974 'the Appeals Commission deliberated that the appeal should stand, withdrawing the respective cut' (ANTT 1971–74: Censorship Process 1286 SNI-DGE, 17 January 1974).

Do we not still hear, from time to time, similar comments about national or foreign public figures, or even the life of our next-door neighbour? This kind of topicality emanating from all the comments made by Mariana Rita Nova Goa seems to corroborate the idea that mentalities are long-term structures and, therefore, the most difficult to change.

In Brazil, starting with the Military Dictatorship, censors were handed censorship guidebooks (1967/68). This, along with specific training in film studies, helped to transform the censorship system. In the Escola Superior de Guerra, those officers with additional academic training would nominate authors and writers to carry out censorship duties. Even so, despite being purportedly better informed, these officers were still highly prejudiced, often expressing a very limited vision. Portugal saw no such initiatives, as can be substantiated by Mariana Rita Nova Goa's appraisal of Robert Bresson's *Au hasard Balthasar* quoted above. In this comment, the censor ignores the fact that ellipsis is both a feature intrinsic to the film and an aesthetic choice in the style of the *Nouvelle Vague*.

In Portugal, during Marcello Caetano's time in office, censors occasionally alluded to and reflected upon their responsibilities vis-à-vis the wider framework of the apparatus of the Estado Novo. The minutes from the Censorship Commission's meetings for the period under Caetano are, in this context, quite revealing. For instance, the minutes corresponding to 16 March 1971 discuss the criteria and their application, but always without questioning the role of the censor:

> His Excellency the President has manifested his concern with the fact that, lately, the Commission has found itself a little disunited, in relation to some of the problems or themes which should be considered a priority in the table of values that it should be defending. Hence, His Excellency has emphasized his desire to appeal for opposition to such a situation. It is obvious that the decisions taken by each individual are always burdened by factors such as age, education, way of life, spiritual temperament, predilections, etc. There is, accordingly, a large slice of subjectivism in every decision taken by the Commission. Still, on the other hand, the Commission's criterion is quite frequently alluded to, a criterion which is abstract and, therefore, inexistent. Thus, what the Commission needs is to apply casuistically certain decisions, which should, nonetheless, be supported by some sort of criterion. And despite the abstractness of this expression, it is really important that an effort is made to define a criterion which is the Commission's, and which in theory should be that of the Government, since the Commission functions as its delegate for a certain remit of responsibility. Therefore, each individual will have to abstract himself as much as possible from his personal criterion and apply as much as possible the Commission's aforementioned criterion [...] By itself, this implies that the censor needs to always evaluate the repercussions of the film or play on the average spectator and, what's more, to think about our people's way of being and to defend those who personify such values, such as the ranks of the army, the priests, the magistrates – all these need to be a priority for the Commission.[7]
>
> (ANTT 1968–71)

Evidence has been assembled in the course of this enquiry to suggest that the role of women in film censorship surpassed that of mere professional censors. When examining the film *A Promessa* (1972), directed by António de Macedo, a quotation by the director emerged which helps to elucidate this suggestion. This had been one of de Macedo's films which had generated the most problems for the Censorship Commission. The director explains these difficulties in detail in his book *Como se fazia cinema em Portugal: Inconfidências de um ex-praticante* (2007).

António de Macedo acknowledges that he made this film in 1972 'as if there was no censorship in Portugal [...] (Censorship existed and it was heavy-handed, it imposed severe cuts to *A Promessa* which I refused to accept, and the battle with this sinister institution was draining and lasted four months until the premiere)' (Macedo cited in Matos-Cruz 2000: 32). When it seemed unlikely that the film could be exhibited without cuts, one last attempt was made, as the director explains: Fernando Lopes, at the time President of the Portuguese Film Centre, requested an audience with the Information and Tourism State Secretary, Moreira Baptista. To try to swing the conversation in their favour, Lopes pledged that no letter of complaint would be written on the condition that the film was premiered without cuts. This is how António de Macedo concludes his account: 'Well, to get rid of us, and because he had run out of arguments, Dr Moreira Baptista agreed' (Macedo 2007: 31–35).

But what were these 'complaint letters' referred to by Moreira Baptista? They were written:

> at the time, by the daughter of the President of the Republic, Américo Thomaz, and by other *bon ton* ladies who had the nefarious habit of going to the cinema with exceedingly sharp owl eyes looking for what could be found to be 'pornographic' and 'immoral', in order to immediately write to the government inconvenient letters, which quite often led to the banning of such films, as is, for instance, the case with *Bitter Rice* [*Riso amaro*, De Santis, 1949] or *The Swimming Pool* [*La piscine*, Deray, 1969], which were removed just a few days after being released.
>
> (Macedo 2007: 34)

The director concludes with a reference to the premiering of his film without cuts and, quite fortunately, without a single lady remembering to write a letter of complaint to the government.

We can therefore conclude that women, inside or outside the Censorship Commission, did play a relevant role in shaping film censorship in Portugal throughout Marcello Caetano's administration (1968–74). The censor Mariana Rita Nova Goa emerges as the most interesting example in this context, not only because she was in her profession one of the most demanding censors, but also because she embodies the subjectivity inherent to censorship methods and practices. Her opinions expose the structuring of mentalities and all the resistance to possible change, which, during Caetano's tenure,was becoming uncontrollable.

Across Europe and even globally, these were decisive years in the sense that a vast and overwhelming wave of cultural dissemination, along with the emergence of the civil rights movement in the United States, and pacifist, counter-cultural, anti-racist and feminist fronts everywhere started to evince change. All these changes continue to have an effect today; but resistance, as encapsulated by censor Mariana Nova Goa's comments, still echoes in this day and age, seeming to point to a perspicacity in censorship that appears to intuit the thoughts of Siegfried Kracauer:

> The films of a nation reflect its mentality in a more direct way than other artistic media for two reasons: First, films are never the product of an individual [...] Second, films address themselves, and appeal, to the anonymous multitude. Popular films or, to be more precise, popular screen motifs, can therefore be supposed to satisfy existing mass desires [...] What films reflect are not so much explicit credos as psychological dispositions, those deep layers of collective mentality which extend more or less below the dimension of consciousness.
> (Kracauer 1947: 5–6)

Through the opinions expressed by Mariana Nova Goa and transcribed above, we can affirm that the censor knew all too well, and therefore feared, this inherent power of national and foreign films to translate and modify mentalities.

REFERENCES

António, Lauro (2001), *Cinema e censura em Portugal*, 2nd ed., Lisbon: Biblioteca Museu República e Resistência.

Arquivo Nacional da Torre do Tombo (ANTT) (1968–74), Fundo do SNI Processos da Direcção Geral dos Serviços dos Espectáculos. Processos de Censura (Torre do Tombo National Archives: SNI National Secretariat of Information and Tourism Deposit General Entertainment Service Administration. Censorship Processes).

——— (1971–74), Livros das Actas da Comissão de Censura (SNI) – Actas das sessões 1971/DGSE Livro 29, Torre do Tombo National Archives: Censorship Commission Minutes Books. SNI – Minutes from the 1971 sessions/DGSE Book 29.

Cabrera, Ana (2008), 'A censura ao teatro no período marcelista', *Media & Jornalismo*, 12:7, pp. 27–58.

——— (ed.) (2013), *Censura nunca mais! A censura ao teatro e ao cinema no Estado Novo*, Lisbon: Alêtheia.

Cabrera, Ana and Costa, Cristina Castilho (eds) (2014), *Atas do Congresso Internacional Censura ao Cinema e ao Teatro*, 2013, Lisbon: CIMJ – Centro de Investigação Media e Jornalismo.

Caetano, Marcello (1974), *Depoimento*, Rio de Janeiro and São Paulo: Distribuidora Record.

Carvalheiro, José and Silveirinha, Maria (2015), 'Acting on the body of the audience: Dictatorship, hegemony, and gender censorship in Portugal', *Feminist Media Studies*, 15:5, pp. 747–62.

Kracauer, Siegfried (1947), *From Caligari to Hitler*, Princeton: Princeton University Press.

Macedo, António de (2007), *Como se fazia cinema em Portugal: inconfidências de um ex-praticante*, Lisbon: Apenas Livros Lda.

Matos-Cruz, José de (2000), *António de Macedo: Cinema, a viragem de uma época*, Lisbon: Publicações Dom Quixote.

Morais, Ana Bela (2017), *Censura ao Erotismo e Violência: Cinema no Portugal Marcelista (1968–1974)*, Vila Nova de Famalicão: Edições Húmus.

NOTES

1. All translations from the Portuguese are mine.
2. Which has resulted in the publication of Morais (2017).
3. For further information about film censorship during Marcello Caetano's leadership, see Morais (2017).
4. The Censorship Commission's books of minutes corresponding to Marcello Caetano's first years in office – between late 1968 and 1971 – have not yet been deposited at the Torre do Tombo according to Paulo Tremoceiro, the Portuguese National Archives film censorship archivist. As Tremoceiro has stated, it is uncertain where these minutes may be, a situation similar to that of other Estado Novo documents, which could be explained by post-revolution turmoil and the methods for dealing with this type of documentation during the revolutionary period. Thus, fifteen standard session books of minutes remain, along with sixteen Appeals Commission minutes records (numbers 109 to 124), with no. 123 of the Appeals Commission minutes missing.
5. Cabrera (2013: 15–77) is a valuable contribution towards a wider understanding of the evolution of film and theatre censorship in Portugal, providing an account of decree-laws and of the main figures in and around the censorship system.
6. The expression '2nd balcony' refers to the public who could not afford better seats to watch the film. This economic situation implied, according to the censor's point of view, that in addition to lack of money, these people also lacked culture and moral standards.
7. For further information and examples pertaining to the difficulties in establishing criteria that could guide what should and should not be censored, see Morais 2017: 42ff.

Costume designers in Portugal: A trade between art and technique, relegated to the status of 'a woman's thing'

Caterina Cucinotta

Introduction

This chapter answers a few questions related to the costume department in Portuguese cinema, an area predominantly occupied by women. The reason why, since the 1990s, costume design has become a department consisting solely of women, as well as the question of its current designation, are key issues concerning the professional and artistic recognition of those who were able to establish the trade in Portugal.

After considerable field[1] and bibliographical research,[2] we are able to state that the costume department in Portuguese film production is currently occupied almost entirely by women.[3] According to research initiated in 2009,[4] both in practical and theoretical terms, we are faced with a history which runs parallel to the great history of women film directors, which is yet to receive due attention.

The position of women in the film industry is an issue that has always mattered to women's studies. Throughout history, women have always been relegated to a secondary role, permanently subject to a failure to see their cultural specificity acknowledged. Whether we are talking about women behind the camera or their performance in front of it, the key issues concern, on the one hand, a shortage of prominent women film directors and, on the other, the representation of women as mere objects for the audience.

An imperative bibliographical reference responsible for opening the door to the history of women filmmakers in Portugal is *Cineastas portuguesas 1874–1956* by Ilda Castro (2000), which is a collection of interviews that include a conversation with a female sound designer. However, we could not help but notice that not a single female costume designer was included in this text. Analysing the issue of women in Portuguese cinema from the current approach of filmmaker theory,[5] we can state that:

> 'filmmaker' is a term which can be applied to any creative professional besides the director (examples include actors and actresses, editors, cinematographers, etc.).
> (Penafria et al. 2016: 10)[6]

If we consider women costume designers as filmmakers in the specific context of Portuguese cinema, we immediately notice that there is an untold history about a department where women have undoubtedly prevailed since the dawn of film.

It is a fact that in Portugal there is no specific literature about costume designers,[7] only occasional references from women directors to their participation in films in that capacity.[8] Nevertheless, the history of costume design is made up of professionals who, alongside directors, set designers and cinematographers, create the visual element of a film. They are more closely linked to the actor's body, working from the on-screen narrative to create a personification of the audience through the characters. Using interviews with costume designers who work or have worked in Portugal, we seek to shed light on a career which is mostly led by women and is still considered by costume designers themselves to be a 'woman's thing'.

In April 2017, together with Nivea Faria de Souza, a colleague from Rio de Janeiro State University, we interviewed several professionals from the costume department in Portuguese cinema. We were able to interview thirteen professionals, from costume designers to assistants, and these results will soon be collected and published. The purpose was to fill an informational, academic and artistic void regarding costume design in Portugal. According to our research, and also in order to appeal to academic interest, it became necessary to determine a few key points of reference as we began to tread a path already initiated by our fellow Italian and Brazilian researchers in the mid-twentieth century.[9]

In Italy, the first volume dedicated to film costumes dates from the mid-1930s and was published by the historian and film critic Mario Verdone (1986).[10] There are numerous academic publications which study costumes and film costume designers while broadening the perspectives on Italian and Hollywood cinema in particular.[11] In Brazil, there are fairly regular publications of texts, essays and volumes dedicated to film costume design within both academic and professional contexts.[12] There are also multiple courses, retrospectives, textbooks and articles which place costumes and film costume designers in an artistic position, closer to that of the director and the cinematographer, for example.

Considering the groundbreaking influence of the anglophone world on these studies, we notice that it has always paid particular attention to this occupation: for example, several of the female Portuguese designers we interviewed had travelled to London in the mid-1990s to attend a costume design for performance course at Central Saint Martins,[13] while some of the most significant academic contributions for the understanding and inclusion of costume design in film analysis originated there as well.[14] Indeed, outside Portugal there is considerable literature about this subject. In our study and analysis, we decided that the first step would be to take a closer look at Portuguese costume designers.

But how can we understand the reason why this and other female-dominated professions in cinema have been forgotten or not rightfully recognized?

Since the beginning of cinema, technical jobs have always been entrusted to women: from editing to colouring and costume manufacturing. While colouring was directly related to cinematography and editing to sewing techniques,[15] in costume departments many clothes were reused theatrical costumes. The women hired by the production companies were essentially required to have some experience in fashion or photography studios: in effect, they had to be skilled at detailed handiwork.

> When speaking of fashion and film, we should first observe that cinema, historically, has been literally 'manufactured': in the silent era and beyond, film was worked on largely by women editors, who labored on strips of film in production houses that resembled fashion houses, where they cut and stitched together materials, mimicking the very process of clothing construction.
>
> (Bruno 2014: 36)

Keeping this perspective in mind, the connection between early cinema and fashion seems simple and natural. To a certain extent, Bruno stresses the intrinsic relationship between fashion and cinema – their 'making' and their surface, or texture – emphasizing the profound importance of appearances in both fashion and cinema, both artistic expressions of visual culture:

> Moving beyond the level of film costume to explore further the interaction between fashion and cinema, it is significant to note the Latin root of fashion – factio – refers to the act of making. The intersection of film – 'making' with this other form of making informs the concept of the 'fashioning' of space, as well as the psychogeographic routes that are built and traversed in the construction of site-seeing.
>
> (Bruno 2002: 158)

These parallel activities existed both in fashion and in cinema, and were related to, on the one hand, women and their role in society and, on the other hand, the more technical aspects of these artistic occupations. These activities are documented by panoramic photographs of the studios in fashion houses where women can be seen working behind sewing machines. These images match the first visual documents of women working in the editing and colouring departments of the film industry.[16]

It is the concept of making (*factio* in Latin) that gives its name to fashion and transforms itself until the fashionizing of space on film an essential premise for knowing more about women costume designers, their lives, their trade and their role in contemporary society. The development of a fresh perception of costume design in Portuguese cinema also provides excellent assistance.

In Portugal, the connection between the costume department itself and fashion is based on the idea of a department made up entirely of women. In fact, through our interviews we can easily perceive how an issue seemingly connected to fashion ends up creating a prison from which even today it is difficult to escape. We discovered that we were dealing with a severe problem when we realized that men head the rest of the departments. Most directors are men, as are most cinematographers[17] and art directors.[18] The situation is the same in more syndicated technical departments, such as grip and electrical.

This recent data presents some immediately obvious irregularities which need to be addressed. In Portugal, the ethos of costume design hints at the notion that anyone can create the 'wardrobe' of a film, the sole requirement being that they ensure the utmost optimization between available resources and final outcome. Therefore, the costume designers we interviewed regularly noticed a disparity between incoming budgets and requested results, constantly labelling their own creative effort as a 'miracle'. Considering the field work[19] we conducted, we cannot help but disclose how dissimilar the materialization of ideas is between different film departments: to a costume designer, the materialization of a director's clothing ideas is definitely an issue related to the materiality of the items selected. In its intersection with costume selection, the fashion universe often determines styles and textures that may not fit into the estimated budget.[20] Our interviews revealed an artistic path which is more connected to domestic economy than, for example, what happens in sound, camera and lighting departments, where the final outcome relies heavily on the creative use of the technical means available.

Georg Simmel (1998) and Giuliana Bruno (2002) agree that fashion has always been an area more associated with the world of women. For Simmel,[21] interest in fashion relates to profound reasons connected to personal and professional fulfilment:

> Historical facts also bring us closer to the concept of fashion as a valve through which women's need for a certain amount of distinction and personal significance finds an escape, as they witness their satisfaction largely denied in other areas.
>
> (Simmel 1998: 40–41)

Simmel does not develop this idea, instead construing fashion as a kind of compensation for the absence of other factors.

Roland Barthes (2009) went one step further than Simmel, stating that fashion has always been a cultural aspect through which women can differentiate their socio-sexual functions. Therefore, it becomes necessary to develop a material history of styles and concepts which is more connected to art history. If we look at film costume design from the point of view of fashion – as a sum of styles and tendencies represented both on and off screen, a collection of ideas evoked between the set and the dressed character – we immediately realize how the analysis of clothes in film might seem isolated, as clothes are seen to merely emphasize psychophysical statuses or underlie the action described in the plot.

Drawing from this idea, Bruno regards fashion as an instrument that women use to know themselves, a valuable tool for introducing themselves to others in a personalized manner, as well as for beginning to explore their inner selves. Thus, Bruno's point of view intersects with the different claims by Roland Barthes and Georg Simmel, who perceived women's use of fashion as having a purely social role. We interpret this interest in fashion not as compensation but as added value: the reflection of a particular curiosity, rather than those isolated analyses suggesting a superficial combination between inner and outer self. In Bruno's words, '[f]ashion, like cinema, thrives on the power of moving form' (2002: 157).

With this in mind, we are able to identify in the fashion/women pairing a curiosity connected to the body and its forms, flowing into a constantly moving self-awareness. If fashion started by being a mirror of modern life, it is easy to recognize in it women's deep-rooted permanent search for movement, development and new visualities. It is no coincidence, Bruno stresses (2002: 157), that in 1904, in the early days of cinema, Simmel compared fashion to the frame of a painting, claiming that it lends character to the work of art and determines the space around it:

> Fashion is like the frame of a painting, characterising the work of art as a unit belonging to itself, an independent world. At the same time, being outwardly adorned, it severs every connection with the surrounding space.
>
> (Simmel 1998: 14)

It is a matter of acknowledging fashion as an essentially cinematographic element which can anticipate the future and that, as an element of modernity, much like cinema itself, thrives on the power of the moving form, 'frames and maps the appearances of the body, redefining sensitivity and energy boundaries' (Bruno 2002: 157).

In Portugal, it has become imperative to understand why costume design has never been researched; why today we still talk about 'rags', 'attire' or 'ensembles', leaving aside the only suitable word; and, finally, the motives that have hindered proper research or, at least, a brief historiography.

Historiography and terminology

In Portuguese, the most suitable term for this occupation is *figurino* (costume design). The first problem to arise concerns the designation of the occupation itself, which seems to have traversed several controversial stages in Portugal. In Portuguese academia, when researchers talk about clothes in a film, they usually refer to their object of study as *vestuário* (clothing), but this term seems to be completely absent from the vocabulary used in the technical environment where clothes and their craft are called *guarda-roupa* (wardrobe) or *figurinos* (costumes). Failing to recognize the difference between these terms is not uncommon, for both 'wardrobe' and 'costumes' are used indiscriminately both in film credits and when referring to the department.

During the interviews conducted, we were provided with extremely valuable points of view on this issue, which may, in fact, solve one of its earliest dilemmas: the question of nomenclature/terminology. Throughout the interviews, the numerous accounts of situations from the period of silent film to the era of Novo Cinema showed an almost complete absence of the costume designer on set. In these situations, professionals took on the role of the film's costume designer through a costume rental company, frequently without appearing on set.

At one point, when cinema in Portugal became an industry, there were a few male costume designers who are remembered to this day. One example is the renowned fashion and theatrical costume designer Alberto Anahory (Tavarede 1906–2000 Lisbon) who, during the 1930s and 1940s, created many costumes for films of that period. Erroneously, we could deduce that Alberto Anahory also worked on set, but our interviews revealed that he owned a costume rental company for film and theatre by the same name, and would eventually design costumes for films upon request from directors. The same thing happened with Paiva, who also owned a costume rental company and featured in the credits of the film *As pupilas do senhor reitor* (Leitão de Barros, 1935) as wardrobe – the costumes were designed by Helena Roque Gameiro (Lisbon 1895–1986).

However, the correct definition for this type of occupation should not be limited to 'costume designer', for their absence on set renders this terminology inaccurate. According to the research we conducted, the nomenclature 'fashion/costume designer' could be a better option, considering that the department itself did not exist in its own right. To this end, there is ongoing research about the role played by the watercolour painter Helena Roque Gameiro, wife of director Leitão de Barros. According to the credits, she worked as a costume designer in the films *As pupilas do senhor reitor* and *Bocage* (Leitão de Barros, 1936). Sandra Leandro states:

> That was also the year (1935) when the film *As pupilas do Senhor Reitor* by Leitão de Barros premiered and for which Helena designed the costumes manufactured by Paiva and the furniture built by Móveis Olaio. In the following year, she was also responsible for the wardrobe of the film *Bocage*. In any case, Helena always closely followed her husband's work.
>
> (Leandro et al. 2016: 19)

On the basis of this interpretation, we are able to establish the relationship between the activity of the costume designer and the name of the department (wardrobe) in Portugal more clearly. During filming, the person responsible for the costumes (dressing, undressing, continuity, storing, transportation, etc.) used to be someone from the technical crew who carried out additional tasks, often assistant directors or production assistants. In fact, the responsibility for storing the clothes on set did not belong to a specifically appointed department that would follow the process through from creation to filming, but to one or more individuals.

Once again, the use of empirical data proved essential for us to be able to proceed with our research in order to thoroughly understand the dissemination of the confusing concepts and terminology 'costumes' and 'wardrobe' in the credits of Portuguese films. Using Brazil as an example, where this department has been widely analysed and has been able to maintain a good balance between creativity and financial resources, we must emphasize obvious differences in terms of terminology in film credits, nomenclature used in academia, and even technical language. In Brazilian cinema, this department is called the 'costume design crew', directly attributing to the term 'costume designer' the creation of the whole team's nomenclature.

If both 'wardrobe' and 'costumes' have been used interchangeably in film credits, in light of the interviews conducted, which filled some of the void surrounding this issue, we were able to determine that the correct term is 'costumes' followed by the professional's name. Most of the costume designers interviewed agree with a more contemporary, conceptual path, accepting this to be the correct designation for this trade. However, there has been some resistance owing to a habit of appearing in film credits simply as 'wardrobe', particularly from professionals able to differentiate between those who create the costumes and those who create the wardrobe.

In one of the interviews, Isabel Branco (Lisbon 1953– present), an art director since the 1980s, states:

> Perhaps costumes are more related to the design, whereas wardrobe comprehends everything from costume rentals to manufacture. Nowadays I am considered a costume designer, despite the fact that I always appear in credits as 'Wardrobe: Isabel Branco'. I think the correct term would be costume designer, for there is no such thing as a wardrobe designer. Either costume designer or wardrobe. This is usually very confusing because Portuguese terminology has never been formally designated.
>
> (Isabel Branco cited in Cucinotta and Faria de Sousa 2017)

Teresa Campos (Lisbon 1947–present), a costume designer since the 1990s, also states that:

> The word wardrobe shows the little value given to costumes in a film. In the old days, people called it wardrobe in the same way they could call it a closet. Wardrobe means closet. And being a department made up of women and clothes, people started calling it wardrobe, because it was where the clothes were stored. When we started working in cinema, Maria Gonzaga, other colleagues and I should have fought for the word costumes. But because we did not value ourselves much, no one did, we kept using the word wardrobe. Now we fight for it, because we do not create wardrobes. I conceive figures. I design costumes from my figures. The term wardrobe was connected to our lack of experience and the way others saw us. 'Take these clothes!' This should end!
>
> (Teresa Campos cited in Cucinotta and Faria de Souza 2017)

Referring to costume designers as 'wardrobe' does indeed denote a depreciation of the work itself. In English, for example, the costume department and wardrobe are two separate departments, the technical aspects of the former being represented by the latter. In contrast to the United States, particularly Hollywood, the confusion leading to this depreciation in Portugal comes from an extremely limited concept of the wardrobe department: both departments, costume and wardrobe, can merge into one because of the lack of professionals dedicated to this craft taking part in filming.

Based on my personal work experience in contemporary Portuguese cinema, there is often a costume designer heading the department who reports to the director about any decisions. Some costume designers devise their own costumes; others use clippings from newspapers, books or magazines, and create the characters' outfits based on artistic or literary quotes.[22] After the costume designer, there is a wardrobe supervisor who, besides being the costume designer's main assistant, closely monitors the assembling and disassembling of the structures on which the costumes are stored, and is also in charge of the continuity book, therefore having to be on set every day. The person who assists the wardrobe supervisor is the costume standby, a key figure during filming who needs to understand the hierarchies of the different departments, always be on set and carefully monitor the video controller to detect any continuity or quality errors.

During this decisive process of adjustment in Portuguese film terminology, another question which is yet to be resolved arose within the artistic departments. In scenography[23] – a department closely linked to costume design but independent in terms of salary,[24] crew and stylistic choices – the person working as head of department is known as the *diretor de arte* (art director). Once again, Brazilian Portuguese helps our research: in Brazil, an art director is a professional who, bringing together costumes and sets, can manage two teams, two budgets and two visual concepts, being careful not to prioritize one over the other. In Portugal, this denomination can be misleading because the costume department is not named using the appropriate terminology: conceptually identifying a set designer as an art director would not raise any issues if, correspondingly, the costume designer were not reduced to the designation wardrobe.

The differences between European and Brazilian Portuguese demand a conceptual distinction while also raising complex issues yet to be settled. Valuing the craft itself also means finding a correct designation: starting out on a path of consolidation and awareness can only help the balance in employment and gender policies in Portugal.

To illustrate the non-acceptance of one department's depreciation over the other, costume designer Teresa Campos, answering the question 'How is the creative process with the art director?', states:

> What do you consider an 'art director'? The set designer? I do not understand the designation: a set designer is as much an art director as I am. Anyone who makes art is an art director!
>
> (Teresa Campos cited in Cucinotta and Faria de Souza 2017)

Based on the empirical data from the interviews, it became clear that in Portugal the use of the term *diretor de arte* (art director) to refer to the set designer started at the beginning of the twenty-first century, and that the term can be applied to the set designer as well as to the combination of both set and costume departments. Concerning the work of artists in Portuguese cinema, the mechanisms of artistic production within these two departments are unexplored areas: not only has there never been theoretical support for the creative process behind artistic objects, but there is also a lack of critical interest in the creators.

As a first and crucial step, we suggest that costume designers, along with set decorators, working in film should be considered material authors of a film – individuals who are able to materialize ideas that are established in a screenplay.

An oral history of costume designers in Portugal

In 2017 we began our journey of interviews based on the only existing document about costume designers in Portugal, which was published by the Portuguese Cinematheque in a retrospective about Jasmim de Matos (1942),[25] a man who worked in the costume department. According to some of the interviewees, whose help was invaluable in documenting Matos' artistic and professional background, Jasmim was taught to sew by his mother, who would often help to manufacture the costumes. During the interviews, the figure of Jasmim stood out as the first costume designer to demand the professionalization of this activity. The professionals we interviewed were unanimous in considering him to be the father of the profession of costume design in Portuguese cinema.

In response to the question 'Do you know any costume designers in Portuguese cinema who might be considered historical references?', the interviewees answered that Jasmim de Matos was one of the most important, both in terms of artistic inspiration and innovative techniques, followed by Teresa Campos, Maria Gonzaga (1951), Isabel Branco and Zé Branco (Lisbon 1951–present). The issue that spontaneously arose relates to how little attention has been given to other active professionals. Not only is there devaluation of the profession, but the most important question is also left unanswered: why should the fact that a department is staffed by women imply that it is less valuable than a department that is staffed by men?

Since its inception in Portugal, cinema has always been an industry characterized by the predominance of men in the so-called artistic departments (particularly directing, cinematography and screenwriting). There are no reports about a constant and distinct female presence engaging in artistic work in the cinematography of the silent film era, for example, as is the case with men. However, countless interesting works have been discovered over recent years that add to the history of both international and Portuguese cinema a few rare female figures whose personal and artistic circumstances we have come to know. Therefore, besides the recently discovered Bárbara Virgínia, there are other remarkable women in Portuguese cinema, as Paulo Cunha highlights:

> the cosmopolitan Virgínia de Castro e Almeida (1874–1945), founder of Fortuna Films (1922–23), screenwriter and producer of *A sereia de pedra* (Lion, 1923),

> producer and editor of *Os olhos da alma* (Lion, 1923); Amélia Borges Rodrigues; or the versatile Beatriz Costa (1907–96), unquestionably 'the most intense female presence' (Costa 1991, 53) in Portuguese cinema and one of its most international faces.
>
> (Cunha 2016: 42)

Similarly, according to recently initiated research, Helena Roque Gameiro can be considered one of the first women costume designers. In fact, her particular case belongs to a typical model of early cinema in which married couples shared tasks in the making of a film. Notwithstanding this, references to the profession of costume designer are scarce, as pointed out by her granddaughter Joana Leitão de Barros:

> Leitão de Barros entrusted Helena with wardrobe and prop research and development. Over the decades, the vast correspondence from José to Helena confirms how she was involved in his prolific activity. In many of the films, parties and parades organized by her husband, she was entrusted with researching and developing wardrobe and props. Helena followed every step of her husband's work.
>
> (Joana Leitão 2016)

After Helena Roque Gameiro, the particular aspect shared by the women who work or have worked in Portuguese cinema is the fact that, in order to join a predominantly male world, they have had to go through secondary channels. Thus, Monica Dall'Asta came up with the following provocative idea:

> the question emerges of how to deal with the much larger number of women filmmakers who, throughout their entire lives, were only able to direct, write, produce, distribute, and so on, no more than a handful of films, or even one single film. Several more questions arise. For instance, why were so many of them also actresses? Could this indicate that women's access to direction, production, and sometimes even screenwriting, was dependent on their previous entry into the film industry in a more traditionally feminine role, such as that of an actress?
>
> (Dall'Asta 2010: 43–44)

Jasmim de Matos joined the Portuguese film business by going directly into the profession he chose, namely costume and set design. However, among the costume designers we interviewed, many of whom began working immediately after Matos in the 1980s, only a handful experienced the same kind of direct path, although many did not have proper training.

In collecting data from the interviews, what stands out is the different treatment received by professionals depending on their gender: Jasmim became a reference in Portugal because he knew how to sew and implement the basic rules of the craft. As for other professionals who came after him, they simply had to train with the master or join the profession through a less direct route. Again, we return to the idea that this activity is a 'woman's thing': if, on the one hand, this fact opened the door to this profession for women, on the other it did not and does not enable a qualitative jump from technical (wardrobe) to artistic craft (costumes).

Teresa Campos claims to have met António da Cunha Telles[26] while accompanying an actress friend who had been chosen for one of his films:

> I remember the film *Retrato de família* by Luís Galvão Teles (1992), with Joaquim de Almeida and Maria de Medeiros. I remember that Jasmim was not around much, so I learned to look after the tasks on set.
>
> (Teresa Campos cited in Cucinotta and Faria de Souza 2017)

Rosário Moreira (Lisbon 1960–present) distinctly remembers having started to frequent film sets as a babysitter; Maria Gonzaga identifies her debut in cinema as the girl who did everything from assistant directing to make-up, also working as a production assistant and even an actress; Isabel and Zé Branco received artistic training in furniture design, but it was their brother, producer Paulo Branco who encouraged them to pursue a career in film. What these stories have in common is a casual and unassuming introduction to the film business, and as Monica Dall'Asta suggests, 'in a way that is more suitable to the feminine role in society' (Dall'Asta 2010: 43–44).

According to the interviews and the valuable oral testimony of the interviewees, the way they entered this profession has a lot in common with women's introduction into the early film business. In the reports about the costume designers who work or have worked in Portuguese cinema, what stands out is that their introduction into a male industry such as cinema was extremely difficult, to the point where the professional role of women could not be considered as important as that of men. Therefore, before our interviews, many interviewees had not realized the meaning attributed to the terms 'costumes' and 'wardrobe'. Nevertheless, there is a new generation who, despite having initiated their professional careers as costume designers, still do not understand the significance of this craft.

In order to write an oral history based on these interviews, it is important to acknowledge their absolute uniqueness, for almost every costume designer who works or has worked in Portugal has never been questioned about key aspects of their profession. For them, verbalizing the art of costume design was the first step towards a structured 'self-consciousness', as opposed to the 'self-inflicted punishment'[27] many of them mentioned. This was the first time these women had verbalized concepts related to costume design, the history of this craft in Portugal and the artistic practices used in their personal process of designing a costume.

In fact, this interview project seeks to reflect on the significance of these women's artistic work: the drawings they prepare to show their ideas to the director; the notebooks filled with creative notes about atmosphere; the items of clothing which, combined with lighting, framing and the actor's body, shape the real film costume; putting theorizations about costumes into practice while turning this profession into a particularly relevant artistic craft within the context of a composite and heterogeneous art such as cinema. Therefore, as a consequence of these interviews, in 2017 the silence was broken, a silence that had been perpetuated not only at the expense of an artistic craft, but also of a few unique personalities in the history of Portuguese cinema.

Conclusion

Reaching this point in the journey of researching costume design in Portuguese cinema, we must not ignore the need to first establish the trade's history: similarly to other film industries, the establishment of an oral history of the costume department is fundamental for future analysis, as well as for new theorizations and hypotheses. In the book *Viagem ao cinema através do seu vestuário* (2018), I articulated an attempt to study costumes in Portuguese cinema by theme units, using the ethnofiction genre as my object of study. Thus I established a connection from theory to practice between documentary and fiction.

An authorial approach to Portuguese cinema means that practices themselves (in addition to costumes, we can include sound, lighting, writing and sets, among others) also have an authorial tendency, made up of little quotes, parallel narratives and visual inlays that, in terms of clothing, are accomplished through the costume designer's work. Research about textures and costumes is not intended to be an approach merely seeking to contribute to the discussion concerning the visibility thus far denied to the craft of costume design. In Portugal, the debate about the position of women working in artistic industries is reaching a crucial point: in contemporary theorizations, the very concept of 'filmmaker'[28] attempts to combine the involvement of the costume designer with the materialization of the film, as an invaluable part of a film's visual work.

As my research on the visual authorship of costume designers in Portugal evidences, through the analysis of interviews, drawings and the contemporary concept of materialities, I ultimately expect to place costume at the centre of the frame, consolidating everything external within the dressed body.

REFERENCES

Barthes, Roland (2009), *Système de la mode,* Turin: Einaudi.

Bruno, Giuliana (2002), *Atlas of Emotions: Journeys in Art, Architecture and Film*, New York: Verso.

——— (2014), *Surface: Matters of Aesthetic, Materiality and Cinema*, Chicago and London: University of Chicago Press.

Calefato, Patrizia (1999), *Cinema e moda: Macchine di senso, scritture del corpo*, Milan: Costa & Nolan.

Castro, Ilda (2000), *Cineastas portuguesas: 1874–1956*, Lisbon: Cultura CM Lisboa.

Castro, Vera (2010), *O papel da segunda pele*, Lisbon: Ed. Babel.

Colaiacomo, Paola (2007), *L'eleganza faziosa: Pasolini e l'abito maschile*, Venice: Marsilio.

Cook, Pam (1996), *Fashioning the Nation: Costume and Identity in British Cinema*, London: BFI Publishing.

Cucinotta, Caterina (2016), 'António Reis e Margarida Cordeiro: Se a estética aproxima-se dos materiais, o ecrã transforma-se em poesia', in M. Penafria, E. T. Baggio, A.R. Graça and D. Correa Araujo (eds), *Ver, ouvir e ler os cineastas: Teoria dos cineastas*, vol. 1, Covilhã: Labcom, pp. 153–75.

——— (2018), *Viagem ao cinema através do seu vestuário: Percursos de analise em filmes portugueses de etnoficção*, Covilhã: Labcom.

Cucinotta, Caterina and Faria de Souza, Nivea (2017), in-person interviews.

Cunha, Paulo (2016), 'Para uma história das histórias do cinema português', *Aniki: Revista portuguesa da Imagem em movimento*, 3, pp. 36–45.

Dall'Asta, Monica (2010), 'What it means to be a woman: Theorizing feminist film history beyond the essentialism/constructionism divide', in S. Bull and A. Söderbergh Widding (eds), *Not So Silent: Women in Cinema before Sound*, Stockholm: Acta Stockholm University, pp. 39–47.

Dall'Asta, Monica, Duckett, Victoria and Tralli, Lucia (eds)(2013), *Researching Women in Silent Cinema: New Findings and Perspectives*, Bologna and Melbourne: University of Bologna and University of Melbourne.

Gaines, Jane and Herzog, Charlotte (eds) (1990), *Fabrications: Costume and the Female Body*, London and New York: Routledge.

Hamburger, Vera (2014), *Arte em cena, a direção de arte no cinema brasileiro*, São Paulo: Senac.

Leandro, Sandra, Valle, Arthur, Júnior, Carlos Lima, Mantero, Ana and Barros, Joana Leitão de (2016), *Flor de Água: Helena Roque Gameiro (1895–1986) – Aguarela e Artes Aplicadas*, Amadora: Casa Roque Gameiro.

Leitão de Barros, Joana (2016), 'Helena Roque Gameiro: Entre dois artistas', *Executiva*, https://executiva.pt/helena-roque-gameiro-entre-dois-artistas/. Accessed 2 September 2018.

Leitão de Barros, José (1935), *As pupilas do senhor reitor*, Portugal: Tobis Portuguesa.

——— (1936), *Bocage*, Portugal: SUS.

Martin, Sara and Re, Valentina (eds) (2017), *Game of Thrones: Una mappa per immaginare mondi*, Milan and Udine: Mimesis.

Penafria, Manuela, Baggio, Eduardo Tulio, Graça, André Rui and Correa Araujo, Denize (eds) (2016), *Ver, ouvir e ler os cineastas: Teoria dos cineastas*, vol. 1, Covilhã: Labcom.

Pierotti, Federico (2011), 'Colorare le figure: Il lavoro femminile sulla pellicola', in *Bianco e nero*, p. 570.

Simmel, Georg (1998), *Die Mode*, Milan: Mondadori.

Street, Sarah (2001), *Costume and Cinema: Dress Codes in Popular Film*, London and New York: Wallflower.

Verdone, Mario (1986), *Scena e costume nel cinema*, Rome: Bulzoni.

Viana, Fausto and Bassi, Carolina (eds) (2014), *Traje de cena: Traje de folguedo*, São Paulo: Estação das letras e cores.

NOTES

1. The empirical data gathered from interviews, field trips and personal work experience were vital resources for this chapter, and will also be crucial to further research on the career of the costume designer in Portuguese cinema. These resources are invaluable due to the nationwide absence of bibliographic material.
2. The bibliographical research includes those texts, articles and reviews about Portuguese cinema where the career of costume designer is mentioned.
3. According to data from a web directory exclusively dedicated to freelancers and Portuguese audio-visual companies, there are only three male costume designers: Cineguia Portugal, https://www.cineguiaportugal.pt/?c=250. Accessed 20 June 2019.
4. In 2009 the author of this chapter began doctoral research about the theorization of clothing in Portuguese ethnofiction.
5. In Portugal, the designation 'Filmmaker Theory' refers to a working group within the Association of Moving Image Researchers (AIM) that since 2015 has presented proposals for reflections based on a broader concept of 'filmmaker'. See http://aim.org.pt/?p=about&sp=workgroups.
6. All translations are mine.
7. The publication most closely related to the work of the costume designer in Portuguese cinema is about theatrical costume design in Portugal: *O papel da segunda pele* by Vera Castro (2010).
8. For example, in Castro (2000: 281) the filmmaker Rita Azevedo Gomes talks about her experience in the wardrobe department in some of Manoel de Oliveira's films.
9. Considering the academic background of the two researchers, both Italy and Brazil have always paid closer attention to issues related to the study of costume design in cinema.
10. Mario Verdone (Alexandria, 1917–Rome, 2009) was a professor of film history and criticism. As Director of the Centro Sperimentale di Cinematografia in Rome (Italian National Film School), he collaborated with some of the greatest international film periodicals.
11. See among others: Calefato (1999); Colaiacomo (2007); Martin and Re (2017).

12. See among others: Hamburger (2014); Viana and Bassi (2014).
13. Whereas in Portugal an art direction discipline is not yet available, the course mentioned here is still active: https://www.arts.ac.uk/subjects/performance-and-design-for-theatre-and-screen/short-courses/costume/costume-design-for-performance-csm. Accessed 24 June 2019.
14. See among others: Street (2001); Cook (1996); Gaines and Herzog (1990).
15. About this topic, see Pierotti (2011).
16. On page 9 of Dall'Asta et al. (2013) we can see a photograph of women workers in the Pathé Color printing room.
17. According to data from the Portuguese Association of Image (AIP) there are only four women in Portugal who have worked as heads of department for more than one film. See http://www.aipcinema.com/. Accessed 20 June 2019.
18. According to data from Cineguia Portugal, there are twenty professionally active women in Portugal. However, based on our interviews, only five of them work as art directors in Portuguese cinema: https://www.cineguia.pt. Accessed 12 June 2019.
19. This refers to the particular attention given to the work experience of the two researchers associated with costume departments in Brazil (Nivea Faria de Souza) and in Portugal (Caterina Cucinotta).
20. Based on our interviews, the final outcome may vary, depending, for example, on whether the costume in question it is made of synthetic or natural fabric, or if it is a tailor-made, rented or borrowed item of clothing. Some of the variables effecting the final outcome are inextricably related to budget issues.
21. This text had three versions: the first was published in 1895, the second in 1904 and the last definitive one in 1911. Interestingly, 1895 witnessed the invention of cinema by the Lumière brothers. Fashion and film emerged as two sides of the same coin: modernity.
22. The materials (notebooks with historical references, set photographs, continuity notes etc.) we gradually discovered are rich in detail and are valuable historical documents that record the creative processes that costume designers follow when they are working on a film.
23. Scenographer is a term used in the theatre to designate the person who creates exterior and interior atmospheres. This denomination is no longer used in cinema, having been substituted by set designer.
24. Concerning parity in the same role, according to the interviews many costume designers complain about a lack of balance in the salaries of so-called 'art directors': if the art director is a woman, it is very likely that her salary is lower than it would be for a man. As a starting point, an art director, head of the set department in Portugal, earns a higher salary than a woman costume designer.
25. Jasmim de Matos was born in Angola in 1942. In 1964 he went to London to study painting at the Slade School of Fine Art, returning to Portugal in 1975. Once in Lisbon, he began his career in set decoration and costume design for theatre and film. Jasmim died in a car accident in 1994 while he was working on the play *Maldita Cocaína* at Teatro Politeama.

26. António da Cunha Telles (Funchal, 26 February 1935) is a Portuguese producer, director and distributor. He is one of the founders of the Novo Cinema movement in Portugal.
27. Alongside the concept of 'miracle', the concept of 'self-inflicted punishment' was also mentioned by some of the professionals with regard to the almost absolute lack of rights in this department.
28. Clarification of this concept can be found in Cucinotta (2016).

PART IV

Historical memory and the gendered archive

Paradigms: Women filmmakers in 1970s revolutionary Portugal – Delgado, Nordlund, Cordeiro and Serra

Érica Faleiro Rodrigues

> *In Portugal, women did not exist in the nineteenth century, during the Republic or the Estado Novo.*
>
> (Pimentel and Melo 2015: 13)

This chapter explores how, following Portugal's 1974 Carnation Revolution, the initial wave of women filmmakers often took their first steps in the film industry organically, as part of a couple or as active members of a co-operative, empowered but also encumbered by a collective spirit of revolutionary camaraderie.[1] It will focus on four films directed either by a woman alone or co-authored with a male partner: Noémia Delgado's *Máscaras* from 1976; Solveig Nordlund's *A lei da terra* from 1977; Margarida Cordeiro's *Trás-os-Montes* from 1976; and Manuela Serra's *O movimento das coisas* from 1979–85. It will also examine issues such as genre, considering if these films are what we could consider traditional documentaries and how they reflect the political turbulence of the times. Furthermore, it will try to shed light on the gender dynamics that governed the making of the films and how this continued to shape female authorship prospects and the career expectations of women directors. It will engage with existing research, but it will also draw on several interviews given to the author by Solveig Nordlund (2016, 2018a, 2018b) and Manuela Serra (2018a, 2018b).

It is remarkable that all four films turned out to be relatively successful with international audiences. João Bernard da Costa, the Portuguese Cinematheque's quasi-mythical director, akin to Henri Langlois, once pointed out that *Trás-os-Montes*, for instance, was exhibited in France '[to] huge international success' (Costa

2007: 43), and *Máscaras* received high praise from the director of the London Film Festival. However, excepting Solveig Nordlund, all these women filmmakers have seen their careers cut very short. This was a time before the budgetary convenience and amenity of digital, when filming meant having to hire expensive analogue equipment and budgeting for film stock. Funding was also allocated by the Instituto Português de Cinema/Portuguese Film Institute (IPC), a scenario that lead to many being starved of funds, as decades later Margarida Cordeiro seems to confirm: 'The reason I did not film was that they allowed for other Portuguese films to be made rather than mine' (Castro 2000: 100).

During the Estado Novo, from 1933 to 1974, women were second-class citizens by law. They had limited access to suffrage and were constrained to journeying from the tutelage of the father to that of the husband for basic rights such as travelling abroad or opening a bank account. Filmmaking was, almost exclusively, a male profession. The few women in the records of Portuguese film history for this period are Alice G. da C. Noronha Granito (agricultural films), Maria Emília Castelo Branco (documentary filmmaker), Maria Luísa de Bivar (documentary filmmaker), Virgínia de Castro Almeida (scriptwriting) and Bárbara Virgínia, the only one to succeed as a feature film director.

When the military coup burst onto the streets on 25 April 1974, the Long Sixties – the cultural revolution, as defined by Arthur Marwick (1998) in his pivotal book *The Sixties* – was already in Portugal. Consequently, with social transformation already on the march, a shifting and rebalancing of sexual and gender boundaries rapidly ensued, in Portugal as in the wider western world. Far left perspectives were the order of the day, and '[i]n the emerging revolutionary context, Portuguese Cinema [became] the motor for the country's transformation' (Costa 2015: 11). This change allowed for the first slate of woman filmmakers to emerge in 'a historic context in which it was possible to foresee an attempt to reinvent both cinema and the country' (Costa 2015: 16). Women making inroads into the film trade reflects what was happening across the country, with female contingents now taking to the streets, occupying factories and entering politics.

Several co-operatives sprung up from this revolutionary juncture: Cinequanon, Cinequipa, Grupo Zero, FilmForm, Prole Film and VirVer. 'All these co-operatives varied in longevity, sustained by dispersed state funding and the production of short and medium length films. In the history of Portuguese film, the 1970s were a relatively long period of a cinema eschewing the need for the traditional figure of the producer, of pursuing alternative forms of creating and producing films' (Cunha 2013: 1). From the start, these film co-operatives had women in their ranks as founding members. Solveig Nordlund and Manuela Serra were, respectively, founding members and leaders of Grupo Zero and VirVer. The idea of filmmakers creating film co-operatives had started in 1969, under the patronage of the

Gulbenkian Foundation, when the Centro Português de Cinema (Portuguese Film Centre, CPC) was born. After the revolution, the CPC would support and finance the films by Margarida Cordeiro and Noémia Delgado discussed in this chapter.

Something that the four films have in common is the fact that they were all filmed in rural areas, outside urban centres. Correspondingly, at the level of policymaking, the Movimento das Forças Armadas/Armed Forces Movement (MFA), through its revolutionary campaign for the cultural dynamization of the countryside, also focused on areas devoid of agrarian reform: the period was also marked by a generalized effort to 'rediscover' the lost or invisible countryside. There was perhaps the realization that, with the agrarian revolution, life in the rural provinces would soon change, fast and dramatically, and the imprint of a certain 'time', still visible in some regions, would disappear – it was imperative to act quickly, to capture a certain moment before profound transformation swept away this rural '*ancien régime*'. These were times of radical revolutionary change in the hinterlands. What shape the future would take no one knew: goalposts where constantly being moved, and how this revolutionary process would insert itself into the rural landscape was one of a few big questions that gripped intellectuals, filmmakers and society at large.

Máscaras, by Noémia Delgado, offers complex readings of gender relations. The title refers to the *Caretos*, the young men wearing the traditional masks and dress of Trás-os-Montes. It depicts pagan traditions associated with the winter cycle, linked to the solstice and involving the passage from boyhood to manhood. Beautifully shot and edited, this is a film that sits comfortably with the best of visual anthropology. And while this was the very first feature film directed by a woman after the revolution, it is also a work purposely dealing with old Portuguese traditions that categorically exclude women.

The fact that the first woman to direct a feature film immediately after the revolution chose to focus on a reality that apparently excludes women as active protagonists is not insignificant. From this we can take two very distant readings. First, this is a film devoid of a burden of representation, one which bears no sense of obligation to address gender inequality in Portuguese society. Delgado had, earlier in her career, trained with Jean Rouch (along with Solveig Nordlund), and it is logical that she would subsequently persist with the ambition of making an ethnographic film. *Máscaras* is carefully planned and shot, full of the detail emanating from the rituals personified by the masked boys, and ancient tradition and celebration. This is an exceptional film in which Delgado captures moments filled with ancestral meaning, and records a naturalistic sound while at the same time placing a soundtrack of classical music over a few scenes, along with the striking recording of a woman singing (recorded by Michel Giacometti, a renowned ethnomusicologist): all of this tends to enfold the action with a sense of timelessness.

It is also significant that Delgado succeeded in entering this secretively patriarchal milieu to record the daily life of men and these complex sets of male rituals.

However, Delgado herself has stated that 'no film is innocent' (Castro 2000: 40). Were we to dissect the film in the light of gender politics, a few issues would arise. First and foremost, this is an ode to exclusively male traditions, as all the women in the film remain bystanders, observing the men, serving them food and displaying a deep respect for the rituals they interpret. Men are the bearers of all ancestral knowledge; they are the carriers of lineal wisdom and therefore hold the key to Totem and Taboo. Prior to the revolution, women were mostly excluded from filmmaking and needed to climb the most difficult heights just to gain the status of an *auteur* in the most varied fields of artistic production. In patriarchal Portugal, they were constantly denied the role of bearer of knowledge (except for domestic wisdom): their work was seldom found in Portuguese museums, bookcases or cinemas, and their relevance was dismissed as secondary to that of men. And yet, paradigmatically, the first woman to direct a feature film after 25 April 1974 elected to depict and celebrate male ritual, and patriarchal knowledge and tradition. We are therefore left with the burning question of why would Noémia Delgado not take the opportunity offered by the revolution to record the rituals, traditions and the wisdom of Portuguese women in these same or similarly remote regions. In making this film, she seems to have released herself from the burden of representation and perpetuated a patriarchal narrative.

In the film, scenes depicting women taking an active part in the narrative are few and far between. One reflects for a moment when, for a few seconds, an old woman dances with one of the *Caretos*. Another depicts women washing wool on a riverbank. Another captures two women arriving from the fields, backs arching under the weight of heavy baskets, while a man carrying an empty basket follows behind, languidly puffing on a cigarette. Finally, a shot catches the *Caretos* chasing young girls. We are left to wonder what female rituals and knowledge could have been depicted and shared had the filmmaker decided to prolong these brief moments.

But it is not solely the representation of women that is secondary or missing. With the exception of a minor joke by one of the *Caretos*, this is a film that renders invisible all the revolutionary turmoil, a film with its back turned on the revolution. And yet it is widely known that Delgado was politically active, that she participated in political discussions about future film policy, that she would often be the only woman to undersign collective revolutionary documents. Also worth noting is the fact that Delgado had been arrested by the Polícia Internacional e de Defesa do Estado/International and State Defence Police (PIDE) and locked up as a political prisoner, testifying years later that it had been in her squalid jail that she had made 'her very first acquaintance with peasant women and female factory workers' (Castro 2000: 50).

Delgado was, by all measures, a solitary women among men, suffering from the gender clichés that materialized in the actions of the CPC co-operative. On patriarchal hegemony within the co-operative, Delgado stated the following:

> the CPC had very little money, and we were all going to a meeting where each of us would decide on doing something which we would not be directing [...] Well, a distribution of duties. And I put myself forward to do editing. We reached the end of the meeting and none of them took any decision to do anything. No one wanted to do anything except directing. That I would do editing, they all agreed on, but that they would do something themselves, no! This exemplifies the state of affairs. This was a group deciding 'let's assume several roles'; directing would be on a rota; and no one stepped up to do anything. This is symptomatic.
> (Castro 2000: 57)

The voice-over in *Máscaras* is that of Delgado's husband, the bohemian poet Alexandre O'Neill in whose shadow she would always remain, in life as well as in death. This would also be her first and only feature film for the cinema, after which she was confronted with an invisible wall, unable to get any of her projects funded – a pattern also damaging to other women filmmakers of her generation. She applied several times for state funding but was never again successful in attaining support, only managing to work for state television.

In an interview at the Portuguese Cinematheque, on 22 February 2016, the Portuguese–Swedish filmmaker Solveig Nordlund mentioned that, during her tenure as film director at the filmmaker's co-operative Grupo Zero, her most relevant directorship had been *A lei da terra*, from 1977. This is a complex and emblematic film, as far as gender representation is concerned, among its post-revolutionary counterparts. The film was directed both by Solveig Nordlund and her then partner, the filmmaker and intellectual Alberto Seixas Santos. It is worth noting that couples filming together during the first post-revolution years was a common phenomenon, a practice that had also been common in other countries in the silent film era. The sheltering provided by being part of a couple seems to have been a means by which women could take their first steps as filmmakers. And yet, while this form of collaboration seems to have allowed women filmmakers to direct and find validation as authors, it also involved the peril of seeing their contribution downgraded to secondary status, overshadowed by its male counterpart. And while such status does not seem to have been conferred upon Solveig Nordlund and the work she accomplished together with Seixas Santos, a very different fate has been shaped out of the relationship between Margarida Cordeiro and António Reis, directors of *Trás-os-Montes* (1976). Margarida Cordeiro's role has been demoted on many occasions, with authorship and even brilliance often allotted solely to António Reis. Collaboration as a couple during these revolutionary times seems to have been a double-edged sword for female authorship: it was often the ticket to directorship, but also, commonly, the major reason for authorial relegation and obscurity.

Going by its credits, we would say that *A lei da terra* can boast a balanced number of male and female contributors, and yet in the film itself representation of gender is profoundly asymmetric. This asymmetry is doubled by the discrepancy between voice-over and images. In what seems to be an unprecedented formal construction, narration is shared between a female and a male voice. All through the film these two voice-overs share equally a similar portion of the cinematic time (sometimes even overlapping): directing and interpreting the narrative, filling out the aural space of the film, seeming to fulfil the great revolutionary ambition of establishing legislative parity between men and women. What takes shape in the soundtrack of *A lei da terra* is the mirroring of this revolutionary ambition and the momentary realization of gender equality. And yet gender representation within the visual and narrative part of the film becomes very different: from beginning to end the frontline protagonists, those who have something to say and are able to voice it, those who carry an opinion about the political situation, those who describe their experiences and enunciate their thoughts, are mainly men; with women more often than not placed in the background, silent, still or just simply nodding.

The gender bias in *A lei da terra* often reaches extremes, as when a couple describes the vicissitudes of poverty and the lack of resources during childbearing, and it is the husband enlightening us about the hardship of giving birth under such conditions instead of the wife, who simply nods her head. In this shot, the husband is facing the camera while the wife remains in profile, reinforcing (no doubt unconsciously) the notion that women are unable to make themselves be seen clearly, or to consciously face the camera. What this scene brings to the fore is not only the repeated cliché of female representation, but also the candid exposure of how gender relations and roles are still subsumed by patriarchy. Knowing their history, we can easily assume that the directors did not intentionally seek to give such an unbalanced portrayal. However, and regardless, this scene is the result of their work, and the situation that was shot and edited is the one that remains, with not a word being uttered by the woman about her own maternity and motherhood. Throughout the film women are more bystanders than protagonists.

There are a few instances in the film when women do become vocal. One is a brief and rather insignificant shot; another is when power of speech is given over to a woman taking a stance against the ethos of the film, an anti-revolutionary character defending the livelihood of *rendeiros* such as her husband. The *rendeiros* were counter-revolutionary types (or had been up to the revolution); as intermediaries between the farmers and the big land owners, they earned up to three times as much as other countrymen, a reward for implementing landowner rule. The *rendeiros* were guardians of profit and were solely male; as the wife of a *rendeiro*, this woman is voicing her support for their actions against farmer co-operatives. With the agrarian revolution, the rendeiros had seen their traditional livelihood suddenly threatened by workers organizing themselves into co-operatives and rendering their role obsolete. The *rendeiros* would, in turn, respond by organizing themselves into several groups with the aim of aborting the agrarian revolution. It is intriguing that a work openly on the side of the revolution and the proletariat gives voice to a woman expressing the views of the counter-revolution. And it is also significant that this is one of the few moments when a female voice is able to puncture the male-driven narrative of the film. The year 1975 was a battleground of revolutionary and counter-revolutionary confrontation.

Towards the end it becomes evident that women are being silenced as active members of the farming co-operatives, that male hegemony is on the rise and unequal conditions are being imposed, with men taking over the leadership of these organizations and voicing without hesitation the idea that work and conditions should be granted disproportionally to male over female workers. This is voiced by men in front of silent women, who listen. The Orwellian adage of 'some more equal than others' materializes again in the re-engineering of the gender gap by men over their fellow women workers.

This is the mood as we approach the end of the film. We watch the scene of an old female farmer candidly voicing her opinion about the injustices that systematically fall upon women. She vociferates that, since they do the same hard jobs, women should be guaranteed equal rights with men. Strong and vocal, this woman faces us while she eats, during what appears to be a welcome break from the hard work in the fields. And it is in this shot that we suddenly witness a reversal of roles: this older woman expressing her opinion based on decades of experience as a farm worker, while all the time she speaks, a younger male co-worker observes, seemingly both respectful and uncomfortable with her truths and the strength of her opinion. The woman goes as far as to unashamedly state that women not only do the same work as men, while receiving less recognition for it, but they also carry the extra burden of having to do all the work at home. After this, no other women will say anything, as all that is meaningful has been eloquently expressed. The film ends with the shot of a crowd, mainly of women workers, raising a fist: despite all the adversities and setbacks, they still fiercely defend the revolution. However – and this should be the image to retain – for most of its narrative *A lei da terra* is a film enforcing gender parity only at the level of narration.

The voice-over is the space for gender equality. But it is also the space of immateriality and idealism, which cannot possibly be reflected by the narrative, whereas all the documental content points to a reshaping of male hegemony and the rise of a counter-utopian reality defined along gender fault lines. Voice-over and footage present two different realities: one revolutionary and idealistic (representing the left-leaning, progressive middle-class views of the authors), the other the revolutionary process as it was turning out to be, outside the control of those who made the film. As militant cinema goes, *A lei da terra* is a complex and rather open object, since (perhaps inadvertently) it presents the ideal of gender parity, as expressed by voice-over and credits, in remarkable contrast with the conservative forces already working their way up into the revolutionary process. It is an idiosyncratic film, one that is erected around an ongoing battle between voice-over and the reality it depicts.

Out of this group of four filmmakers, Nordlund comes out with the most positive assessment of the time she spent in the film co-operatives: 'The life of an independent filmmaker is very lonely. I miss the time of the film co-ops in Portugal, when we all worked as part of a group and discussed things together. We were all part of a structure' (Castro 2000: 148). In conversation, Nordlund has confessed that what has helped her sustain momentum and secure a career as a woman filmmaker has been her dual Portuguese–Swedish citizenship, since she has always managed to find support for her films between the two countries. Rather contentedly, Nordlund points out: 'I have never had massive commercial success, but all of my films have been released in cinemas' (Castro 2000: 160).

Quite a contrasting example as far as gender representation goes is given by *Trás-os-Montes*, a film that João Bénard da Costa considered to be magical realist and which documents villagers going about an extraordinary array of tasks, from real documentary scenes, to the staged re-enactment of their thoughts and daily activities, to the representation of completely fictional scenes. In this film, female presence is strong and prominent throughout. Many moments in women's lives are presented, as we listen to the stories told by grandmothers to mothers and daughters and watch female rituals of weaving the wool, setting the fire or passing oral traditions on to the young. In *Trás-os-Montes* women are represented in all moments of their daily lives, with their thoughts and in the conversations and activities that propel the narrative. Financing for *Trás-os-Montes* was raised thanks to the generosity of Paulo Rocha, who, in true co-operative camaraderie spirit, 'gave up, for the second time running, the funding made available to the film *A Ilha dos Amores*, and proposed that in Plan III of the CPC, his film be replaced by *Trás-os-Montes* (Costa 2007: 40). In 1974 Paulo Rocha had already stated that 'from all the films proposed this seems to me the most promising and urgent' (Costa 2007: 40).

The soundtrack to *Trás-os-Montes* drifts from naturalistic sound to a visually empowering silence, with the use of classical music in order to accentuate feelings of ancestry and a history that is rooted in the distant past (as also seen in Noémia Delgado's *Máscaras*). But this is also a film granting the roles women play their due attention, as in a scene in which an older woman, experienced in the art of the loom, is weaving quickly and efficiently on an old wooden machine, the strong sound of her work transitioning from where the action is taking place to another shot of a man riding, always overpowered by the sound of the woman working. By bringing a female narrative to the forefront, this is obviously a feature documentary making a difference in terms of gender representation. But it is also a work that uncovers what is often kept hidden: women active in the workplace, and the workplace as both the home and the workshop or the fields. Female work is represented as double, both inside and outside domesticity. Women carry the babies and look after the children and yet they still find the time to cook, weave and work in the fields.

While not addressing or mentioning the revolution directly, *Trás-os-Montes* deals with important social issues of the time, such as when the camera records conversations about forced migration to find work and a better life, a recurring tribulation across generations. We learn that migration spreads both to the environs of large Portuguese cities as well as abroad. Levels of illiteracy among peasant women are also exposed. In one scene, an elderly unschooled woman requests that a young boy write a letter for her. In another scene a second woman is incapable of reading a letter and it is a boy who reads it for her. The film exposes how disadvantaged women had been by the dictatorship and how frequently women in villages were denied the opportunity to learn to read and write, even more so than men.

With *Trás-os-Montes* it is also worth remembering that, imbued with revolutionary spirit, the filmmakers had organized film sessions with the community they had filmed, screening the final version for them. The villagers, when confronted with this final cut, were highly critical of the film, failing to recognize themselves in the picturesque and impoverished vision the film had made of them, believing that it had made them look poorer and more outdated than they considered themselves to be. Scenes such as that (completely fictional) of a family starving to such an extent that they resort to eating snow probably contributed to this feeling. Watching the film, it is easy to conclude that the villagers were willing participants, but because this is a collage of so many different moments and scenes, only when confronted with the edited work did they manage to grasp the entire narrative and the overall gist of it. As expressed by Cordeiro: 'We recorded a staged reality because that is what is filmed – placing a camera in a certain position, we are already conditioning a point of view – but we did not make a documentary. We controlled the way in which we would gather the images and sounds' (Castro 2000: 96).

In a bizarre twist, the population's strong criticism of the film, in turn, led to a robust criticism of their attitude towards it from intellectuals and film critics.

As part of this argument, it was stated that the locals were unable to realize what a work of art the film was. It is without a doubt ironic that villagers and critics diverged so much in their opinions of the film. This clash of meaning and purpose is often found in many other instances of the revolutionary process. What the intellectuals considered to be the appropriate cultural products to be enjoyed by the people and what the people wanted often diverged irreconcilably. The people and the revolutionary elites would often find themselves on opposite sides, the manifestation of an ever-present class struggle.

Cordeiro only managed to shoot two more films, also in partnership with António Reis. She never again managed to secure funding, although she applied continuously for ten years, her career eventually coming to a halt with the death of António Reis. As she states: 'What hurt me the most was to have to stop working. One starts to master a way to express oneself in film and suddenly we are forced to stop because of a power beyond our control' (Castro 2000: 97).

Manuela Serra cut her editing teeth on the mythical revolutionary film *Deus, Pátria, Autoridade* (1976) by Rui Simões, working through a profuse amount of footage. Serra was a young woman just arrived from a few years of exile in Belgium, where she had managed to take her first steps in filmmaking by securing a place in the selective Belgian Film School. At that stage a single parent, Manuela Serra found in charismatic filmmaker Rui Simões the partner who could ensure that her return to revolutionary Portugal could be both viable and stimulating. Serra spent days on end in the dark, organizing the materials that had been shot all over the country. Her work in the editing room gave her the strength to start the co-operative VirVer together with Simões. The revolution was everywhere and, for a while, the utopia of the film co-operatives blossomed. But only in 1979, with the revolution already crumbling and the co-operatives in crisis, did Manuela Serra manage to start filming on her own, in the north of Portugal. Her single feature film, *O movimento das coisas*, is a production marked by misfortune.

The main details of what happened were recorded in an interview on 8 June 2018 at her home in Lisbon. Serra's production ran for fifteen days initially, in November 1979. As her budget ran out, she could only resume filming for a further two weeks one year later in 1980. Following this, she had serious problems obtaining the remaining funding for editing and to finalize the film, something she only achieved in 1985.

Both personal and institutional constraints were responsible for Serra's hardship. As well as being the founders of film co-operative VirVer, Rui Simões and Manuela Serra were partners. Life, work and idealism were so intermingled during those revolutionary times that the co-operative functioned from the house they both lived in with children from previous relationships. The equipment, the editing facilities and the co-operative meetings were all at this house – an intense situation in which the personal and the professional intermixed. Manuela Serra was last to film as part of the co-operative and, as her relationship with Rui Simões came to an end, the co-operative also came to have an uncertain status, propelled by a meeting where all except Serra voted to dismantle it. What happened to VirVer is similar to the fate of other co-operatives: 'the manner in which the co-op CPC and other similar groups functioned only worked when the number of members was relatively small. With expansion and new members the co-ops became unmanageable, since the budget available was not sufficient for all the individual projects' (Cunha 2013: 7). Beyond this, for Serra the erosion of her relationship with Simões became the major factor that sealed the end of VirVer.

At the beginning of the 1980s Serra's disenchantment with the ideals held by the collectives was at its peak, and this was further enhanced by years of bureaucratic battles with the IPC. Serra realized that two other members of the co-operative had withheld a substantial amount of money granted by the IPC to *O movimento das coisas*, a fact unknown to her at the time. This pushed her into a battle that lasted several years to prove that she was innocent of the legal difficulties she had faced as a result and that the money had been diverted into the wrong hands. She had to wait several years for the funds that would finally allow her to finalize her work.

Initially, Manuela Serra had intended to film in the Alentejo. But while travelling with another woman companion in search of locations, she found in the places she visited in the south of Portugal a surprising hostility towards her, as a young female urbanite. This pushed her to start looking for locations in the north of Portugal, until she found Lanheses, a village still immersed in ancient traditions but also one with factories lurking nearby. Engaging with the village priest and having him explain at mass that she was a filmmaker, she managed to convince the people, who would become the participants in her documentary feature. The community embraced the project.

O movimento das coisas is a film in which the camera is allowed to linger over the details and mundanities of the day-to-day lives of several women, from preparing for work, to cleaning, to childcare, to making bread, to working with the animals and in the fields, to working in a factory. It is a film that captures female work and female daily routines with an observant and delicate eye, allowing us to witness the life of the villagers. In an interview on 8 June 2018, I asked Manuela Serra to what extent the shots were staged and she recalled that most shots were acted, choreographing the events which would typically take place. Serra replied laughing, saying that, as we should all be aware by now, to make fiction is to try to capture reality and to make documentary is to fictionalize a moment of it.

A unique aspect of this film is its soundtrack, which seldom features dialogue but instead records the mumblings and noise arising from the activities unfolding before our eyes, intermixed with the natural sounds of the space. Diegetic and non-diegetic sound mix smoothly between passages, giving us notions of proximity between actions and of a continuity between the activities of different characters. The music by José Mário Branco brings a feeling of uncanniness, of what is and is not. In Lanheses, old traditions are forced to share a space with the new ways: next to the factory, carts pulled by animals sit beside modern cars.

In *O movimento das coisas* detail is key to the fluidity of the narrative. One of a few women villagers we follow, Isabel, is captured in several dimensions: fixing her hair, eating breakfast, walking to work, working in a factory, returning home, eating with her family, shopping, singing at a popular festival. Isabel's life is captured, but by a sympathetic camera that moves to study its object with delicacy and respect. Isabel, along with the other men and women portrayed in the film, are filmed in their daily movements, close up but also in wider shots and takes that integrate them into the surrounding landscape, as if this were a village symphony.

Serra's film never had commercial distribution but was nevertheless successfully received by many a film festival around the world. The IPC told her that 'by 1989 it was the Portuguese film that had been shown at the most film festivals' (Castro 2000: 186).

After concluding the film, Manuela Serra felt emotionally and financially exhausted. *O movimento das coisas* was repeatedly screened at film festivals, but at some point she started to feel that it was a gimmick to continue with film and plunge deeper into debt. Serra decided to stop and did not film again.

If, initially, these works could be considered straightforward documentaries, further scrutiny, and the interviews given by the authors, provide new insights and lead us to the realization of how staged the portrayal of these realities is. All four films are, to a greater or lesser extent, choreographed, exploring the blurred lines between documentary and fiction. All feature carefully planned photography and sound, and all offer a singular and distinctive reading of the process and the outcome of filming in politically convoluted times – perhaps a way for these young women to maintain a certain level of control when entering the difficult world of filmmaking.

This chapter is meant to offer a wide-ranging perspective on the cinema made by women filmmakers at the start of a new democratic era in Portugal. These non-traditional documentary works nevertheless differ substantially in what they depict and the aesthetic mechanisms they employ. And yet all four films respond to the beat of a country experiencing the transition from dictatorship to democracy. Although they contain many common aspects, such as the director's gender or their emphasis on rurality, these are markedly different films. Furthermore, the careers of these four filmmakers are also widely different, despite some common blueprints between a few of them. This leads us to the idea that generalizations should be left out of the picture, and that the study of women filmmakers in Portugal in the years surrounding the revolution is necessarily a dynamic and complex field. The four films included in this succinct chapter are, however disparate, only a small sample. Wider and deeper research on the topic is therefore needed.

REFERENCES

Castro, Ilda (2000), *Cineastas portuguesas 1874–1956*, Lisbon: Lisboa Câmara Municipal Cultura.

Cordeiro, Margarida and Reis, António (1976), *Trás-os-Montes*, Portugal: Instituto Português de Cinema (IPC).

Costa, João Bénard da (2007), *Cinema português: Anos Gulbenkian*, Lisbon: Fundação Calouste Gulbenkian – Serviço de Belas Artes.

Costa, José Filipe (2015), *O cinema ao poder! – a revolução do 25 de Abril e as políticas de cinema entre 1974–76: Os grupos, instituições, experiências e projectos*, Rio de Janeiro: UERJ.

Cunha, Paulo (2013), *Um cinema sem produtores? As cooperativas como modo de produção*, Atas II Encontro Anual AIM 47, http://aim.org.pt/atas/indice/Atas-IIEncontroAnualAIM-47.pdf. Accessed 5 November 2019.

Delgado, Noémia (1976), *Máscaras*, Portugal: Instituto Português de Cinema (IPC).

Geada, Eduardo (1977), *O Imperialismo e o Fascismo no Cinema*, Lisboa: Moraes Editores.

Marwick, Arthur (1998), *The Sixties: Cultural Revolution in Britain, France, Italy and the United States, c.1958–74*, Oxford and New York: Oxford University Press.

Nordlund, Solveig (1977), *A lei da terra*, Portugal: Grupo Zero.

——— (2016), interviewed by Érica Faleiro Rodrigues, Portuguese Cinematheque, Lisbon, 22 February.

——— (2018a), interviewed by Érica Faleiro Rodrigues, Portuguese Cinematheque, Lisbon, 22 February.

——— (2018b), interviewed by Érica Faleiro Rodrigues, Lisbon, 6 March.

Pimentel, Irene Flunser and Melo, Helena Pereira de (2015), *Mulheres portuguesas: História da vida e dos direitos das mulheres num mundo em mudança*, Lisbon: Clube do Autor.

Serra, Manuela (1979–85), *O movimento das coisas*, Portugal: VirVer.

——— (2018a), interviewed by Érica Faleiro Rodrigues, Lisbon, 8 May.

——— (2018b), interviewed by Érica Faleiro Rodrigues, Lisbon, 8 June.

NOTE

1. A publication, far from consensual, but which nevertheless provides a relevant insight into the first years of post-revolution filmmaking in Portugal, is O *Imperialismo e o Fascismo no Cinema* (Geada 1977).

The mother awaits: Woman and landscape in Galician non-fiction cinema

María Soliña Barreiro González

Landscape lies at the heart of non-fictional representations of the Galician territory.[1] Documentaries and features portray Galicia according to a set of recurring compositional, temporal and symbolic tropes that end up creating an imaginary for the collective recognition of a space in memory that is not conflictual; a space that tries to become the emotional physiognomy of Galicians.

In this space, the mother plays a key role, as this figure links the mother and the motherland at a psychological level to generate a 'guilty conscience over departure' (García-Caballero and Area Carracedo 2007: 91) in migrants for leaving the mother/land. Migration as a fundamental wound in Galician society is of relevance when constructing an immutable and shared space that neither betrays memory nor compromises the possibility of returning. This shows that space is not important because of its physical-geographical features, but rather anthropologically, because what this mythic space represents is, to some extent, the motherland. Both await. In this sense, some of the discourses we find in non-fiction films[2] become a sort of collective autobiography for discussing loss: of the land and of the mother who is left behind.

Women in communion with the land can be seen in films such as *Galicia y Buenos Aires* (Gil, 1931), where Galicia is described as 'the devoted mother [who] waits for you with her loving bosom', or in *Un viaje por Galicia* (Arís, 1958), where the director films his own mother, sharing an intimate space of his imaginary with the whole Galician community, at home and abroad, thus maintaining the delusion of actively belonging to the same group.

The mother as a symbol of loss in suspension is the leitmotif of this chapter as seen through migration films, promotional films and films produced on the borders of the territory in the twentieth century. In some cases I will use *auteur* films or documentaries for comparative purposes. The heterogeneity of the sample has led me to use the term non-fiction to encompass all the examples cited.

Stereotypes around landscape and identification

The configuration of the contemporary landscape imaginary in Galicia is the sum total of images produced through nineteenth-century Romantic travel writing, Galician landscape painting, photographic iconography and the first films about this region. These films are made up of snapshots showing beautiful nature and chubby, folksy types; both the takes and the editing are archaic, and sequences of juxtaposed neutral overviews reveal an absence of experience in the territory. Such representations aim to create a non-conflictual landscape of common recognition, a landscape stereotyped according to past contributions (by photography, painting and literature) and others now introduced by films.

The takes in *Un viaje por Galicia* (Alonso, 1929), *Un viaje por Galicia* (Arís, 1958), *Nuestras fiestas de allá* (Gil, 1928), *Galicia y Buenos Aires* (Gil, 1931) and *Galicia y sus gentes: ayer y hoy de las Tierras Meigas* (Reig and Anwander, 1951) follow one another like a journey, devoid of any meaning except for that of the itinerary itself. Cities with their monumental spaces, calm estuaries and wild seas, green forests, mountainous landscapes, some pleasant shots of people tilling the land or working at sea and some romantic sunsets: these views are chained together to create an animated postcard of the territory, using no more than a fixed camera and panning.

A sort of scopic regime of distance is created, a regime of accumulation and objectivism that is closely linked to perspective. It serves to establish representative icons that are easy to recognize and that, as postcards, fix the memory of the territory for travellers, migrants, locals or foreigners. These icons seem to remain unchanged because they are alien to the whole economic, social and historical experience of the place. They have been repeated throughout contemporary times and have thus become a sort of emotional physiognomy for an identity that is non-conflictual, for a community communion through which we identify ourselves and are identified.

The process of literalization and socialization (Pageaux 1995) nurtures and disseminates these stereotypes, which, in turn, allow for the emotional expression of a bond with the land and of nostalgia. The impossibility of facing loss felt by migrants freezes stereotypical spatial memories and creates an ideal and immutable land that awaits the migrant once he has left it. This self-deception through the imaginary had already been described by Celso Emilio Ferreiro[3] in his 1973 poem *O añoiro*, an epitaph for a migrant who never accepted expatriation:

> Here lies an exile who said:
> Galicia is a thing
> Unreal, far away.
> But living in exile

is a real thing that hurts me
Deep inside.

(Ferreiro 1989: 153)[4]

The imaginary of the Galician landscape is generated by the overlay of previous re-creations, local and foreign, repeated and ritualized throughout the nineteenth and twentieth centuries. In time, they created an imaginary that became an 'organization that institutes reality', an imaginary that allows for the landscape to become 'the sender of images that facilitate transition from the conscious to the unconscious' (Pageaux 1995: 94). This imaginary of the landscape is socialized through culture and works in the 'organization and domain of collective time in the symbolic plane' (Pageaux 1995: 89). The history of representation, in this case of the landscape, can be understood in the field of a history of ideology in Marxist terms: the awareness of a given objective situation that was falsely represented by the work of an ideology through the images of the landscape.

In the case at hand, and considering the importance of migration in Galicia, this becomes even more relevant, as the imaginary is created as an image in absence, as a simulacrum that uses referential realities – because absence enables affective commitment to become more important in socialization than critical reflection on the images. This analysis will help us to understand the links with the real and how they were systematically hidden in these idealized and frozen images of Galicia.

Cultural representation constitutes Galician communities, because all memory has its foundations in a social environment, in an ideology understood as an unconscious expression of the ideas derived from a concrete social situation. Halbwachs reflected on this in *The Collective Memory*, claiming that individuals always use social frameworks when they remember, and that these frameworks possess a specific temporality (Halbwachs 2004). Such social frameworks are reflected in the way the landscape and the mother are used in films as a promise of return. One of the essential figures in the construction of these internal Galician frameworks was Rosalía de Castro.[5] Núñez Seixas interpreted this in relation to the poetic images used by the poet:

> Rosalía was an image [... who] managed to combine a rebellious tone with the sensitive recreation of an inherent feeling to any migrant: longing, nostalgia or *morriña*, with all the connotations of that period [...] as an individual experience of those who depart, as a subjective interpretation of absence and the communion with the physical and, we could say, anthropological environment [...] Rosalía de Castro thus embodied the almost telluric image of the bond between migrants and the land they left behind.
>
> (Núñez Seixas 2016: 42)

This was so much the case that the images and structures used by de Castro ended up being the way in which migrants expressed their experience:

> Many migrant reminiscences about the land presented images taken from the works of Rosalía (internalised through a sort of *habitus*) and used the structures of some of her poems to express what leaving Galicia had meant for them [...] The literary images forged by Rosalía became the mirror regularly used to understand their own migration experiences, thus becoming the appropriate format in which to convey them.
>
> (Núñez Seixas 2016: 49–50)

Landscape, the motherland and Rosalía de Castro ended up merging in an idealized imaginary of Galicia, alien to the social and economic experience of the territory. This is why this chapter investigates what is behind those images, behind those social imaginaries that require some specific visual (and poetic) structures to represent a territory, or more specifically to possess that territory, to recognize it, to make it one's own and to express oneself as a group through a non-conflictual imaginary of self-recognition and recognition by others. Identifying the ideological and economic elements that underlie the representation will also reveal the reasons behind the formal configuration of these images, because the territory is a physical, economic and ideological configuration resulting from the clash between capital and labour (Harvey 2015).

Our historiographical proposal uses the analysis of cultural products of a certain period from the contemporary historical perspective; this will shed light on a constellation of aesthetic representations that will make the relationship between the imaginary of the Galician landscape and the social and economic setting behind it legible, albeit 'written in invisible ink' (Benjamin 2005: 478 [N11, 3]). We will see that reality is diverse and not homogeneous; in spite of this, it is presented in an iterative pattern in the representation of the landscape. In this way, we will be in a position to develop a sort of theory of mentalities and to understand the specific historical perception of migration, a fundamental phenomenon in the configuration of contemporary Galician society, identity and art.

The films that will be studied are features and/or documentaries with different purposes: promotion of the territory or its industries, capturing amateur memories, visual correspondence with migrants and the strengthening of identity through television broadcasts. Exceptionally, and as a counterpoint, we will analyse some films describing struggles over the territory or *auteur* films. The choice to focus on non-fiction films in order to study the Galician emotional physiognomy through landscape was made for several reasons. First, hardly any Galician fiction films were produced throughout the first half of the twentieth century; documentaries were easier to develop. Second, migration films seem to be a very specific Galician format.[6] Finally, in these films the territory leaves its own imprint and is presented without fictional mediation. This imprint, though phantasmagorical and mediated by the author and technical procedures, still creates an emotional link that is stronger from being linked to ideas of authenticity. Non-fiction images establish a sort of telluric connection with the territory that, even if they are produced at diverse times and in diverse spaces, generates in the spectator an updated experience of return, in the case of migrants, through the image of the real.

The shots of the films analysed are characterized by an aseptic and institutionalized composition that enables recognition and the bond between one's own memory and the image. But what is most important is that, through the landscape and the mother, these films construct an emotional autobiography, built by a country of migrants to lessen the loss, to elaborate in the least painful way the abyssal loss of migration and exile. The space is mythicized and acquires an almost anthropological nature in order to 'elaborate loss': the loss of the mother, of the motherland.

The anthropological landscape: The motherland awaits

> Galicia is a motherland
> a motherland of soil and time
> leaning on the deepest night,
> bearing children of nostalgia and numbness.
>
> (Ferreiro 2018: n.pag.)

Galicia is represented in many literary, pictorial and cinematographic works as the mother, the motherland. This element is deeply rooted in Galician culture, as is an understanding of matriarchy as a society in which women ensure the survival of the household, its continuity when others migrate: women are those who faithfully wait. Although the migration of single women is a fact, most Galician migrants were men; in this sense, the icon of the woman who waits is created, the widow of the living, who takes care of all the tasks, of the land, the property and the home.

In Galicia, the population hardly increased in the twentieth century due to continuous mass migration. Between 1850 and 1930, 55 per cent of Spanish migrants to Argentina were Galician (Núñez Seixas 2001: 11); between 1911 and 1915 alone, 136,645 people officially departed from the port of A Coruña as migrants (Cagiao 2001: 112). Between 1946 and 1960, 286,437 Galicians left for the Americas, 45 per cent of Spaniards living overseas during this period (Fernández Santiago 2001: 181–82). If we look towards Europe between 1962 and 1976, 257,229 people migrated to the rest of the continent (Rivas 1990: 62). In order to give some context to these tragic figures, we need to remember that the Galician population was around 2.5 million inhabitants. It is therefore with minimal exaggeration that some say that during that century, the number of people who left Galicia was almost as many as the number who stayed. All in all, if we focus on the statistical series of the Spanish Statistics Institute (INE) from 1900 to 2000,[7] we can see how the population boom of the century's middle years was not felt in Galicia due to the constant flow of migrants towards other countries. The region finished the twentieth century with a population increase of less than 800,000 (1,980,515 in 1900 to 2,720,445 in 1991).

This population debacle is reflected in Galician culture in the figure of widows of the living, characterized by Rosalía de Castro in her poem *¡Prá á Habana!* (1880), which used its vindicatory and melancholic tone to speak about the economic, social and emotional repercussions of migration:

> This one went, that one's going
> and all, all of them go,
> Galicia, you're without men
> to work your soil.
> You have orphans instead
> and empty fields;
> and mothers who are childless
> and children without dads.
> And you have hearts that suffer
> life-long absences,
> Widows of the living, widows of the dead
> whom nobody will console.
>
> (Rosalía de Castro [1880] 2016: 214)

The development of this image over time is not only found in literature; in painting, Castelao and Luís Seoane renewed the image in the second half of the twentieth century, updating it to the social and political evolution of the concept of Galicia resulting from migration and exile. This figure shows some set features: grief that cannot be consoled; the overlapping of past, present and future; she is embodied in the female farmer who awaits, with an aged and spectral body,[8] but who is at the same time the supporter of the house, of the land. This figure tries to activate collective memory: 'the widows of the living, as they are a representation and not real women, become another spectre that suffers and speaks about the history of the people, of the disinherited, of a bereavement that is quiet and silenced but present at the same time' (Garrido González 2015: 262).

A lonely woman can be seen in other works such as *Conversas* (Seoane 1946), where it is only women who seem to occupy the fields; she is also seen as the elderly woman who waited her whole life to see her son die in the album *Nós* by Castelao ('Eu non quería morrer alá ¿sabe, miña nai?', 1920); or already merged with the idea of the motherland in *Mater Gallaeciae* (Seoane 1961) or *Galicia Mártir* (Castelao 1937). According to Ana Garrido, Castelao and Seoane 'already use an updated selection of historical facts and characters; they see migration as an epic odyssey, the spectres and the figure of the woman waiting as the representation of the nation' (Garrido 2015: 258).

Travellers coming to Galicia and writing their chronicles also contributed to the construction of this image of the lonely woman who waits while she takes care of all the work. Travellers were scarce due to the remote geographical location of the region on the Iberian Peninsula – it was a place that led nowhere. This was also because the railway did not connect Galicia to the rest of Spain until 1883 and to Portugal until 1886. Travellers around Galicia in the nineteenth century agreed on some aspects relating to Galician women: they were worn and aged prematurely due to excess work. Richard Ford began his journey around Spain in Seville in 1841 and in 1845 he published his impressions. This is his description of Galician women:

> When the Gallician [*sic*] men migrate, the females do all the drudgery at home in house and field, and a painful sight it is to see them labouring at the plough: in the field or out of it, their hands are never idle, and the *rueca* or distaff is as much part and parcel of a Gallega, as a fan is of an Andaluça. A fare hard as they work, coupled with exposure to an uncongenial climate, nips their beauty in the bud; few, indeed, are born with much, nor do the fortunate ones retain their charms long; aged before thirty, they soon seem models for witches, and look as if they never could have been young, or had anything of the feminine gender; they look like mummies or cats found starved behind a wall, objects of skin and bone.
>
> (Ford 2008: 16)

Silveira da Mota visited Galicia when the railway was inaugurated and wrote *Viagem na Galiza* (1889). The book shows the Romantic imprint of Rosalía de Castro in the way it conceives the land: it criticizes the economic inequality of the interior and the coast, and highlights the similarity between the lands of O Miño in Galicia and O Minho in Portugal. Women, in particular, are to Silveira da Mota's eyes, very much alike in Galicia and Portugal – they are all submission and sacrifice, crushed by work:

> Their features, saddened by the hardness of the work, lose their vigour and freshness early; moral life, however, remains inaccessible to equal damage, their souls remain good, loving, sincere. An example of holy abnegation, the Galician woman accepts deprivation, her hard life and brutal disrespect without complaint; she bends, like a loving servant, before her father, her brothers, her husband and her children, before all who near and far are her family; and be what it may the pain that oppresses her, she listens, sweet and compassionate, to the pleas of the forlorn and shares with them the salary she gets.
>
> (Mota in Cerqueira Pascoal 2017: 13)

In the common imaginary of migrants, the idea of the woman-motherland that awaits remained; and filmmakers, who were often commissioned to make the films by migrants, went to great lengths to present a Galicia that matched their memories. Overseas, the fear of change was therefore exorcised by visiting the cinemas, and going back to the places of memory that confirmed this image of Galicia as the eternal motherland and projected the delusion of active belonging and the anticipation of a potential return without conflict.

José Gil was commissioned by the Sociedad Progresista Hijos de Fornelos y Anexos (Progressive Society of the Children of Fornelos) in Buenos Aires, Argentina to film *Galicia y Buenos Aires* (Gil, 1931) and show the opening of the Community Hall of Sindicato Agrícola y Ganadero de Fornelos (Fornelos' Farmers Trade Union). The film is divided into two parts: the first shows the traditional lifestyle of the area, and the second, the inauguration of the trade union's facilities and the festival that followed. The rhetoric of the mother who awaits appears in the final sequence of the film, as the emotional climax created by the intertitles by Saturnino Piñeiro, interspersed with the speech by Daniel Rodríguez, representative of the El Progreso society, who, 'evoking absent comrades, says: As I cannot share the blessings of this "terra meiga"[9] with you, comrades overseas who remember your "lar" with love and tenderness, please receive through this peculiar format the wish of a bunch of brothers for your speedy return to Fornelos where a devoted mother is waiting for you with her loving bosom'.

Mother and motherland are psychologically linked to generate a 'guilty conscience over departure' in migrants as they equate leaving the land with leaving their mothers, according to Alexandre García-Caballero and Ramón Area Carracedo in their study *Psicopatoloxía do retorno* (2007). The insistence on remaining in the mother/land, of both waiting on the other side of the ocean and the warm welcome the migrant will receive despite their previous departure, are symbolic elements that are often seen in migration films. They are produced to show the world as if nothing had happened, as if the space could not have changed because the space is not physical, it is anthropological, and that is the reason why, for these films, showing fixed, unchanging and familiar landscapes is so important: 'The fantasy of an encounter and merging with the object lead to a situation in which any elements that alter a feeling of origin (physical changes in the landscape, children, alteration of values ...) produce negative feelings in the face of an impossible restitution' (García-Caballero and Area Carracedo 2007: 91).

Analysing the psychiatric pathologies developed by migrants who have returned, García-Caballero and Area Carracedo confirm that the type of loss embodied by migration is ambiguous and not standardized. That is why it is so difficult to find closure and, when grief 'finds no closure, it is passed on from one generation to the next as family-based, collective myths' (2007: 109). The discontinuity of space and family tries to find closure through the second generation in films such as *Porriño en Buenos Aires* (González, 1929). In this film, we find a lateral tracking shot of the children of a migrant community and an intertitle explaining that they are '[t]hose who shall perpetuate our name and virtues on American soil tomorrow', thus foreclosing return. On other occasions the wish is maintained, and a visual imaginary is used to give continuity to the generational link between the children and the motherland on both sides of the Atlantic; *Galicia y sus gentes* (Reig and Anwander, 1951) is dedicated to '[t]hose who, on the other side of the sea, still dream of their motherland'. Furthermore, if we look at the symbolic structure opening this film, we find a low-angle shot of a *cruceiro* (stone cross) lit from behind (by heaven and the dead), an *hórreo* (traditional barn) in front of the *ría*, a vessel at sea (the memory of migrants), a descent from the sky to the wheat fields, and then a song with words from Rosalía de Castro's 'Ariños, ariños, aires'[10] starts playing. In this poem the migrant woman prays for the winds to take her back to her homeland because sadness follows her, and because she is afraid that if she does not return soon, she will be a foreigner in her own land:

> Oh, if you don't soon lift me upward,
> Little breezes of my land,
> If you don't lift me, little breezes,
> No one will recognize me soon.

(Intertitle from *Galicia y sus gentes*, Reig and Anwander, 1951)

The need for nothing to change is also found in this opening.

The generational transmission of the guilty conscience of the migrant, and the divergence and idealization that stopping time supplies, are habitual in the films we discuss, but find their discursive, formal and authoritative counterpoint in the film *Bs.As.* by Alberte Pagán (2006), where the divergence of family members due to migration is addressed differently. Pagán portrays, through conversations and letters, the dislocated loss of two generations; it is a loss that has been mythicized by both sides and a wound that is reopened because of an inheritance. The film addresses the loss of the great-grandmother – she even loses the memory of her name – the suffering of the second generation – the grandmother reveals the bitterness of her life as a migrant: the money, the deception, the illiteracy, the alcoholism, the lies, the pain – and the third generation – the cousins who send each other letters (one of them is the author of the film) and who build common ground for memory in the family's history, myths aside.

Migration and travel films, however, highlight the awareness of grief amid a certain paralysis in form and content. The form in which they are shot (static snapshots), their content (stereotypical and familiar postcards of the most important landmarks in Galicia) and their feeble narrative structure (in the shape of a journey or itinerary in the widest sense) suggest a concrete time, a static time, which is necessary for constructing an eternal landscape. The aesthetic form of these films speaks of this myth and its atemporality. If for the migrant 'the changes produced in the village of origin are like scars that show the passing of time' (García-Caballero and Area Carracedo 2007: 92), these films try to avoid this through their aesthetical construction of the landscape.

Manuel Arís Torres, a Galician migrant who left for Uruguay as a child, travelled to Galicia three times between 1953 and 1958 and filmed different monuments and landmarks, editing them later and premiering the film in Buenos Aires in December 1958 under the title *Un viaje por Galicia*. The film was shown in theatres for two and a half months due to the large number of migrant Galicians who went to the cinema to see their towns and villages, to check that the object of their memory and *morriña* still existed (CGAI n.d.).

Un viaje por Galicia accompanies this journey through Galicia with a soundtrack including a voice-over and a musical repertoire of *alboradas*, *muiñeiras* and *comparsitas*. Arís combines music from and for the migrant community with popular Galician songs such as 'Queixumes dos pinos, A Rianxeira' (very popular in Galicia but originating in Argentina) or the *Alborada de Veiga*. The most important role of this music was to evoke emotions and to generate an atmosphere of communion with the memories of the land left behind. There is, therefore, a stark contrast between the connotative and emotional sound and the bland and objectifying image. Memories are triggered by the sound, which each person decodifies using the images and their own memories; in this way the image is neither real nor experiential and it does not contradict this mythicized memory.

The images of Manuel Arís move centripetally, they close in on themselves and are self-referential as they address the same audience that produces them. The film is always sufficiently distant and minimally grounded in the land of origin in order to prevent a real – not petrified – living film from emerging. If this were to happen, the idealized memory of the land would be disturbed, as migrants would see a place that is changing without them. The music evokes their own memory, while the image neutralizes and reaffirms the myth. In the film *Un viaje por Galicia* we can see how this scopic archaism materializes, on the one hand, in a loving sequence of mythification of the mother and, on the other, in some tokenistic sequences praising some form of progress, exclusively in urban Galicia.

The distance Arís maintains changes when he comes to the landscapes of his own region and he is reunited with the imaginary of his tender years. The filming is different: closer, with the intimate complicity of amateur films, of tapes that can only be deciphered by close relatives. 'A eira da miña casa' (my home's threshing floor), says the voice-over in Galician, in a film narrated in Spanish, showing images of the *malla* (traditional threshing), the washerwomen in the river, workers spraying sulphate in the vineyard (the traditional form of manure used) and his mother ploughing the land. Then he comments: 'This lady working so hard, I am going to introduce her to you: she is my mother.'

This sequence contains one of the most decisive moments in the development of the film's relationship with the audience and their gaze. With these familiar images, Arís assimilates the migrant Galician community into his own family, and he shares with them the intimate space of his childhood, giving a collective sense of his personal return: everything has remained the same, the mother awaited his arrival. The familial liberties taken by Arís were criticized by Seoane, who thinks they are inappropriate interferences in the filmic representation of Galicia.[11] Seoane is right, but this was not Arís' intention : he did not want to create a real reflection, but to sustain the myth that the community had developed without modifying their memory. With the gift of this sequence with his mother, he invoked anybody's mother: with 'my mother' she became the mother of everybody, the fortune of returning to the mother/land. The empathic connection was ensured: the mother of Manuel Arís embodied the aspiration of all those present in the cinema in Buenos Aires to return and see their own mothers again.

As we have already seen, the Galician collective conscience is, for better or worse, dependent on the imaginary developed by Rosalía de Castro, a fact which is even more true for the migrant community, to the point that the identification between the mother and the motherland becomes the motherland Rosalía. The last stanza of the 1968 poem by Celso Emilio Ferreiro *Miña matria Galicia* (Galicia, my motherland) ends up reinforcing the idea that the redemptive spirit of the motherland is Rosalía:

Women, they are pristine springs
for our insatiable thirst for homeland
flesh of anguish, powerful clay,
they await the judgment day of the nation created.
What word can I use for so much foam?
What phrase can I use, in just one name,
to describe the love, the strength, the warmth,
the appealing light of the family home?
I would like to use one word
the old finesse
the flower that does not wither,
the quiet evening,
the peaceful dove,
the light of faith, in the never-ending darkness.
I will say, Rosalía.

(Ferreiro 2018: n.pag.)

Woman, territory and economic transformation

In the immobility of Galician landscapes and the mythification of the mother/land, migrants reflect their own sense of time. They are immersed in a 'sacrificial model' of the present. The sacrificial model that García-Caballero and Area Carracedo (2007: 93) refer to had already been described by John Berger in his book on migrant workers *A Seventh Man*. The sacrificial model is based on a temporality torn off the present: suspended in time until – if ever – they return, migrants are displaced in time and space (Berger 1975: 241). Berger spoke of a paused temporality in the life of the migrant in which '[t]he past acts as a Wall which prevents the present entering the life's time; or, if it filters in, it is transformed immediately into terms of the past' (Berger 1975: 178).

Thinking about going back to the land of the migrant worker 'sacrifices the present for the future under circumstances which continually confound his sense of continuity. Scarcely anything he experiences or witnesses confirms the value of his sacrifice' (Berger 1975: 187). In this sense, all the images of their memories from the past and the future stand still, 'the rest of his life is reduced to a series of fixed images relating to past and future [...] for he believes that by saving his wages he will be able to rejoin these images and animate them' (Berger 1975: 171).

The aesthetic of Galician landscape films falls into the temporal model of the migrant worker described by Berger. The migrant worker would be like a hero travelling, but a hero in a constant state of waiting, a hopeless hero. The adventure of migration has a temporality, like any other adventure, that stands apart from daily life, with a clearly defined beginning and end, and anything that transcends this remains suspended (Kracauer 1995). But in the end the adventure becomes uncommunicated life, and migrants cannot return to the real life they left behind. Their life remains, therefore, temporarily suspended; they sacrifice the present for the future, and understand a present of sacrifice, of hard work and loneliness as a tribute, as a 'parenthesis in life' (García-Caballero and Area Carracedo 2007: 45).

Stopped time in landscapes seems to exist to 'elaborate loss'. The landscape has a time anchored in memory and built before departure. The idea that life will be restored and that images will come to life again when the migrant worker returns, encourages them while they are abroad. If there are changes in their village, in their anthropological landscape, the whole migratory narrative operation, the sacrifice, will be in vain and identity will become a wound. That is why time has to be stopped in the aesthetic construction of the landscape.

This proposal of suspended time in the psychological and visual sense is related to the suspended hero. This means, in fact, the negation of adventure, because the time of travel is not lived: one lives for the future, sacrificing all for a return that is not guaranteed, and that, if it ever happens, will lead the migrant to find a country that will not match their distorted imaginary, which has been set in stone during the years of absence. We thus have a heroic countersense, not a daytime hero, active and ready to take action. The state of migrants is that of waiting. It seems that life only moves forward for whoever stays behind, for the women who are supposed to await the return of their sons and their husbands. Only they can live outside suspended time; only they, with their presence and their words, can keep the house and the motherland standing. On both sides, waiting traverses the construction of the imaginary. Action remains absent.

The Galicia that brings together the mother, the motherland, the landscape and Rosalía still is, in the twentieth century, a rural society of pre-capitalist structures; these structures mean that the process of original accumulation did not find total fulfilment in its transition towards capitalism. If we follow the analysis of Silvia Federici (2010), women maintain their role in production and reproduction without being stripped of the value of social reproduction or household work. This means that the labour of women in Galician society, as they were not employed, was not torn between paid and unpaid; that is, their role in social reproduction was still not considered 'a natural resource or a personal service' (Federici 2010: 20).

Women had a key social position in the economic and social structure of Galician rural homes, without this supporting the idea of a mythical matriarchy. This was so because the economic structure, based on small land tenure, was not prone to industrialization and land seizure. Migration put the almost pre-capitalist production style that was present in Galicia on the road to extinction. What happens in the films from real Galicia, in which the widows of the living were not consumed by waiting and moved forward? In the Galicia that fought against the capitalist expropriation of traditional resources? There, the representation of women, the landscape and even language is radically different.

The landscape-territory we see in *O monte é noso* (Soler, 1978) is lived through rest, work and struggle. It opens with a woman sitting in a clearing, speaking of the traditional uses of communal forests, and with a panning shot of wonderful mountains with valleys divided into grazing land; the voice-over in Galician clearly shows how the landscape is going to be presented:

> their natural resources determine the relationship between the men who work and inhabit it, Galicia, land and country in which the sea, the land and the cattle are the most important wealth, crippled by the satyrs of centralism. Our political dependency and *caciquismo* are still the most important examples of the most crushing[12] internal colonisation. Our forests are one of our most important wealth reserves, with two million hectares, one third of the country.
>
> (Soler, 1978)

The voice continues speaking about the history of communal forests, while we see cows and rural women crossing the territory-landscape, the houses and the paths, the *hórreos*, the *palleiros* (haystacks); territory and landscape intertwine. The mess caused by the usurpation of common forests during the Francoist era and migration is communicated; we see derelict villages falling down, filled with brambles and silent as death.

The demonstrations to get back the common forests also happen in the landscape and they are filled with women. Life happens in the landscape, which is seen as a territory to live in and not to depart from. One year before this film was shot, Llorenç Soler had already filmed the struggle for the territory in Galicia in *Autopista, unha navallada á nosa terra*, in which he shot 'an attack on the land and on a thousand-year-old way of using our resources in the construction of the habitat' (Ledo 2012: 189). The landscape of Galicia is the habitat. With its population distribution there is not an inch that is untouched by the hand of man (Portela in Rivas 1990: 23). This is so true that in order to build a highway, not only was the agricultural lifestyle of the place fractured, but houses were also torn down and the autonomy of the women supporting them was destroyed, as Soler shows in a beautiful sequence moving from the outside to the inside of a woman's house that was almost destroyed when they built the highway: 'the leap towards the deep crack in the walls of the house leads us from the exterior to the interior, from light into the wound, from tactile textures to a live attack' (Ledo 2012: 190). In the end, the landscape is also inside: not a phenomenological exploration of natural beauty, but the way we have developed to live it.

The ritualization[13] of the landscape in literature, in painting and cinema was articulated around a paralysed time, for both those who left and for those who stayed. Under this phenomenology of the landscape, a poisonous myth lurked to mitigate the pain of those who left, but which also meant giving up rebellion and accepting the comfortable call of resignation, thereby leaving its symbolic and economic weight of permanence to the mother who awaits.

REFERENCES

Alonso, Luis R. (1929), *Un viaje por Galicia*, Spain: Diputaciones gallegas.

Arís, Manuel (1958), *Un viaje por Galicia*, Spain: privately funded production.

Beiras, Xosé Manuel (1972), *O atraso económico da Galizia*, Vigo: Xerais.

Benjamin, Walter (2005), *Libro de los pasajes*, Madrid: Akal.

Berger, John (1975), *A Seventh Man: Migrant Workers in Europe*, New York: The Viking Press.

Bruno, Giuliana (1990), 'Streetwalking on a ruined map', dissertation, New York University. http://www.nyu.edu/projects/wke/dissertationsSite/indices/phd_graduates/bruno_giuliana.php. Accessed 13 August 2019.

Cagiao Vila, Pilar (2001), 'Género y emigración: Las mujeres inmigrantes gallegas en la Argentina', in X. M. Núñez Seixas (ed.), *La Galicia austral: La inmigración gallega en la Argentina*, Buenos Aires: Biblos, pp. 107–39.

Castro, Rosalía de (2016), *New Leaves* (trans. E. Moure), Sofia: Small Stations Press.

Cerqueira Pascoal, Sara (2017), 'Carmens e Lolas: Representações da mulher espanhola na literatura de Viagens portuguesa da segunda metade do século XX', *E-Revista de Estudos Interculturais do CEI-ISCAP*, 5, May.

CGAI (n.d.), 'Un viaje por Galicia: Filmes recuperados polo CGA', https://cgai.xunta.gal/es/filmes/un-viaje-por-galicia. Accessed 20 September 2018.

Chao Rego, Xosé (1989), 'Mito e configuración do carácter galego', *Filología Románica*, 6, pp. 111–18.

Federici, Silvia (2010), *Calibán y la bruja: Mujeres, cuerpo y acumulación originaria*, Madrid: Traficantes de sueños.

Fernández Santiago, Marcelino X. (2001), 'Asociacionismo gallego en Buenos Aires (1936–1960)', in X. M. Núñez Seixas (ed.), *La Galicia austral: La inmigración gallega en la Argentina*, Buenos Aires: Biblos, pp. 181–203.

Ferreiro, Celso Emilio (1989), *Antoloxía*, Vigo: Xerais.

——— (2018), *Miña matria Galicia*, Vigo: Fundación Celso Emilio Ferreiro.

Ford, Richard (2008), *Manual para viajeros por España y lectores en casa: Galicia y Asturias*, Madrid: Turner.

García-Caballero, Alexandre and Area Carracedo, Ramón (2007), *Psicopatoloxía do retorno*, Vigo: Galaxia.

Garrido González, Ana (2015), 'Viúvas de vivos: La representación desde el exilio gallego de la vulnerabilidad y la violencia en el cuerpo de la mujer que espera, a partir de la obra de Luís Seoane y Alfonso Daniel Rodríguez Castelao', in M. Garrera Garrido and P. Mariola (eds), *Violencia y discurso en el mundo hispánico*, Seville: UMCS and Padilla, pp. 251–70.

Gil, José (1928), *Nuestras fiestas de allá*, Vigo: Galicia Cinegráfica.

——— (1931), *Galicia y Buenos Aires*, Vigo: Galicia Cinegráfica.

Halbwachs, Maurice (2004), *La memoria colectiva*, Zaragoza: Prensas Universitarias de Zaragoza.

Harvey, David (2015), *Espacios de esperanza*, Madrid: Akal.

Kracauer, Siegfried (1995), 'Travel and dance', in *The Mass Ornament: Weimar Essays*, London and Cambridge, MA: Harvard University Press.

Ledo, Margarita (2012), 'Galicia en V.O. El cine militante y el lugar de Llorenç Soler en la construcción del cine gallego contemporáneo', in M. Francés (ed.), *La mirada comprometida: Llorenç Soler*, Madrid: Biblioteca Nueva, pp. 183–98.

Núñez Seixas, Xosé Manuel (ed.) (2001), *La Galicia austral: La inmigración gallega en la Argentina*, Buenos Aires: Biblos.

——— (2016), *O soño da Galiza ideal: Estudos sobre exiliados e emigrantes galegos*, Vigo: Galaxia.

Pagán, Alberte (2006), *Bs.As.*, Spain: Pagán.

Pageaux, Daniel-Henri (1995), 'Littérature génerale et comparée et imaginaire', *Anuario de la Sociedad Española de Literatura General y Comparada*, 9, pp. 81–95.

Piñero, Chano (1984), *Mamasunción*, Galicia: Luciano Piñero Producións Cinematográficas.

Plantinga, Carl (2005), 'What a documentary is, after all', *The Journal of Aesthetics and Art Criticism*, 63:2, pp. 105–17.

Reig, Alberto and Anwander, Christian (1951), *Galicia y sus gentes: Ayer y hoy de las Tierras Meigas*, Madrid: NODO.

Rivas, Manuel (1990), *Galicia, el bonsai atlántico*, Madrid: El País/Aguilar.

Seoane, Luís (1958), *Galicia emigrante*, 35, 14 July.

Soler, Llorenç (1977), *Autopista, unha nevallada a nosa terra*, Spain: Soler.

——— (1978), *O monte é noso*, Spain: Goordinadora de Montes Comunais.

NOTES

1. Galicia is a territory located in the north-west of the Iberian Peninsula. It is a Spanish autonomous community with a language of its own, Galician, which is similar to Portuguese.
2. Due to the heterogeneity of the sample, we use the category 'non-fiction' as defined by Plantinga (2005: 105): 'A non-fiction film is any film that is not fiction, for example, instructional films, advertisements, corporate films, or historical or biographical documentaries.'
3. Celso Emilio Ferreiro (1912–79) was a Galician poet and a political prisoner during Franco's dictatorship. He wrote in Galician and was a migrant himself.

4. All translations by María Reimóndez.
5. Rosalía de Castro (1837–85) is the most important poet in the Galician language. Her book *Cantares Gallegos* (1863) was the first work published in Galician language after centuries of written silence during the so-called 'Dark Centuries'. This book became a milestone in the history of Galician written culture.
6. The phenomenon of film migration letter – films that were commissioned by those travelling between the two Galicias – only finds its counterpart in Italy, as Giuliana Bruno proved in her dissertation of 1990.
7. See http://www.ine.es.
8. *Mamasunción* (Chano Piñeiro, 1984) is a short film that is key in the use of the Galician language in cinema. It portrays the widow of the living as a spectral mother who can only wait.
9. Intertitle written originally in Spanish but these words – *terra meiga* and *lar* – were written in Galician. We keep the Galician words to highlight the intention.
10. 'Little breezes, breezy breezes.'
11. *Galicia emigrante*, 14-XII-1958.
12. The study of the landscape in this film is economic and social; it is in line with the analysis Xosé Manuel Beiras presented in 1972 in O *atraso económico da Galiza.*
13. 'Space signifies, in its full intensity, only if it is ritualized. This is a socio-cultural unavoidable relativity, time is the most vertebral of spatial dimensions' (Fernández Rota in Chao 1989: 113).

Exploring the Portuguese memory through appropriation film: *A toca do lobo* (Mourão, 2015)

Elena Cordero-Hoyo

Thus the life of someone whose existence has somewhat preceded our own encloses in its particularity the very tension of History, its division.

(Barthes 1981: 65)

Introduction

Esfir Shub's statement written in the Soviet Union in 1928, pointing out that '[n]onfiction film became a reality and, despite the absolute inequality, is conquering the screen', is now possibly truer than ever (Shub in Kostina and Dyshlyuk 2016: 20). Documentaries are experiencing a golden era, having spread from specialized festivals and circuits to a broader audience thanks to video-on-demand platforms, DVDs and specialized movie theatres. The year 2004 was important for documentary films with the October editorial of *Cahiers du Cinéma* being devoted to this phenomenon (Ortega 2007: 17). After the great commercial success of *Fahrenheit 9/11* (Moore, 2004), *Super Size Me* (Spurlok, 2004) and later *Pina* (Wenders, 2011), several artistic and industrial initiatives began to introduce contemporary documentary practices to a wider public. For example, distribution platforms such as Netflix have updated their catalogues to include more documentaries as well as producing their own. With increased investment, non-fiction cinema[1] is now expanding its aesthetic, poetic and technical diversity. With this shift, women filmmakers are gaining more recognition and important works and documentarians such as Esfir Shub, Germaine Dulac, Nicole Vedrés, Agnès Varda and Chantal Akerman, among others, who have been largely ignored until now, are entering the canon. In addition, archival films are assuming an important position in the world of non-fiction filmmaking (not only documentaries but also more experimental and artistic audio-visual products).

Fostered by the democratization of digital technologies and the re-appreciation of archival material, we are seeing an emergence of found footage films, many of them made by women directors and editors. For that reason, in 2016 the Italian scholars Monica Dall'Asta and Alessandra Chiarini edited an issue of the *Feminist Media Histories* called 'Found Footage Film: Women without a Movie Camera', in which they contradict the long-repeated essentialist theories that explain women's proclivity towards film editing due to its similarity with tailoring and sewing. The above-mentioned scholars argue that one of the reasons for having a higher proportion of women directors devoted to found footage film than other kinds of industrial cinema filmmaking is partly because it enables them to undertake research and embark on projects that can be developed as both individual and intimate work:

> [W]omen, in the absence of directorial opportunities within the frame of institutional cinema, may have elected [*sic*] the practice of found footage as a way to build an autonomous space of creativity that allows them to transform limitations into a stylistic peculiarity [... T]hese filmmakers usually keep working beyond the borders of mainstream narrative cinema, that is, in the fields of documentary, experimental, or animated cinema.
>
> (Dall'Asta and Chiarini 2016: 4)

Documentaries have historically been a place where women directors have enjoyed more freedom, as it is a practice of filmmaking which is less industrialized and requires less economic investment in comparison with mainstream fiction films. In addition, found footage is a cheaper genre within documentary films because its production can be focused on selecting previous content and editing them to give a new significance to the images, as will be discussed below. However, the reasons for choosing to work in this way are not merely economical. There are also artists who choose this kind of filmmaking for aesthetic, political and/or ethical reasons.

Laura Mulvey, author of the groundbreaking article 'Visual pleasure and narrative cinema' (1975), was the speaker for the course 'Women and film: An approach through representations of the mother in image and narrative' at the film festival Filmadrid (12–15 June 2017).[2] The programme included the projection of and commentary on four films (two melodramas and two compilation films) related to the topic of motherhood. Among the films exhibited was Alina Marazzi's documentary *Un'ora sola ti vorrei* (2002).[3] This film explores the tragic story of the filmmaker's mother, Luisa Hoepli/Marazzi (Liseli). She came from an Italian upper-class family and was married with two young children. As she suffered from depression, she was interned in a mental health institution until she committed suicide in 1972, when she was only 33 years old and Alina Marazzi (her daughter) was 7 years old.

While watching *Un'ora sola ti vorrei* it is difficult not to be reminded of another documentary with similar characteristics: *A toca do lobo* (Mourão, 2015).[4] In this film, the filmmaker also tries to reveal family secrets: her uncle's imprisonment by the Salazar regime, but mainly those that surround the figure of her own grandfather, the Portuguese writer Tomaz de Figueiredo (1902–70), who was also confined to a mental health institution due to his depression when Mourão's mother was 11 years old, causing her to suffer from abandonment trauma.

The resemblances do not only arise because both are documentaries that aim to have a healing effect by re-examining the familial memory and experience of mental institutions, but also because they illustrate a bigger picture: the historical and political context of the country. For that reason, this chapter aims to analyse Mourão's *A toca do lobo* and its function as a political essay on the collective memory of the Portuguese dictatorship, following a comparative methodology with Marazzi's *Un'ora sola ti vorrei*. As mentioned above, this latter documentary has been the object of Mulvey's feminist analysis as an interesting depiction of the hidden constrictions of the female life experience (Mulvey 2015b).

Mulvey analysed Marazzi's ability to take the footage filmed by her grandfather that idealized their bourgeois way of life and the beautiful women in his life – his wife and daughters. Editing it, she gave another meaning to the images, showing the decline of a family and the loneliness and isolation of her mother. On the other hand, *A toca do lobo* is an effective criticism of the Salazarist dictatorship and the harmful effects that its repressive institutions, such as schools, prisons and hospitals – most of them ruled by the Catholic Church – had on Portuguese society for generations.

A toca do lobo is the sixth film by Mourão, who is forging a notable career as a documentarian having also worked as the producer, writer, editor and cinematographer for this film. All her documentaries have in common a very personal dimension in which the filmmaker's involvement can be clearly felt. In 1998 Mourão founded AporDOC, the Portuguese Documentary Association, and with her projects she is continuing the genealogy of women documentary-makers in Portugal. Before her, filmmakers such as Noémia Delgado, Solveig Nordlund, Margarida Cordeiro, Manuela Serra and Susana de Sousa Dias,[5] among others, made documentaries which illuminated different facets of Portuguese history.

Documentaries have been falsely contrasted to fiction films as 'non-played' cinema depicting real-life events. The division between documentary and narrative cinema fiction is blurred and there is no consensus on the definition of a documentary film. Even more confusing is the distinction between the films that use archival material and those that use new footage. Several scholars, with one of the first examples being Wees (1993), have established their own categories including found footage film, compilation film, appropriation film and collage film, among others, trying to define them according to the level of experimentation, subjectivity or fictionalization in these films (although none of these concepts are well defined by academia). For that reason, in her book *The Archive Effect* (2014), Jaimie Baron points out that there is a lack of consensus.

According to Baron, this differentiation, as well as the proliferation of terminology, 'often seems to be based on the personal preference of the theorist rather than on a substantial theoretical foundation'. For that reason, she proposed the use of the term *appropriation film* based on a new way of conceptualizing filmic objects by their mode of reception and the effect that they produce on the spectator, which she calls 'the archival effect' (Baron 2014: 8–9). This chapter will use Baron's proposed terminology, and we will also use the term 'appropriation film' because we want to highlight the political dimension of the transgressive act of appropriating and editing archival material committed by the filmmakers. However, as we are using Laura Mulvey's analytical pattern, we will also respect her preference for the term 'compilation film' whenever we use her terminology or examples. In any event, this chapter's focus is not on classifying the films but on analysing the filmmaking process and 'the archival effect' that *Un'ora sola ti vorrei* and *A toca do lobo* have on the spectator.

Acknowledging the lack of academic agreement on the definition of compilation film, appropriation film or found footage film and the subjectivity in the choice of terminology that is used, rather than establishing a system of categorization in this case study, this chapter aims to identify common elements by comparing *A toca do lobo* with *Un'ora sola ti vorrei*. Our hypothesis is that, although both films differ in their content, form and approach, they contain the three characteristics identified by Mulvey when reflecting on compilation film and, therefore, they are comparable and can be considered part of the same genealogy of documentaries. This also makes Mourão and Marazzi members of the same lineage of contemporary female filmmakers.

Women, families and history from below

Mulvey (2015b: 27) argues that compilation film is a special genre that fits the position in which women have been historically placed. Researching history from fragments of sources was denominated 'history from below' in the 1960s, with reference to the social history of the common subjects who were considered unworthy to be part of hegemonic history because of their class, gender or sexual orientation, or for ethnic reasons, among others. Therefore, in order to write counter-histories that recognize and comment on women's experiences which have been denied by official history, New Historicism confronts them and focuses on individual experiences based on the unique, the particular and the personal (Baron 2007: 15). This allows the fragmented narration of multiple alternative histories and the patterning of time to subvert the linear structure of the single *absolute* history. According to Dall'Asta and Chiarini:

> Found footage and original shots are combined in counterpoint to offer a critical reflection about history that calls into question the causal and chronological linearity of official historiography, thus revealing unforeseen connections between past and present, individual and collective.
>
> (Dall'Asta and Chiarini 2016: 6)

Although men have been more active in documenting family activity in the act of photographing or filmmaking, women have always played an important role as the memory keepers and storytellers, being responsible for collecting and transmitting personal and family documents through generations. Grandmothers, mothers or aunts have historically been the living archive of family history. Private documents have been disregarded from a positivist and scientific view, but with the rise of New Historicism, previously neglected sources such as diaries, letters, old photographs and, most importantly for this chapter, home movies have become useful documents for historiography. Therefore, critical movements such as feminist scholarship are partly responsible for the recent recognition of the use of 'the family archive' to comment on history from a subversive perspective, and also to explore its possibilities as a creative and artistic practice.

In that sense, both, Mourão and Marazzi are young filmmakers interested in discovering their family secrets, but, at the same time, in commenting on some of the historical aspects of their countries. Therefore, through *family archaeology* they link the private and the public; the individual and the social; the intimate and the collective. Consequently, what these two filmmakers are doing with their films has been called 'the politics of intimacy' by the editor of *Un'ora sola ti vorrei*, Ilaria Fraioli (Fraioli in Dall'Asta and Chiarini 2016: 137). The feminist activists from the late 1960s had already defended 'the personal is political' perspective, because bringing private experiences to a public level and discussing the problems of the family institution in a social sphere has political consequences, as will be explored in this chapter.

The recycled found footage that Mourão and Marazzi use in their documentaries (apart from some newsreel in *A toca do lobo*) are their families' own home movies. Their use as historical sources, and their possible combination with original filmed footage, offers a game in which the director plays with the different mediums and materiality of the archival documents. In that sense, Mourão and Marazzi 'turn film into document' (Labandeira Moran 2015: 93). They give forgotten home movies a second life by using them for interrogation, analysis and comment, and by transforming the found footage into part documentary film, part historical discourse.

A hypothesis developed by Jane Gaines points out a 'pattern of precarious relations between the historical past and the present moment [...] to ask how each present needs the very past that it proceeds to make' (Gaines 2018: 3). Therefore, there exists the possibility that through using the archives (composed of still images, home movies, found footage, sounds, objects and memories) as their source, the filmmakers may have acted as historians re/constructing their own historical past in order to answer their present anxieties as part of their subjective position in the film.

This kind of film constructs a parallel between the exhibitionism of the filmmakers, who expose their family secrets on screen in a profound and naked way, and the voyeurism of the spectator, who becomes almost part of the family, feeling a complete and unreal intimacy with the artists. In that sense, both Marazzi and Mourão must accept screening and criticism not only of their work but also of their personal and familial relations. Being professional filmmakers and, at the same time, being personally involved in the story, they establish a bridge between the home movie and the political documentary in a special way.

In *A toca do lobo* almost all the testimonies happen on a domestic/familial level in which Mourão's mother, aunt or daughter, or even Mourão herself, are the most important interlocutors. Mourão constantly appears on screen as part of the narration, being a testimonial subject and interviewer. She is playing a part of the collective family memory by positioning herself as an active researcher, a guiding narrator, but also as a passive spectator. While Mourão's objective is to overcome the pre-established family mediation obscured by silence, absence and mythology, and to create a genuine relation between her grandfather and herself as granddaughter, her documentary adds another layer to the subjective narratives that surround the figure of Tomaz de Figueiredo. The documentary, trying to understand, reveals and archives his personality through a filmic medium, and makes it even more difficult to access his true self in a non-mediated way.

In comparison, in *Un'ora sola ti vorrei* Marazzi only appears on screen as a child in the home movies. The filmmaker is confronted with the old version of herself. She is looked at through the eyes of her grandfather's footage and is referred to in her role of daughter from her mother's perspective in her diaries.

This transition, from passively having her life narration conducted by others and mediated by her mother's writing to being the active author of the film through editing it, creates a paradoxical situation that is solved by the presence of 'adult Alina Marazzi' as a voice-over embodying her mother's words and guiding us through the film. Marazzi has the emphatic capacity to incorporate her mother's maternal experience, which was full of doubts, and to reflect about the role that she herself played (as her daughter) on Liseli's will to end her own life, breaking the illusion of perfect daughter, housewife and mother that is represented in the found footage.

Either by using the voice-over (in Marazzi's case) or by the guiding physical presence of the filmmaker on screen (in Mourão's case), both films 'tend to integrate – documentally or fictionally – the flux of the images' (Alonso 2007: 22).[6] Applied to appropriation films, the integrative effort, taken by Luis Alonso from the study of the origins of cinema or 'primitive cinema', reveals the tension between the past and the present as one of the common elements between these two documentaries.

Palimpsest: Dialogue between past and present

The first concept identified by Mulvey is her description of the compilation film as a *palimpsest*. This comes from the idea of the inscription of a new text onto another – a past one. In this sense, the original meaning of the archival material is erased to be used for a new narration creating a double-temporality and a double-authorship.

In the process of constructing the documentaries, as well as reconstructing an emotional relation with those family members that they barely or never knew, Marazzi and Mourão open a fruitful dialogue between present and past. Their documentaries illustrate a counter-story of their families as respected, bourgeois and unproblematized structures. They also disrupt the narratives of modernity during the twentieth century in Italy and Portugal. With hindsight both filmmakers are able to step back and see the bigger picture, relating their familial stories to political and sociological aspects of their national histories that reveal two different kinds of repression. Collecting and recycling archival material from the past, they are able to add another layer of meaning, creating a literal *palimpsest*.

Therefore, Mulvey's identification of the *palimpsest* effect is produced by using past archival material in contemporary documentaries (Mulvey 2015b: 28). Marazzi and Mourão inscribe a totally new meaning on the used documents (home movies, diaries, official documents, photographs, sound recordings, etc.), creating a double-temporality and pointing out the gap that exists between the past and the present. But appropriation films create a palimpsest not only of double-temporality but also of double-authorship. By editing pre-existing materials, the filmmakers subvert the original authorship and overlap a new authority over the footage – a female one. Therefore, women filmmakers directing appropriation films are in fact taking not only an artistic or personal position, but also a political one, challenging the hegemonic order and repositioning themselves from the margins to the centre of historical discourse. They let the past talk to the future, but under their direction and mediated by their individual female experiences.

Even in telling a very personal and familial story, the filmmakers used still and moving images, as well as documents and verbal descriptions, as sources of historical collective knowledge portraying a social experience of the Portuguese dictatorship (*A toca do lobo*) and the female domestic experience in upper-class Italian families (*Un'ora sola ti vorrei*). While Marazzi's film sustains the tendency identified by Dall'Asta and Chiarini (2016: 2) 'to employ the past to produce an allegory of the present', Mourão does the opposite by filming and mixing archival images with present original footage to access and interrogate (in a literal and metaphorical way) the past. In both cases the palimpsest is produced by the inscription of the filmmaker's commentary on the past through her editing of the archival material.

In the case of Marazzi's film, the political reading of her familial story concerns the oppression and depression that women felt before the women's liberation movement emerged during the 1970s. This experience has been described as 'the problem that has no name'. The expression was coined by Betty Friedan (1963) in her book *The Feminine Mystique* to denote the pervasive feeling of unhappiness and dissatisfaction that white middle-class housewives were feeling without understanding why. In the case of *A toca do lobo*, it was the temporal distance of Catarina Mourão from the Salazar dictatorship – 'full of silences and omissions', as it was described by Mourão's mother in the documentary – which allowed her to be the narrator of her family story. She managed to unravel the different family narratives and points of view, as well as to connect the apparently disconnected stories of each family member to some of the hardest years of the dictatorship in her country. In both cases the repression was inflicted on individuals who were exceptional and outside social norms, and, coincidentally, the result was very similar for Marazzi's mother and Mourão's grandfather: they were forced into mental health institutions. The medical treatments of the time (such as isolation, electroshock therapy, strong medication and martial routines) were applied to force them to conform to society's expectations and 'to cure their depression'. In both cases these treatments produced tragic results.

Gleaning: The archival practice

The second concept applied by Mulvey to compilation film is the concept of *gleaning*, which is probably the most well known (Mulvey 2015b: 29). Coined with a filmic meaning by Agnès Varda in her documentary *Les glaneurs et la glaneuse* (2000), the term reflects on the ability of filmmakers – such as Mourão and Marazzi – to visit the archives where memories are stored (both familial and public ones) so that they can revise, collect, select and recycle pre-existing materials.

Baron structures her classification of contemporary documentaries depending on their relation with the archive and the filmmaking process (Baron 2007: 13). She identifies those documentaries that make use of archival materials (such as film footage, photographs and other artefacts) as illustration or evidence for completing the narration, as could be the case with *A toca do lobo*. By contrast, *Un'ora sola ti vorrei* belongs to the category of those documentaries that rely exclusively on found footage.

The visual language of *Un'ora sola ti vorrei* is completely composed of 8mm home movies shot by Marazzi's grandfather, old photographs of the family and new static shots of diaries, letters and newspaper pages. The soundtrack comes from old vinyl records, Marazzi's voice-over reading her mother's personal writings, sound effects and music. The most valuable aspect of this documentary is its achievement in creating a perfectly coherent narrative that produces a very strong and emotional reaction in the spectator almost without shooting new footage or writing a single new line of dialogue (Dall'Asta et al. 2016: 119). In this particular case, the Italian film could be consistently designated as a *found footage film* for having chosen an experimental and challenging editing option.

A toca do lobo is formally part of a more classical genealogy of documentaries that mix historical footage with present-day footage. An important element which gives strength to the film comes from the newly filmed material and the contemporary family interviews, which give a new time dimension to the story and relate the past events with today's familial relations and daily lives (appearing in the form of dreams, fears and traumas). In this case, the found footage of public television interviews with Tomaz de Figueiredo and the 9½mm family home movies are edited together with other elements including original footage, new audiovisual testimonies, fictional recreations, archive documents and so on. Therefore, Mourão's objective as a filmmaker is not to produce an especially original piece of art, but to solve an intimate puzzle, give sense to family secrets and heal her mother's trauma through the camera and the editing room.

In addition, Baron reflects on the relation that the filmmakers have with the archive and the degree of exposure that they want to give to their research practice during the final montage. These two differences highlighted by Baron are very useful in the comparison and differentiation of Marazzi's and Mourão's documentaries:

> In the past few years, however, a number of independent documentaries have entered into a new relationship with archives and archival practices [... They] simulate for the viewer the experience of being in an archive, of following and trying to make sense of fragments and traces. More specifically, these documentaries begin by mobilizing material or textual objects to which the filmmaker has some personal connection and follow not the defined trajectory of a journey but, rather, the tentative movements of an exploration. This exploration is often indirect, dispersed, and nonlinear. It foregrounds process, digression, and discovery rather than a straightforward recovery of 'the facts'.
>
> (Baron 2007: 14)

In this sense, and in contrast with the experience of watching *A toca do lobo*, Marazzi and Fraioli are hidden behind the editing process – which can in any case be a very invisible endeavour – and their authority over the documentary is not necessarily acknowledged by the spectator, who is able to feel a direct and non-mediated relationship with Liseli, getting to know her and her life-story, with a sense of first-voice narration. This is because *Un'ora sola ti vorrei*'s only (but powerful) tool of subjectivity is editing without directly manipulating the text or the image and respecting the original spirit of the found footage, following what Fraioli called 'the ethics of re-appropriation':

> Any shot is a fragment that can be extracted from its original context and reinserted into a new narrative, which can modify or even subvert the image's original meaning. In appropriating any piece of material, it was important for us to abide by the rule of preserving the original spirit of the film in which it had first appeared.
>
> (Fraioli in Dall'Asta and Chiarini 2016: 127)

In contrast to Marazzi's hidden personal process of recovering, recollecting and reconstructing, Mourão shows her previous research work in her documentary. The spectator follows her in the process of researching through the archive (the familial, the literary, the political and the medical) in an attempt to reconstruct her family memories. The spectator witnesses the non-linearity of her progress, the obstacles, the emotions and the frustrations with the feeling that they are meeting her grandfather, Tomaz de Figueiredo, at the same time as she does.

The figure of Mourão's mother is the most vulnerable, in exposing her personal process of healing the trauma (understood by Mulvey as something left behind that comes back to the present) with her own father. Her 'real' reactions during the film transmit a level of sincerity that produces a sensation of unintended voyeurism in the audience, giving us the impression that we were not supposed to witness these personal moments. However, as spectators we know that we are not seeing anything that was not purposefully shown to us, given that our experience is mediated by the filmmaker. Mourão is consciously manipulating and guiding our journey and is herself creating the illusions that cinema produces. In that sense, she does not hide herself, the sources or the materiality of the medium, and she exposes the discontinuous *gleaning* and construction of the unstable filmic narrative. In one scene the home movies are projected onto her body, and onto the walls of her working space (and probably her living space, too) in which she is arranging previously gathered photographs, documents and notes, trying to make sense out of the disorganized combination of sources. The scene unravels a kind of fragmented picture, a puzzle or, more precisely, a project for a future (or work-in-progress) documentary film.

A toca do lobo's authorial mediation and subjectivity cannot be overlooked as Mourão enters into a personal dialogue with the found footage. She and the progression of her research appear constantly on screen because, in fact, *A toca do lobo* is mainly about the process of discovery. The filmmaker also reflects on the incommensurability of the archive and the impossibility that it will fill the absence of and holes in knowledge: 'the archives provoke more an absence than a presence' (*A toca do lobo* 00:52:12). Ricardo Vieira Lisboa analyses a scene in which the filmmaker's shadow hovers over the wall where images of her grandfather in Radio and Television of Portugal (RTP) found footage are projected, creating the suggestion of physical contact: 'the filmmaker's shadow over the RTP images fills this absence of the archival material, manipulating and appropriating them and, in that way, updating family and national memories with what before was an inane celluloid' (Vieira Lisboa 2016). In this way, the filmmaker reveals to the audience her vulnerability and her despair that she could ever fill the gaps.

For example, the impossibility of Mourão being able to enter the family house in Casares, where her grandfather grew up, lived and died, and which nowadays has become the official museum for the memory of Tomaz de Figueiredo, guarded by Mourão's aunt (Mitó), reveals the *gleaning* process. The documentary shows how her aunt denied the filmmaker (and therefore us) access to Casares and, consequently, access to the *family archive* where the heritage (both physical and memorial) is in storage. According to Derrida's notions developed in his article 'Archive Fever' (1995), Casares has become the Archive and Mitó (the aunt) the Greek *archon*:

> On account of their publicly recognized authority, it is at their home [the archon's home], in that *place* which is their house (private house, family house,

> or employee's house), that official documents are filed. The archons are first of all the documents' guardians. They do not only ensure the physical security of what is deposited and of the substrate. They are also accorded the hermeneutic right and competence. They have the power to interpret the archives.
>
> (Derrida 1995: 10, original emphasis)

Therefore, Mitó takes on the role of administrator who blocks access to the documents and becomes the only sanctioned interpreter of the familial, political and social historical past. Following this logic, Mourão reflects in the film: 'suddenly I thought of Casares as a prison where my grandfather was still locked away with my aunt or by my aunt' (*A toca do lobo* 01:27:47–01:28:00). This blocking is so aggressive and direct that it makes a symbolic connection with the oppression of the Portuguese dictatorial past. Being a faceless guardian of the house (as she only appears on screen as an image in old photographs), Mitó becomes in the spectator's mind an oppressive figure of Salazarism: a metaphor of the prison guard, the psychiatric priest and the school nun responsible for Mourão's uncle's imprisonment, her grandfather's confinement, and her mother's internment at school.

Acting as the keeper of the family archive and memory, the female domestic figure of the aunt (with limited power over her private sphere) transitions before the spectator's eyes into a male public agent ruling over the political sphere. It is this unexpected mutation that reveals the power of the archive through which personal documents and experiences of the past become a present source of public interest simply by placing them into a narrative. As Shub had already claimed in her text 'From my experience' in 1927: 'it is important to understand that each little piece of newsreel filmed nowadays has to be considered a historical document for the future' (Shub in Kostina and Dyshlyuk 2016: 18). For this reason, the importance of preservation and documentation is revealed by the use that artists or researchers might make of archival materials, collecting, gathering and recycling them in order to give them a second life as the source of important historical knowledge.

Mulvey recognized the importance that *gleaning* has for the compilation film practice. For example, Marazzi had to gather the images and writings that were useful for her to tell her mother's story when she entered her grandparent's attic where the diaries, letters and home movies were stored. Equally, Mourão managed to construct a narrative out of discarded material that had been omitted from the official archive of Casares and from the censorship that made access to her grandfather's mental health documentation and her uncle's trial difficult. Finally, during the last scene of the movie she appears tidying up some objects that were owned by her grandfather but that were stored and forgotten in family members' wardrobes and boxes. Therefore, she ends the film by revealing her gleaning skills not only for images or information, but for physical objects too.

Detournement: The memory

Finally, the Debordian concept of *detournement* used by Mulvey in this context is based on 'Lev Kuleshov's intuition about the signifying power of montage by reworking pre-constituted materials that had been originally produced to respond to a completely different, and sometimes even opposite, ideological project' (Dall'Asta and Chiarini 2016: 1). The filmmakers choose which fragments of the discarded material are still valuable and they edit them with a clear, self-conscious determination to construct a narrative from their own perspective that is sometimes in opposition to the intended one.

The first time we hear or read the name of the protagonist Tomaz de Figueiredo during the film it is mediated by aseptic, disembodied and neutral voices such as that of a GPS navigator or the street signs of residential streets in peripheral neighbourhoods. In that moment, we, as spectators, are situated *in media res* of a family story searching for the figure of the grandfather, the one that answers to the name we have just heard. Figueiredo's memory as a writer is absent in his national culture and his memory as a father is absent in his family history.

In the film Mourão reflects on fact and fiction; on sign and content; on the conscious and the unconscious; and the memory and perception of our senses; the presence and absence of images, and so on. One of the aspects that interests her is the existence of old family photographs that keep secrets, play with perception or have visual effects. For example, her mother is seen in a photograph in which a reflection on water gives the impression that she had a longer ponytail; in two other photographs one of her legs is behind the other, giving the impression that she only has one; in another she pretends that a salt mound is made of snow; and finally there is one in which she feigns sleep, although she is clearly aware of the presence of the photographer. In these moments Mourão makes parallels between the images and her family: full of *trompe l'oeil*, absences and falseness. 'At first sight, the photo albums of my mother's childhood, like most of the family albums, show snippets of happiness. The captions catalogue the family, making it the same as any other. Established and normal. But listening to my mother talk about each photograph, I realise the illusions they create', Mourão explains in the film (*A toca do lobo* 00:09:30–00:10:20).

Just like the home movies that constitute *Un'ora sola ti vorrei*, those that we see in *A toca do lobo* present the leisure time of an upper-class bourgeois family. But there is a great difference: in Marazzi's home movies Liseli is undoubtedly the protagonist. She is filmed in diverse situations, in close-ups exuding true admiration and love. The visual representation shows a totally different narrative to the one we hear through Liseli's testimonies. This contrast between what we see and what we hear or what we know in *Un'ora sola ti vorrei* is produced in the editing of the film. According to Mulvey, it is the dichotomy between the faked happiness of the found footage and the revealed unhappiness of the writings that produces the *detournement* effect in Marazzi's movie.

Meanwhile, Tomaz de Figueiredo does not appear even once in Mourão's home movies. His absence in the images of the family and their leisure moments is as significant as Liseli's prominent central position. Furthermore, Mourão's mother's family album is full of gaps in the places where the photographs of the grandfather used to be. The *detournement* effect in Mourão's film is produced precisely because the absences are transformed into presences by the filmmaker's editing. By filming the gaps, Mourão is referring to the moment in which someone decided to remove Tomaz de Figueiredo's photographs from the family album, meaning total erasure, not only from national memory but also from family memory. This produces absolute silence, absolute oblivion, absolute exile. Only memory keeps a human being alive and consequently, through making *A toca do lobo*, Mourão is offering a second life to her grandfather, Tomaz de Figueiredo, by gathering, collecting and creating an artistic project for his memory.

As Mulvey (2015b: 37) points out, compilation films always have a spectral dimension through the recycling of archive material and breaking of the temporal linearity between the past and the present. In *A toca do lobo* the phantasmagorical figure of the filmmaker's grandfather is present throughout the film in his writings, in his photographs and in his absence. The circularity is perfectly closed in one of the central moments of the film when Mourão remembers a conversation that she once had with her grandmother, who told her that Figueiredo had left a message for her on a Portuguese television broadcast. 'He died months after I was born; why would he have something to tell me?', Mourão asks herself (*A toca do lobo* 00:19:00–00:19:04). After searching the television network archive, she discovers an old interview in which her grandfather was showing his collection of cigar bags and talking about his unborn granddaughter. Quoting Tomaz de Figueiredo:

> But who's to say … that one day … my granddaughters won't find this collection in one of my drawers? It's possible that one of them, her name, for example, might be Catarina, I love the name Catarina … it's possible that one of them, might fill theses pouches with little shells. And maybe it will occur to her to say … she may never have seen me, but maybe she'd say: 'it's funny, Grandpa Tomaz, how did he collect these things, these pouches for us to play with now'.
>
> (*A toca do lobo* 00:21:45–00:22:30)

Interpreted by Catarina Mourão as an effort by her grandfather to communicate with her from the past in a phantasmagorical way, this is the moment in which the relation between the filmmaker and Tomaz de Figueiredo is no longer intermediated by the presence of their mother and daughter (respectively), but an independent relation between them is created. The message, surprisingly, has indeed travelled across time and space and has reached his granddaughter Catarina, overcoming her professionalism as documentary filmmaker and restoring the possible personal relationship between them in an emotional way that could not be achieved through any other medium. In addition, Figueiredo noted the limitations of the filmed image compared to the brain because the audience could not see the colours or smell the smell. However, it is because of cinema that the grandfather is given the possibility to come back from the dead to talk to his granddaughter. This moment of the film is one of those in which the function of cinema as a time machine is revealed.

Closing remarks

We can establish at least two different genealogies of which these two films are part: the genealogy of appropriation documentaries and the genealogy of contemporary female filmmakers. However, those are very broad categories, so the place in which both films intersect is in their political commentary on the family. Other female filmmakers, such as the Canadian Sarah Polley, the Spaniard Carla Subirana[7] or Helen Hill from the United States, also use different documentary practices with home movies to comment on their own families and politics. In fact, Josep M. Catalá adopts the term 'melodramatic documentary' for those filmic essays that 'explore public and private affective memory: that is, a memory that brings those values together and produces innovative visuals' (Catalá 2009: 314–15). So, taking a greater risk, we could claim that Alina Marazzi's and Catarina Mourão's films are not only part of the same genealogy within the documentary category, but that they can also be considered *melodramatic appropriation films* that produce an 'archive effect' on the spectator.

Mulvey identifies 'the tensions in the family, and between the sexes and generations' as one of the points of departure for melodrama (Mulvey 1989: 40). She argues that melodrama addresses female marginalities centred on family and domestic spaces through speaking to female spectators about their overwhelming silence in patriarchal societies. The political and the cinematic also come together through melodrama. However, far from being limited by the traditional genre rules attached mainly to family crises and female experiences, contemporary melodrama is exploring and foregrounding a wide range of other genres and forms. According to Catalá, the melodrama documentary 'is not about communicating emotion or poeticizing visual realities, but instead about displaying emotions from the archive of the real' (Catalá 2009: 318). Or as Christine Gledhill describes it, 'in materializing the fusion of individual and society, melodrama reveals the work of emotion and personality in social and political processes' (Gledhill and Williams 2018: 2). For that reason, it is coherent that melodrama could have been intertwined with appropriation film in such an effective way, as Marazzi and Mourão are interested in commenting on the individual and social, domestic and political, and contemporary and historical aspects of their families and countries.

The family as a typically female sphere collides in these documentaries with the family as a typically male institution. Therefore, family memory attains a different level of significance if we apply it to appropriation film. Forgotten home movies can transform themselves into documents that are open to a new creative process in which women finally have the means, the technology and the opportunity to transform content from the past to speak to us in their own voice and to tell their own version of history. Can there be anything more transgressive than physically finding, selecting and transforming (understood as *palimpsest*, *gleaning* and *detournement* by Mulvey) old patriarchal/archival documents (the *patriarchive* coined by Derrida) and working on them to tell a new feminist counter-history?

As Labandeira Moran posits, the filmmakers 'offer a counter-statement, a possibility for resistance, which instead of just imposing a new understanding opens a dialogue with the representation of the historical event and its means of representation'. The value of the feminist perspective applied to history is that it does not 'necessarily lead to a negation of previous understandings, although it might, but prevents from taking [*sic*] *official* images and *official* discourses at face value, creating a space for complexity and contradiction' (Labandeira Moran 2015: 99, original emphasis). Giving space to doubt, to insecurity, to absence, to failure and to contradiction, among others, Mourão and Marazzi highlight important ideas about how each family's story reflects the political structures of the countries and their tensions, and also the circularity of memory and time.

Both films discuss and interrogate the individual and social, domestic and political, and contemporary and historic aspects of their families and countries without giving conclusive answers: what would have happened to Liseli if she had survived until the women's liberation movement emerged in Italy? And to Tomaz de Figueiredo if he had lived until the Carnation Revolution in Portugal? Telling her family history, Mourão is also enacting her own revolution against the dictatorship and the effect that it had on intellectuals, children and families in general, and she does it without interrogating political or social figures. She only interrogates her own personal and familial figures, whose testimonies are descriptive of a political moment. This aesthetic and filmic revolution that arises through appropriation film could only happen after the political and social revolution that took place on 25 April 1974. Without the liberation of Portugal, censorship, oppression and silence would have acted to close the archives and prevent the critical message delivered to patriarchal institutions and hegemonic history in *A toca do lobo*.

REFERENCES

Alonso, Luis (2007), 'Sobre el cine aficionado, entre sumisión e insurrección', in J. A. Ruiz Rojo (ed.), *En torno al cine aficionado*, Guadalajara: Centro de la Fotografía y la Imagen Histórica, pp. 15–33.

Baron, Jaimie (2007), 'Contemporary documentary film and "archive fever": History, the fragment, the joke', *Velvet Light Trap*, 60, pp. 13–24.

——— (2014), *The Archive Effect: Found Footage and the Audiovisual Experience of History*, New York: Routledge.

Barthes, Roland (1981), *Camera Lucida: Reflections on Photography*, New York: Hill and Wang.

Catalá, Josep M. (2009), 'El documental melodramático de María Cañas: Ética y estética del *collage*', in S. García López and L. Gómez Vaquero (eds), *Piedra, papel y tijera: El* collage *en el cine documental*, Madrid: Ocho y Medio, pp. 301–30.

Dall'Asta, Monica and Chiarini, Alessandra (eds) (2016), *Feminist Media Histories*, special issue: 'Found footage film: women without a movie camera', 2:3.

Dall'Asta, Monica, Grespi, Barbara, Lischi, Sandra and Pravadelli, Veronica (2016), 'A politics of intimacy: A conversation with Alina Marazzi and Ilaria Fraioli', *Feminist Media Histories*, special issue: 'Found footage film: women without a movie camera', 2:3, pp. 119–41.

Derrida, Jacques (1995), 'Archive fever: a Freudian impression' (trans. E. Prenowitz), *Diacritics*, 25:2 (Summer), pp. 9–63.

Friedan, Betty (1963), *The Feminine Mystique*, New York: Norton.

Gaines, Jane (2018), *Pink-Slipped: What Happened to Women in the Silent Film Industries?*, Urbana, Chicago and Springfield: University of Illinois Press.

Gledhill, Christine and Williams, Linda (2018), *Melodrama Unbound: Across History, Media and National Cultures*, New York: Columbia University Press.

Hatzmann, Hanna (2014), 'La memoria líquida: Imaginarios colectivos y sus interrelaciones con la historia familiar en la obra de tres documentalistas españolas', in P. Feenstra, E. Gimeno Ugalde and K. Sartingen (eds), *Directoras de cine en España y América Latina: Nuevas voces y miradas*, Frankfurt: Peter Lang Edition, pp. 293–311.

Kostina, Anastasia (trans.) and Dyshlyuk, Liubov (intro.) (2016), 'Esfir Shub: Selected writings', *Feminist Media Histories*, special issue: 'Found footage film: Women without a movie camera', 2:3 (Summer), pp. 11–28.

Labandeira Moran, Sibley Anne (2015), 'From waste to worth: Recycling moving images as a means for historical inquiry', unpublished Ph.D. thesis, Getafe: University Carlos III of Madrid.

Marazzi, Alina (2002), *Un'ora sola ti vorrei*, Italy and Switzerland: Venerdi, Bartlebyfilm, Radiotelevisione Sviezzera Italiana.

Moore, Michael (2004), *Fahrenheit 9/11*, USA: Fellowship Adventure Group, Dog Eat Dog Films.

Mourão, Catarina (2015), *A toca do lobo*, Portugal: Laranja Azul.

Mulvey, Laura (1975), 'Visual pleasure and narrative cinema', *Screen*, 16:3, pp. 6–18.

——— (1989), 'Notes on sirk and melodrama', in *Visual and Other Pleasures: Language, Discourse, Society*, London: Palgrave Macmillan, pp. 39–44.

——— (2015a), 'Gleaning, "detournement" and the compilation film: Some thoughts on *Un'ora sola ti vorrei* (Alina Marazzi, 2002)', research seminar chaired by Catherine Grant, 14 December, https://www.youtube.com/watch?v=LqQlqxYl6xU. Accessed 10 December 2018.

——— (2015b), 'Women making history: Gleaning and the compilation film', in M. Albeit and I. Christie (eds), *Where Is History Today? New Ways of Representing the Past*, Olomouc: Palacký University Olomouc, pp. 27–38.

——— (2017), 'Women and film: An approach through representations of the mother in image and narrative', lecture delivered at Filmadrid, Madrid, 12–15 June.

Ortega, María Luisa (2007), *Espejos rotos: Aproximaciones al documental contemporáneo norteamericano*, Madrid: Ocho y medio.

Spurlock, Morgan (2004), *Super Size Me*, USA: The Con.

Varda, Agnès (2000), *Les glaneurs et la glaneuse*, France: Ciné Tamaris.

Vieira Lisboa, Ricardo (2016), '*A toca do lobo* (2015) de Catarina Mourão', À Pala de Walsh, 3 November, http://www.apaladewalsh.com/2016/11/a-toca-do-lobo-2015-de-catarina-mourao/. Accessed 16 December 2018.

Wees, William (1993), *Recycled Images: The Art and Politics of Found Footage Films*, New York: Anthology Film Archives.

Wenders, Wim (2011), *Pina*, Germany: Neue Road Movies.

NOTES

1. As the name suggests, the category of non-fiction film, in which the documentary is included together with other experimental or art films, is defined by what it *is not*, instead of having its own affirmative definition like the category of fiction film.
2. Although this talk is not available online, see the similar talk given in Mulvey (2015a).
3. *Un'ora sola ti vorrei* (2002), Italy, Switzerland, Venerdi, Bartlebyfilm and Radiotelevisione Sviezzera Italiana, 55 min., 16mm, 8mm and Digital Betacam. Crew: Alina Marazzi (director) (producer) (voice-over) (idea); Ilaria Fraioli (editor); Gianfilippo Pedote, Giuseppe Piccioni, Francesco Virga (producers); Benni Atria (sound edit); Alessandro Feletti (voice recording); Paolo Segat, Remo Ugolinelli (mixer), Daria Sorrentino (titles). Winner of the 2002 Locarno Film Festival (Special Mention – Video); 2002 Best Italian Documentary Film at the Torino Film Festival; Award for Original Vision of the 2003 Newport Film Festival in Rhode Island; and 2006 Special Award for Best Documentary of the Italian Online Movie Awards.
4. *A toca do lobo*, 2015, Portugal, Laranja Azul. DCP, 102 min. Crew: Catarina Mouão (director) (producer) (idea) (editor) (cinematography); Pedro Duarte (editor); Maria Ribeiro Soares (producer); Bruno Pernadas (music); João Ribeiro (cinematography); Armanda Carvalho (sound); Irma Lucia (post-production). 2015 Audience Award at IndieLisboa.

5. For more information on these Portuguese filmmakers, see Chapter 10 'Paradigms – women filmmakers in 1970s revolutionary Portugal – Delgado, Nordlund, Cordeiro and Serra' by Érica Faleiro Rodrigues in this volume.
6. The translations of this and all other quotations are mine.
7. For more on Spanish family documentaries by female filmmakers, see Hatzmann (2014).

Notes on contributors

María Soliña Barreiro González holds a Ph.D. in social communication. She has conducted research for ARIAS (Atelier de recherche sur l'intermédialité et les Arts du spectacle, CNRS, ENS, Sorbonne III). She is a film researcher specializing in avant-garde, documentary, silent film and cinema in minority languages. She has published several articles and book chapters on these issues, including 'Filmar a terra: A paisaxe como cuestión de clase', in Margarita Ledo (ed.), *Marcas na paisaxe: Para unha historia do cinema en lingua galega* (Vigo, 2018). She works as a full professor at University of Santiago de Compostela where she is a researcher at Estudos Audiovisuais (USC) and Presence and Representation of Women in Early Cinema (University of Girona, HAR201566262-P).

Elena Cordero-Hoyo is a Ph.D. student carrying out a research on 'Women's access to silent cinema in Spain and Portugal' in the PhDCOMP (University of Lisbon, KU Leuven, University of Bologna), receiving a FCT scholarship (PD/BD/128075/2016). She is part of the research projects 'Iberian and Ibero-American Dialogues' and 'Cinema and the world' at Centro de Estudos Comparatistas (Centre for Comparative Studies) from the School of Arts and Humanities, University of Lisbon, and of the research group Presence and Representation of Women in Early Cinema (University of Girona, HAR201566262-P). She is also an editor of *Secuencias*, an online peer-reviewed film history journal.

Caterina Cucinotta has a Ph.D. in film studies (2015) from New University of Lisbon (FCT fellowship) with a thesis on 'Costumes in Portuguese ethnofiction movies'. Her doctoral thesis was published in 2018 with the title 'Viagem ao cinema atraves do seu vestuario'. She is one of the coordinators of the working group Materiality and Cinema at AIM (Association of Researchers on the Moving Image). Since 2017 she has been a post-doctoral researcher (FCT fellowship) at IHC (Contemporary History Institute) at Lisbon University researching 'Portuguese cinema of the last 50 years in its relationship with fashion theory, sartorial philosophy and materials aesthetic'.

Adriana Martins is assistant professor of culture studies at the Faculty of Human Sciences (Universidade Católica Portuguesa) in Lisbon, where she teaches 'Culture and globalization', 'Portuguese film', 'Portuguese culture' and 'Portuguese as a foreign language'. She is also a senior member of the University's Research Centre for Communication and Culture Studies (CECC). Her main research interests are culture studies, film studies and intercultural communication. Her latest book is *Mediations of Disruption in Post-Conflict Cinema* (co-edited with Alexandra Lopes and Mónica Dias, Palgrave, 2016).

Ana Bela Morais has a Ph.D. in theory of culture. Among other publications, both national and international, she was one of the editors of the book *Los límites del hispanismo: Nuevos métodos, nuevas fronteras, nuevos géneros* (Peter Lang, 2017) and author of another, published by Edições Húmus (2017), which corresponds to her post-Ph.D. research: *Censura ao erotismo e à violência: Cinema no Portugal marcelista (1968–1974)*. She is currently an auxiliary researcher and lecturer at Centro de Estudos Comparatistas (Centre for Comparative Studies) at the Faculty of Arts, University of Lisbon. At the same university, she teaches 'Cinema and literature'.

Katarzyna Paszkiewicz is a lecturer in English studies at the University of the Balearic Islands and a member of ADHUC–Research Center for Theory, Gender and Sexuality (University of Barcelona). Her primary research is in film studies, cultural studies and gender studies, with an emphasis on film genres and women's cinema in the USA and Spain. Most recently she has co-edited, with Mary Harrod, *Women Do Genre in Film and Television* (Routledge, 2017, winner of the BAFTSS Best Edited Collection prize) and has published her monographs *Rehacer los géneros: mujeres cineastas dentro y fuera de Hollywood* (Icaria, 2017) and *Genre, Authorship and Contemporary Women Filmmakers* (Edinburgh University Press, 2018).

Ana Catarina Pereira is cinema and cultural studies professor at University of Beira Interior. She has a Ph.D. in communication sciences, with a published thesis titled 'A mulher-cineasta: Da arte pela arte a uma estética da diferenciação'. She is a researcher at LabCom.IFP, and is also the co-author of the book *Geração invisível: Os novos cineastas portugueses*.

ÉRICA FALEIRO RODRIGUES is a Ph.D. candidate at Birkbeck College, University of London, with a thesis proposal on cinema, gender and politics in the years surrounding the Portuguese revolution of April 1974. At Birkbeck, she was also Assistant Tutor in the School of Arts. She is the recipient of a Millennium Award Fellowship granted by the British Government for her work as a documentary filmmaker. She is the author of the chapter 'Representations of sexuality and gender in Portuguese cinema during the late Estado Novo and the Carnation Revolution', in the book *Consumption and Gender in Southern Europe since the Long 1960s* (Bloomsbury, 2016). Faleiro Rodrigues has also worked extensively as an international film curator.

ANNETTE SCHOLZ is international coordinator at ALCINE – Film Festival of Alcalá de Henares (Madrid). She holds a Ph.D. from the University of Passau (Germany) and is the founder of the Spanish Film Festival in Tübingen-Stuttgart. She has collaborated with several film festivals and international distribution projects. She continues her research on contemporary Spanish cinema, a topic on which her doctoral thesis also focused. In 2016 she co-edited the third volume of the series *Aproximaciones a las culturas hispánicas el cortometraje español (2000–2015): Tendencias y ejemplos* (Vervuert).

BEGOÑA SOTO-VÁZQUEZ is professor of media history and cinema theory at the Universidad Rey Juan Carlos (Madrid), where she directed the MA and Ph.D. courses on Spanish cinema studies. She is the Spanish coordinator of the Women Film Pioneers Project. She was the founder and director of the Film Archive of Andalucia and has collaborated with film restoration projects within Filmoteca Española and Filmoteca de Catalunya. She is part of the research group Presence and Representation of Women in Early Cinema (University of Girona, HAR201566262P) and a member of the Asociación Española de Historiadores del Cine and Domitor.

ESTELA VIEIRA is associate professor in the Department of Spanish and Portuguese at Indiana University. Her teaching and research areas include Lusophone literature, culture and film. She is author of *Interiors and Narrative: The Spatial Poetics of Machado de Assis, Eça de Queirós, and Leopoldo Alas*. Her current research focuses on nineteenth-century Portuguese women's writing as well as on historical memory in film.

RICARDO VIEIRA LISBOA was born in Lisbon in 1991. He holds an undergraduate and master's degree in applied mathematics and computer science and a master's degree in cinema. He works as a film programmer for IndieLisboa – International Film Festival and is a regular curator for the Calouste Gulbenkian Foundation. He is also a film critic for the À Pala de Walsh website and a film director of experimental short films and video essays. In 2017 he co-edited the book *O cinema não morreu - crítica e cinefilia À pala de Walsh.*

www.ingramcontent.com/pod-product-compliance
Lightning Source LLC
LaVergne TN
LVHW060728310826
846742LV00016B/53